THE LEGAL ACADEMIC'S HA

The Legal Academic's Handbook

Edited by

CHRIS ASHFORD

AND

JESSICA GUTH

First published 2016 by
PALGRAVE

Palgrave in the UK is an imprint of Macmillan Publishers Limited,
registered in England, company number 785998, of 4 Crinan Street,
London N1 9XW.

Palgrave Macmillan in the US is a division of St Martin's Press LLC,
175 Fifth Avenue, New York, NY 10010.

Palgrave is a global imprint of the above companies and is represented
throughout the world.

Palgrave® and Macmillan® are registered trademarks in the United States,
the United Kingdom, Europe and other countries.

ISBN 978–1–137–43428–9 paperback

This book is printed on paper suitable for recycling and made from fully
managed and sustained forest sources. Logging, pulping and manufacturing
processes are expected to conform to the environmental regulations of the
country of origin.

A catalogue record for this book is available from the British Library.

A catalog record for this book is available from the Library of Congress.

Printed and bound by CPI Group (UK) Ltd, Croydon, CR0 4YY

Contents

Notes on the Contributors

Emily Allbon is a lecturer at the City Law School, City University London. She is an HEA National Teaching Fellow and is creator of the Lawbore website. Previously a law librarian, she was awarded the Routledge/ALT Teaching with Technology Prize 2013.

Chris Ashford is Professor of Law and Society at Northumbria University. He edits *The Law Teacher: The International Journal of Legal Education, the International Journal of Gender, Sexuality and Law* and is Chair of the Association of Law Teachers. He is also a former Secretary of the Socio-Legal Studies Association.

Rosemary Auchmuty is Professor of Law at the University of Reading. She writes about gender and law, sexuality, property law, legal history and children's books.

Karen Barton has published widely and carried out a number of funded research projects in legal education, professionalism and professional learning and is the Head of UH Online, the University of Hertfordshire's Centre for Online Distance Learning.

Vera Bermingham is Visiting Lecturer at Kingston Law School. She has authored and co-authored a number of tort textbooks and published articles on a variety of aspects of legal education and law teaching.

Paul Bernal is a lecturer in IT, IP and media Law at UEA Law School, has appeared on national and international television and radio and in print in the UK and abroad. He blogs at paulbernal.wordpress.com and tweets as @paulbernalUK.

Alison Bone is a principal lecturer at the University of Brighton. She originated the National Law Teacher of the Year Award and is a former chair and current committee member of the Association of Law Teachers.

Anthony Bradney is Professor of Law at Keele University, having previously been Professor of Law at the University of Leicester and the University of Sheffield. He has published widely on, amongst other things, university legal education, religion and law and law and popular culture.

Graeme Broadbent joined Kingston Law School in 2002. He has written and spoken extensively on aspects of legal education. He has a close association with LERN and was a member of the editorial board of *The Law Teacher* and its book reviews editor 1994–2009.

Michael Bromby is a Reader in law at Glasgow Caledonian University and was seconded to the Higher Education Academy from 2011–2013 as the Discipline Lead for Law.

Kevin J. Brown is a lecturer in Law at Queen's University Belfast. He is a member of the Executive Committee of the Socio-Legal Studies Association. He is widely published on the subject of the regulation and governance of anti-social behaviour.

Deveral Capps is Head of Leeds Law School at Leeds Beckett University. Deveral was a member of the consultation steering panel for the recent Legal Education and Training Review (LETR). He is a practicing barrister and holds a door tenancy at Trinity Chambers in Newcastle.

Jane Ching is Professor of Professional Legal Education at Nottingham Law School, Nottingham Trent University. She is interested in the learning of practitioners, particularly in the workplace.

Richard Collier is Professor of Law at Newcastle Law School, Newcastle University. He has published widely in the areas of law and gender, with a particular focus on questions of men and masculinities in family law, criminology and legal education. His most recent book is *Men, Law and Gender: Essays on the 'Man' of Law* (Routledge 2010).

Tim Connor has recently retired from his position as lecturer at the School of Law, University of Bradford. Before that he completed his PhD by publication.

Dave Cowan is Professor of Law and Policy at the University of Bristol Law School. He was Vice-Chair of the Socio-Legal Studies Association from 2001–2003. He is a member of the editorial board of the *Journal of Law and Society* and an editor of *Social and Legal Studies*. He is also the series editor of the Palgrave Macmillan Socio-Legal Series.

Fiona Cownie is Professor of Law and Pro Vice Chancellor (Education and Student Experience) at Keele University. She is the author of several books and numerous articles on legal education, including *Legal Academics: Culture and Identities* (Oxford, Hart Publishing, 2004).

Fiona De Londras is Professor of Law at Birmingham University. She is joint editor-in-chief of the *Irish Yearbook of International Law* and co-editor of *Legal Studies*, the journal of the Society of Legal Scholars of the UK and Ireland. Fiona is also a member of the Executive Committee of the Society of Legal Scholars, a Global Affiliate of the Vulnerability and the Human Condition project based in Emory University and a member of the advisory boards of the Centre for Comparative and European Constitutional Studies at the University of Copenhagen, the UCC Department and Faculty of Law and the Centre for Global Public Law at Koc University, Turkey.

Hugo De Rijke practised as a criminal barrister for a number of years before joining Plymouth University, where he is Associate Head of the Law School. He is interested in all aspects of innovation in legal education and especially in the relationship between law, literature and film.

Karen Devine is a lecturer at the University of Kent. She teaches on the medical law and ethics and obligations undergraduate programmes and has published in socio-legal work. She was voted the Oxford University Press National Law Teacher of the Year in 2012.

Jonathan Doak has been Professor of Law at Durham University since February 2012. He is particularly interested in the theoretical and socio-legal dimensions of criminal justice and transitional justice.

Nigel Duncan is Professor of Legal Education at The City Law School, was, for 20 years, Editor of the *Law Teacher* and is now Consultant Editor. He is a member of the Editorial Advisory Boards of the *International Journal of the Legal Profession* and the *Legal Education Review*. He publishes regularly on issues of legal education and legal ethics.

Rachel Fenton is a senior lecturer at the University of the West of England (UWE) in Bristol. Her areas of expertise cover bystander interventions, sexual offences and gender in law.

Ben Fitzpatrick is Professor and Head of Law at the University of Derby. He was formerly Director of Learning and Teaching at York Law School, where he played a leading role in the design and implementation of a law curriculum built on a core of problem-based learning.

Chris Gale is Dean of the Faculty of Social Science, Law and Technology at GSM London. Prior to that he was Head of Bradford University Law School and, before that, Head of Undergraduate Studies in Leeds Law School. He has had nearly 20 years' experience of being an External Examiner and over 15 years of undertaking performance reviews.

Richard Grimes is Director of Clinical Programmes at York Law School, University of York. He has published widely on legal education in general and clinical legal education in particular. The focus of his work is to link advances in learning to better access to justice for the wider community.

Jessica Guth is Head of Law at the University of Bradford where she has worked as Lecturer and Senior Lecturer since 2007. Her research interests are legal education and the legal academy as well as aspects of EU and equality law.

Robert Hiscocks is a lecturer and tutor in criminal law at BPP University. He has a particular interest in teaching part-time and mature students, on both face-to-face and online classes.

John Hodgson is a Reader at Nottingham Law School. He edits *Carriage by Road and Rail* in the *Encyclopaedia of Forms and Precedents*, and has contributed to legal journals such as the *CILEx Journal*, *The Litigator*, *New Law Journal* and *Solicitors Journal*, and non-legal journals such as *Structural Survey* and the *British Journal of Nursing*.

Rosemary Hunter is Professor of Law and Socio-Legal Studies at Queen Mary University of London. She is a prominent international feminist legal scholar and is the Chair (2011–2017) of the Socio-Legal Studies Association.

Becky Huxley-Binns is Professor and Vice Provost at the University of Law. Widely published in criminal law, English legal system and legal education, Becky is a National Teaching Fellow, former Chair of the Association of Law Teachers and was Law Teacher of the Year 2010.

Annabelle James is the Subject Leader for Law, Policing and Investigation at Teesside University.

Michael Jefferson MA (Oxon), BCL is a senior lecturer at the School of Law, University of Sheffield. He was the first Director of Teaching in the School and the first Director of Learning and Teaching Development in the Faculty.

Karen Jones is Associate Head of the School of Law, Accounting and Finance at the University of South Wales and a legal practitioner with a current practising certificate. Karen's teaching and research interests include civil litigation and dispute resolution, employment law and clinical legal education.

Francis King is a senior lecturer in property law at the University of Westminster. She is passionate about property; teaching and researching the 'property-related' aspects of tort, as well as land law.

Jackie Lane, Senior Lecturer at the University of Huddersfield, has particular interests in the rights of students with disabilities to be treated equally, and the rights of the disabled and other disadvantaged groups in the workplace.

Ben Livings is a senior lecturer at the School of Law, the University of New England, Australia. He has previously held academic positions at the University of Sunderland, UK, and the Université d'Angers, France.

Chris Maguire is Dean of Academic Affairs at BPP University. He has held a number of external appointments, including: Chair of the Association of Law Teachers, Chair of the Lithuanian SPCK Review of Degrees in Creative Industries, British Council consultant to the Cypriot Government, consultant to the Nigerian Council of Legal Education, Chair of the UKCLE funded Phineas Gage Group on Neuroscience, member of the European Union Stage Experts Committee and member of the advisory committees for the UK Centre for Legal Education.

David McArdle is Senior Lecturer in Law at the University of Stirling. He read law at the University of Wales, Aberystwyth and worked in legal publishing before commencing his PhD studies in 1993 under the supervision of Steve Redhead at Manchester Metropolitan University.

Paul McKeown is a senior lecturer at Northumbria University. He works in Northumbria University's award-winning clinic, the Student Law Office. He has experience in various models of clinical legal education, including Street Law programmes.

Ben Middleton is the Head of the Law School and Principal Lecturer at the University of Sunderland. Outside of legal education, his research interests include public law, broadly construed, with a focus on counter-terrorism law and human rights.

Sarah Morse is a senior lecturer at Northumbria University. She works in Northumbria University's award-winning clinic, the Student Law Office. She has experience in various models of clinical legal education, including Street Law programmes.

Edward Mowlam is a lecturer in law at the University of Bradford teaching and researching in the fields of criminal and European Union law. As a student he was the student law society president and he is now the student law society staff liaison.

Richard Mullender is Professor of Law and Theory and Director of Research at Newcastle Law School, Newcastle University.

Victoria Murray is a teaching fellow and programme leader of the M Law (Exempting) degree at Northumbria University. She is a clinical supervisor in the multi-award-winning Student Law Office and co-editor of *A Student Guide to Clinical Legal Education and Pro Bono*.

Elizabeth Mytton is Professor of Legal Education at Southampton Solent University. She is a former Chair of the Committee of heads of University Law Schools (CHULS) and has worked extensively in the area of course design and curriculum development, as well as quality assurance, in the UK, the former Soviet Union, China, Sweden, Switzerland, Greece, Israel and the Channel Islands.

Christopher J. Newman is Reader in Public Law at the University of Sunderland. He has a diverse practitioner background having worked with the Metropolitan Police and as a solicitor in private practice. As an academic Chris has experience of external collaboration with organisations in both the public and private sector that has informed both his research and his teaching.

Rory O'Boyle is a solicitor and is based at the Law Society of Ireland. He was previously a lecturer at Northumbria University's School of Law.

Mark O'Brien is Head of the School of Law at Oxford Brookes University. A specialist in Civil Liberties and Cyberlaw, previously he worked at the University of Reading, Sheffield Hallam University and most recently the University of the West of England, where he was the Director of Law.

Dr Liz Oliver is a lecturer in work and employee relations at Leeds University Business School. She completed her PhD at the University of Leeds and has also worked as a lecturer at the University of Liverpool.

Jon Reast is the Pro Vice-Chancellor (International Development) at Northumbria University.

Philip N.S. Rumney is a professor of criminal justice at the University of the West of England. His teaching and research focuses on sexual offences, the use of interrogational torture and freedom of expression.

Helen Stalford is a full-time Professor of Law at the University of Liverpool. She has five children and just does the best she can.

Philip A. Thomas is Emeritus Professor of Law, Cardiff Law School, Cardiff University and the founding and current editor of the *Journal of Law and Society*. He is also a visiting professor at Northumbria Law School, Northumbria University, Newcastle upon Tyne.

Chloe Wallace is an Associate Professor and admissions tutor at the School of Law, University of Leeds.

Gary Watt, Warwick Law School, is a National Teaching Fellow and was named Law Teacher of the Year 2009. He is co-editor of the journal *Law and Humanities* and the author of books on equity, trusts, Shakespeare and dress.

Matthew Weait is Dean of the Faculty of Humanities and Social Sciences at the University of Portsmouth. He was previously Professor of Law and Policy at Birkbeck, University of London. His research centres on the impact of law on HIV prevention, and on people living with HIV and AIDS.

Lisa Webley is Professor of Empirical Legal Studies at the University of Westminster and Senior Research Fellow at the Institute of Advanced Legal Studies. She is author of *Legal Writing* and teaches legal research and writing at a range of levels from first year undergraduates to early career researchers.

Sally Wheeler is Professor and Head of School at Queen's University, Belfast. She edits the *Northern Ireland Legal Quarterly* and in 2012 became a Fellow of the Academy of Social Sciences. In 2013 Sally was elected to the Royal Irish Academy. Sally is also a former Chair of the Socio-Legal Studies Association.

Donna Whitehead is Pro Vice-Chancellor and Executive Dean of the Faculty of Business and Law at UWE, Bristol. She was previously the Head of the School of Law, Accounting and Finance at the University of South Wales. Her teaching and research interest is family law – specifically non-traditional modes of family life and parenting.

Laura J. Wilkinson is a chartered librarian, working at the University of Sunderland. She provides subject support for Law, and maintains authentication and discovery systems for the university library's e-resources. She is a member of the UKSG Research and Innovation Committee, and blogs at darkarchive.wordpress.com.

Carol Withey is a principal lecturer in criminal law at the University of Greenwich and a University Teaching Fellow. Carol has developed criminal law revision videos, where LEGO® characters play the role of defendants and victim. These videos are available on YouTube and are free to view.

Introduction

This book is intended as a guide to colleagues who are new to their roles as legal academics or new to particular aspects of their roles. This book is not a rule book or even a definitive how to guide but rather an attempt to share our experience, and the experience of colleagues, with you. We hope that in doing so you can build on that experience and perhaps avoid making some of the mistakes and falling into some of the traps we did. We have tried to do justice to the fact that there is no typical legal academic and no typical role. We all do slightly different things in slightly different institutions and we all have slightly different backgrounds, career paths and ambitions.

We have therefore imagined four legal academics with four different career paths in four different institutions and tried to imagine how their journeys might play out and what advice they might find useful along the way. The book is structured around these four people: Meg, who has some experience of legal practice and has a job at a research-rich institution; Anton who joined a private provider leaving a career as a city lawyer behind; Jack who has significant teaching experience and works in a teaching intensive university; and Nadia who has completed a PhD and is starting her career in a research intensive university.

You might recognise a particular career path as close to your own or you might see elements of all four in your own situation but the structure of the book and the short nature of the contributions on each topic should help you find what you are looking for.

Our careers stories reflect our individual journeys and these stories – although fictional – are combined with the experiences of real academics to offer advice on the various challenges and opportunities that you might encounter on that journey.

Meet our characters

Meg

Meg is 30 when we first meet her. She works in a research-rich institution, with engagement with business and the professions. Meg joined the institution after spending five years in legal practice as a solicitor. This is her first academic post. She has one young child at home and is planning for another. Meg is naturally a worrier and is concerned about doing a good job and about not annoying people by saying no. She is therefore likely to agree to most requests by colleagues and managers.

She has a relatively high teaching load but is also expected to deliver research outputs. She is struggling to fully understand and meet the many demands the institution is placing on her and is particularly struggling with the institution's requirement that all staff should be working towards a PhD, she thinks more training in terms of teaching might benefit her more.

As Meg's career progresses we see her becoming involved in Street Law activities, setting up a law clinic, dipping her toes into empirical research and writing for publication for the first time and eventually enrolling for a part-time PhD. We also see her developing as a teacher and trying to engage with a wider audience by sharing her ideas through social media channels. Meg is a good teacher and competent researcher but is beginning to realise that she enjoys management aspects of her role such as module leaderships and she wants to build on this. We see her taking on programme management responsibility and explore possibilities of committee work within the university.

Meg seeks opportunities for management roles at a variety of institutions but the lack of research track record is stopping her from progressing. She does eventually secure a senior role in a teaching-focused institution heading the law programmes in a larger faculty.

Anton

Anton has worked as a solicitor for ten years in a national and, later, a city firm. He also previously worked in quality assurance for a European legal services regulator. He's now joined a private-sector legal-education provider following a number of years of requests to join from his new employer. They are rapidly expanding and want to draw upon experienced practitioners with major city connections. Anton is an accomplished practitioner but is new to education. He believes passionately in training the next generation of lawyers through a practical and employment-focused approach to their education. He holds little interest in academia and what he believes are antiquated methods of working and an inherent inability to appropriately respond to a fast changing marketplace.

Jack

Jack is 25 when we first meet him. He works in an institution that regards itself as 'teaching focused' with an emphasis on widening participation; providing opportunities for students who might not otherwise have experienced higher education. Jack has spent three years teaching courses part time at similar institutions in the region, and also taught on the CILEX programme at a nearby college of further education. Jack is keen to develop his teaching profile and is considering doing a PGC offered by his institution. He is keen to try out different teaching techniques and on using technology in his teaching but is fairly clueless when it comes to what is available. Jack spends a lot of time with students, giving feedback and acting as personal tutor. He sees pastoral care as really important and a key motivator for his career in education.

Jack was drawn to the role for the extra freedom he anticipated compared to his previous employers – particularly compared to his time at the local college. Jack is motivated by a sense of social justice and enabling people from whatever background to become economically and socially mobile through education. He would also like to seek recognition for his teaching and is considering writing a textbook.

Jack is seeing the number of students at his institution fall, and increased pressure to respond to the National Student Survey – which his institution scores well in. Jack's institution is also keen to distinguish itself from private providers and Jack's former employer, the nearby college, which is growing their higher education (HE) provision. To do this, the institution is increasingly asking Jack to develop his – by now – impressive record of teaching innovation into a research agenda. Jack is developing Legal Education research but feels he is too often under-resourced with funds to attend conferences and lacks sufficient time to do his research. He is also struggling to balance this demand with his continued desire to develop high-quality teaching materials, and to support his students. He's increasingly frustrated and unhappy.

Nadia

Nadia is 27 when we first meet her. She finished her PhD a year ago and is now working as a research assistant. She has now applied for (and will get) a lectureship at an institution that describes itself as 'research focused'. Nadia teaches undergraduate students who have a strong academic record, and is also teaching an increasing number of postgraduate (PG) students, particularly from Asia. Nadia mostly teaches tutorials on courses which already exist and are led by others but is asked to develop her own PG course. She is keen to explore socio-legal and contextual approaches to law and legal study and incorporate those into her teaching.

She has research targets both in terms of income generation and in terms of outputs and is trying to develop a book proposal based on her PhD work. Nadia is a focused researcher and wants to apply for a substantial research grant and gain experience in managing research teams including international collaborations. She will in due course join an editorial board of a leading journal, edit special issues of top journals and take on editorship as overall editor. She is excited about the possibility of supervising her own PhD students.

She will need to demonstrate some administrative roles and external activities in order to progress to senior lecturer (SL) at her institution and eventually to reader/ professor. She has made enquiries about how to get onto the executive of various professional associations.

Nadia's strengths are her research skills and academic/intellectual ability and her enthusiasm for her work. She tends to work long hours and her main priority is her research. She has confidence in her abilities as a researcher but is far less sure about her abilities as a teacher. She is a competent administrator but sometimes struggles with university processes. She is not particularly interested in a management career in HE, she wants to be a research professor although she accepts that some management responsibilities are inevitable – she wants them to be research focused, though.

How to use this book

We do not intend for you to read the book from cover to cover (although we would be thrilled if you did) but we have structured the contributions for each of our fictional legal academics in such a ways as to hopefully show the progression through their career and the various difficulties and opportunities that they might encounter. You may therefore like to look through the chapters relating to a particular character. You might however be looking for specific advice in which case the contents pages or index should help you locate the information you are looking for. Each chapter has a very brief summary of the situation our fictional academics are seeking advice on which is followed by the advice. Each chapter ends with some key messages or tips and where relevant a short list of further resources you might find helpful. We have also included a short glossary.

We hope you find this book useful as you start or continue your academic journey, and we'd love to hear your feedback on this book.

Chris Ashford and Jessica Guth
July 2015

PART I

Meg

Meg is 30 when we first meet her. She works in a research-rich institution, with engagement with business and the professions. Meg joined the institution after spending five years in legal practice as a solicitor. This is her first academic post. She has one young child at home and is planning for another. Meg is naturally a worrier and is concerned about doing a good job and about not annoying people by saying no. She is therefore likely to agree to most requests by colleagues and managers.

She has a relatively high teaching load but is also expected to deliver research outputs. She is struggling to fully understand and meet the many demands the institution is placing on her and is particularly struggling with the institution's requirement that all staff should be working towards a PhD; she thinks more training in terms of teaching might benefit her more.

As Meg's career progresses we see her becoming involved in Street Law activities, setting up a law clinic, dipping her toes into empirical research and writing for publication for the first time and eventually enrolling for a part time PhD. We also see her developing as a teacher and trying to engage with a wider audience by sharing her ideas through social media channels. Meg is a good teacher and competent researcher but is beginning to realise that she enjoys management aspects of her role such as module leaderships and she wants to build on this. We see her taking on programme management responsibility and explore possibilities of committee work within the university.

Meg seeks opportunities for management roles at a variety of institutions but the lack of research track record is stopping her from progressing. She does eventually secure a senior role in a teaching-focused institution heading the law programmes in a larger faculty.

CHAPTER 1

From Legal Practice to Academia

KAREN JONES

> Meg has been working in legal practice as a solicitor for about five years and is now considering a move into academia. She doesn't really know what to expect or whether she has the skills and knowledge necessary to make the switch.

So you are considering moving from legal practice to academia. Perhaps you dream of a more flexible lifestyle, a more intellectually challenging role, the offer of an opportunity to impart your experience and knowledge or you are simply drawn by the thought of no longer having to record your working life on a timesheet. Some, if not all, of these things lure legal practitioners to apply for academic law jobs. Before continuing, it is worth noting that there are two main types of academic jobs and practitioners can and do apply for both. However, the expectations of these roles do differ somewhat and although it is possible to move from one to another once in academia or to move onto different types of roles, for example management, it is worth considering which type you wish to apply for as your initial choice on application will impact on how and what you should do to prepare.

Legal education in England and Wales takes different forms but courses roughly fall into two camps: those which are professional training courses – courses such as the Legal Practice Course (LPC) and the Bar Professional Training Course (BPTC) – and those which are academic courses, for example the three-year law degree or a master's in law. Many universities have a range of these courses and in many institutions academics are expected to and do teach across both professional and academic courses. It goes without saying that initial enquiries as to the nature and expectations of any role are a must when applying for an academic role from legal practice. The ability to tailor an initial application will ensure not only a good chance of being shortlisted but also a head start in the interview process.

Before applying, an excellent starting point is to consider – and if possible some time in advance – how to best equip yourself for a possible transfer into academic life. As stated above, preparation very much depends on what type of role you are considering, as a practitioner/clinician-type role, where the expectation is to deliver professional courses, requires slightly different preparation from a research-focused role with minimal teaching. Practitioners tend to veer towards the former role but there are those who have been very successful in the latter role too.

Universities now see quite large numbers of applicants for posts and the new applicant, particularly the practitioner, needs to find a way to stand out in that process. Teaching experience, quite sensibly, is now an essential criterion for all posts and for some legal practitioners this can seem like a challenging criterion. If you are seriously considering a move to academia, it is advisable to test out both your teaching skills and whether it is really for you. One of the best ways to do that is to obtain some hourly paid work at a local institution. Many universities use hourly paid lecturers for delivery of modules and this can be a great way of not only introducing yourself to teaching, and what is expected, but also getting a head start in the application and interview process.

Often regular hourly paid work is not an option, particularly if you are working full time. There are however other options, particularly if you know someone in academia or are still in contact with your alumni institution, and this includes delivering practitioner-focused guest lectures either on specific topics or on career development. Both of these will provide you with an insight into academia, however small, and give you ammunition for your application. If you have no such access to delivering sessions then consider engaging in the training of more junior members of staff or getting involved in client training events, all of which can enhance your CV in preparation for the move.

Teaching is only part of the role. Institutions operate in a highly competitive market and the legal-education sector is no different. There are a number of very large private providers of legal education in the market and institutions are therefore looking at key selling points. If you can bring something different or additional to the role then this is of benefit not only to the institution but also to you in the application process.

Employability and preparing students for the world of work are key buzzwords in academia and as a legal practitioner you will have the skills to develop students in this way. You may want to consider carrying out some pro bono work or volunteering in a university or other law clinic before applying. Most institutions have their own clinics or work-based learning modules in order to enhance both the student experience and their employability skills and it will give you a real edge in the process if you have this type of experience.

Research is also key. You may decide that you wish to take a more clinician's approach to research or to focus on the more traditional subject-based research. Whatever you decide to do, you will be required to engage in some scholarly activity and you therefore may wish to engage in some publications or business engagement before entering academia. Practitioners' texts and commentaries and conference events give you ample opportunity to develop a research and business engagement profile, however small.

You may want to also give thought to how you wish to present your areas of expertise. You may be a litigation or employment specialist but you will still have the core knowledge to teach tort or contract law and you need to play on these strengths in your application.

Finally, be prepared to have some knowledge of the higher education landscape and legal education developments. Higher education is a fast-changing world and whilst it may be some time since you last had contact with it, find out more and keep abreast of issues that affect legal education. Make contacts in the sector – networking, as in the legal profession, is key!

The key messages for Meg and other practitioners considering a move into academia:

1. Be realistic. Suitable academic posts are not commonplace and the competition is fierce. It will take time so give yourself an advantage in the application process.
2. Make contact with your local institution and get yourself some teaching experience. If you can't do this, offer your services for guest lecture spots or get involved with staff and client training.
3. Take on some pro bono work or volunteer at a law clinic.
4. Start to build a research profile. You can start in practitioner texts and by the time you move into academia you will already have a profile which you can build on.

FURTHER READING

BOOK

Cownie, F. (2004) *Legal Academics: Culture and Identities*, Oxford: Hart Publishing.

WEBSITES

Association of Law Teachers. http://www.lawteacher.ac.uk/default.asp

Higher Education Academy. https://www.heacademy.ac.uk/discipline/law

Institute of Advanced Legal Studies. http://ials.sas.ac.uk/lern/lern.htm

CHAPTER 2

Lectures

ANTHONY BRADNEY

> Meg has successfully secured her first academic post, working in a research-rich institution. She has now been told that she will be teaching large groups of students in lectures.

Lectures are the cheapest way of efficiently conveying information to large numbers of students. Providing you have the appropriate facilities a lecture to 100 students is much the same for the student as a lecture to 550 students and costs the law school the same. Since many law schools are busy places, lectures have huge attractions for law schools as a means of delivering teaching. Notwithstanding the deficiencies that lectures have, these attractions are genuine. Law schools have finite resources. Academic staff have a duty to provide effective teaching, contribute to the administration of their university, take part in the wider life of the legal academic community and, not least, undertake research. Using teaching methods which are so cost-intensive as to make teaching the only thing that the law school can do does not signal a devotion to the needs of students. Instead it betokens a failure to understand the complexities of academic life. Good teaching needs to be done so that good learning can take place but that should never be the only thing that law schools are doing.

The most important danger with the use of lectures is that they can contribute to students acquiring only a superficial understanding of material. No lecturer can speak with the precision that they can write. No student can completely concentrate for 50 minutes on an argument that is being presented to them whilst, at the same time, taking a note of that argument. Written material can be read again and again until understanding is achieved. Lectures are ephemeral affairs that have to be consumed immediately.

There are many things that can be done to improve on traditional lectures. However, the efficacy of anything that is done has to be measured against the advantages that lectures have for the law school. Lectures always have to be cost-effective.

One way to improve on traditional lectures is the lecture handout. Handouts have a number of significant advantages. References, quotations and figures can be reproduced accurately. The lecturer no longer needs to laboriously repeat basic facts. The student can focus on ideas rather than information. But handouts take time to write. If they are to be loaded to a module's website or Virtual Learning Environment (VLE), further time is involved. If they are reproduced and given to students, this involves time before the lecture as well as time in the lecture. Reproduction itself means a cost to the school.

PowerPoint presentations also have advantages and disadvantages. They can convey information more precisely than the spoken word. If posted on a module website they become points of reference. Slides break lectures up, varying a presentation and thus assisting with student concentration. However, particularly if done well, they take a significant amount of time to prepare. More than this, slides can become as much a distraction in lectures as a help. PowerPoint slides mean that the student is now being asked to listen to the lecturer, think about what they are saying, take notes and also look at visual presentations. Slides can help but they can also hinder learning. The effort in preparing slides has to be measured against the fact they are not necessarily good when it comes to learning, even though students usually like them.

Lectures are inevitably a performance. The only question is whether they are a good or bad performance. The performance in lectures should be designed to convey information and argument in such a way as to maintain the students' focus on that information and argument. Simply, accurately presenting material does not make for the best lecture. Following oral presentations, whilst at the same time critically thinking about them and taking an accurate note of them, is a very difficult skill. To do so for a period of 50 minutes is tasking, and when this is the third or fourth lecture that you have listened to in a day, it is even more tasking. Lectures need to be broken up to help students. Asides, changes in tone and even irrelevancies, amongst many other things, if used judiciously, can all help. Yet, whilst all lectures are a performance, the performance should never become simply entertainment. Equally, the lecture not the lecturer ought to be the most important thing. Lectures are part theatre but if the lecturer wants to be in a theatre they should find a different job.

Lectures should always be a participatory experience for students. In principle, critical reflection by students on the material that they are being presented with constitutes the most important part of their participation. In practice, for students, lectures often become inherently non-participatory. In contrast to seminars or tutorials, students have permission to be silent. Indeed, if the lecture is to be effective for the majority of the students, students must be largely silent. However, silence can quickly become absence either intellectually or physically. There are numerous ways of trying to break this pattern. Asking students to prepare material before lectures, asking direct questions in lectures and stopping a lecture to divide students into groups to look at an individual issue are all ways of getting away from what can be, for students, the monotony of lectures. But, if this is to be done, both the advantages of lectures as a vehicle of course delivery and the practicalities of the individual module have to be considered. Apart from considering the merits of the extra preparation time that has to be undertaken, the logistics of the group being taught need to be taken into account. If a cohort numbers several hundred, how is prior preparation to be monitored? If individuals are questioned, how will they feel about being singled out? How will other students feel about the fact that they have not been singled out? If there is group work, does this mean that extra lectures will be needed to compensate for lost time? If so, is this good for either the lecturer or the students? More lectures are not necessarily a good thing. More teaching, even in small groups, is not necessarily a good thing.

Learning, in the end, is always a lonely, solitary matter. What space is the lecturer leaving for individual student learning?

Unless law schools are given a very big increase in their resource level, lectures are always going to be a mainstay of course delivery. The problems that they produce for learning can be mitigated. However, care needs to be taken in not causing longer-term problems for the law school in seeking to improve the quality of lectures.

The key messages for Meg and other academics considering lectures:

1. Law schools have finite resources.
2. Lectures are good at cheaply delivering teaching to large numbers of students.
3. Lectures can be bad at making students active learners.

FURTHER READING

BOOKS

Brown, S. and Race, P. (2002) *Lectures: A Practical Guide*, London: Routledge.

Harland, T. (2012) *University Teaching: An Introductory Guide*, Abingdon: Routledge, chapter 3.

Thomas, P. (2000) *Learning About Law Lecturing*, Warwick: UK Centre for Legal Education. http://www.ukcle.ac.uk/resources/personal-and-professional-development-and-cpd/thomas/

JOURNAL

Cockburn, T. and Matthew, A. (2006) Lecturing Law with Powerpoint: What is the Point?, *eLaw Journal*, 13(1), 113–140. https://elaw.murdoch.edu.au/archives/elaw-13-1-2006.html

Marking

BECKY HUXLEY-BINNS

> Meg has just been given her first batch of exam scripts and coursework to mark.

Marking student work is difficult, lonely, time-consuming and often frustrating work, but it can also be very rewarding, and it always, always matters. It matters because assessing student performance gives the student, the school, the institution and the sector an objective judgment on the student's level of achievement.

Marking is difficult because tutors usually have a great many answers to mark within a tight deadline and it requires great concentration to read, absorb and judge the strengths and the weaknesses of the work. It is frustrating because students may have spent hours and hours writing the best answer they can, and the tutors have only 30 or so minutes to mark the work and give a fair and objective judgment on its quality, as well as meaningful and constructive feedback. Further frustration comes from the repetition of common mistakes and in particular from repeated common mistakes about which the students have been repeatedly warned and from lack of effort or attention to detail, such as a simple and avoidable misreading of the question. It is also very frustrating, and also unfortunately not uncommon, to find student work is plagiarised. On the other hand, marking is rewarding when students crack the answer, apply beautiful logic and well-expressed critical reasoning to a complex problem or assertion, and at its best, marking involves pleasure from reading well-constructed and well-argued legally sound prose.

We use the word marking here to mean assessing student written work, including coursework and examinations and also oral performances including moots. Assessing involves making judgments about the level of achievement against set and, preferably, published criteria. The criteria should be written clearly and be easily understandable to the students and the assessors. They should also be level specific (by which we mean written in such a way as to relate to the level of study the student is undertaking, whether at undergraduate or postgraduate level, and at undergraduate level, more finely grained to the Quality Assurance Agency (QAA) for higher education levels 4, 5 or 6). The module or course leader should provide the assessment criteria, and if you are in any doubt about the criteria, their existence or meaning, they should be your first port of call for enquiry. If assessment-specific criteria are not available for any reason, you should instead use the learning outcomes for the module which can usually be found in the unit or module specification documentation. If that documentation is not available, you are advised to use the QAA's Law Subject Benchmark statement and make a judgment on the students' work using the benchmark as the yardstick.

Marking student-written work

Sit comfortably in a well-lit and well-ventilated space, and try to ensure minimum distractions. Make sure you are confident about what the question is asking, and the contents of the model/outline/suggested answer. If you are part of a topic/unit/module team a pre-marking or standardisation meeting can be useful to discuss strategies for assessment and dealing with common and foreseeable mistakes. Agreeing the characteristics of a typical 2:1 or 2:2 answer helps the tutor who is marking reach a decision more quickly and helps ensure a degree of consistency across the team which can be validated during the post-marking moderation processes.

The author of this chapter has some marking habits that seem to make the marking process less painful, such as setting a target of four coursework or full exam scripts to be done before a quick chocolate break, or ten before a good weed in the garden (breaks from marking should really involve moving, and not sitting and watching the TV or answering emails on a computer screen or even reading a book. During the summer exam period, I spring clean my whole house, including the skirting boards and the vegetable drawer of the fridge). There is no right or wrong way to mark. It is a personal torture. When I am marking exams, I tend to do all the popular answers (e.g. the non-fatal offences against the persons/consent question in criminal law) first and I mark that answer for the whole cohort so I can try to achieve consistency in my judgment about level and content. As I move through the questions to the least popular (joint enterprise), there is relatively speaking less to do and the light at the end of the tunnel is now visible. Whenever I feel my concentration levels have dropped so low I cannot tell the difference between this answer and the one before, I stop marking and have a walk or do some yoga until my mind is clear enough to give the credit due to this student's effort and achievement. I never have music playing in the background because for me it is a distraction and does not help me focus (I am more likely to conduct the orchestra or have a dance than focus on marking). I have certain annotation habits too: a tick for a very good point, a squiggle in the margin for an irrelevance, a question mark for an unclear point and an insertion triangle for an undeveloped point. I make fewer comments on exam answers than coursework as the former are less likely to be seen and read by students than the latter, and in the event that a student seeks feedback on the former, I talk the student through my thinking in person.

There are inevitably doubts in tutors' minds about levels and fairness in making judgements against criteria. As an experienced marker and examiner I would say that every marker has those doubts and they are normal; but being consistent in your marking is more important than any other factor when it comes to the post-marking moderation process (marks can be increased or decreased across your cohort to bring you into line if you are consistently too harsh or too generous but if you are out of line and inconsistent, the only solution is to remark the whole cohort). Don't be fooled by the number of case names that the student cites; it is what they do with the authorities which counts. Are they applying valid law from an authoritative source? Quality not quantity.

Assessing oral performances

Presentations and moots are now a common method of assessment, and a good thing too, to have law students showcase their oral abilities. Assessing oral presentations and moots is tiring because of the high levels of concentration needed and, unlike the weeding or the fridge cleaning, fewer opportunities arise for a break. The advantage though is, if you are sufficiently organised and quick at taking legible notes, the assessing is done and finished during the presentation (bar perhaps a bit of tidying up) and there is little, if anything, to take back to your desk. The assessment criteria should, as with the written assessment, be published in advance and, for moots, the rules on content and etiquette should be well known to students in advance. The main difference between the written work and the oral presentation is that judicial/assessor questions and interventions are expected in the latter and can work to the student's advantage if they are able to listen and respond well. This gives them an opportunity to clarify and improve an answer given previously or in writing in a skeleton argument. Tutors should be aware of their responsibility to ask students questions that give them another opportunity to improve and perform to the best of their ability.

The key messages for Meg and other academics embarking on marking:

1. Marking can be frustrating but it is also rewarding and an important part of our work.
2. Make sure you are clear about the marking criteria and how they are to be applied.
3. Set yourself targets to help you stay focused.
4. Pre and post-marking meetings with module teams (or colleagues if there is no team) can help ensure consistency.

FURTHER READING

JOURNALS

Bennett, M. (2010) Assessment to Promote Learning, *The Law Teacher: The International Journal of Legal Education*, 34(2), 167–174.

Wallace, C. J. (2010) Using Oral Assessment in Law: Opportunities and Challenges, *The Law Teacher: The International Journal of Legal Education*, 44(3), 365–377.

WEBSITES

Archived UKCLE Resources on Assessment and Feedback. http://www.webarchive.org.uk/wayback/archive/20130109231023/http://www.ukcle.ac.uk/resources/assessment-and-feedback/

CHAPTER 4

Gender Issues in Teaching and Learning – Difficult Situations with Students

RACHEL ANNE FENTON

> Meg has now been teaching for a few weeks, and is concerned that some students are not taking her as seriously as she would like. She is now reflecting upon how gender may be playing a part and shaping the learning and teaching experience.

Gender may create difficult situations with students in teaching and learning in several different ways. Female academics, particularly young female academics, may face reluctance, resistance and even hostility (Farley 1996, 341) to their role as law teacher on the part of, mostly, male students but sometimes also female students. The combination of perceptions of law as a discipline as being rational, objective and neutral, opposite to characteristics or values commonly associated with women (Farley 1996; Wells 2002) and assumptions that attribute authority and power to males in society may lead to women law teachers being perceived as less authoritative and less competent than their male counterparts. This will vary between institutions, teaching teams and cohorts of students and may be more pronounced when students come from a culture where women are regarded as subservient or inferior. Gender bias may manifest itself in direct challenges to authority in terms of questioning knowledge, creating a '"prove-it" class dynamic' (Farley 1996) and in classroom disruption. Gender expectations and undermining of women law teachers' credibility may also be manifested in more subtle ways such as through student feedback. Farley's research demonstrates that women receive less positive feedback than men, and that that feedback is gendered (for example, a male who speaks too fast is evidencing his superior intellect, a female speaks too fast because she is nervous). Different language is used about men and women: women are praised for their approachability, accessibility, being nurturing and caring but are criticised when they do not conform to these gendered expectations, whereas men are praised for their subject mastery and knowledge. Women receive personal comments about their appearance and personal advice, men do not (Farley 1996, 336–343). Farley's research may date back almost two decades but her findings are without doubt similar to the experiences of women law teachers today.

The gendered expectations of students that women academics are nurturing and caring may lead women to be overly approachable in their concern not to be criticised and to be popular and liked. Students with pastoral as well as academic issues are more likely to gravitate towards accessible women and as women get older, possibly the more 'motherly' women within a department. The knock-on effects will be on workload and time management as well as the way 'nurturing' female academics are perceived negatively by other, predominantly male academics, perhaps particularly in research-focused institutions, where being student-friendly and being a good researcher might be seen as mutually exclusive. Additional unsought pastoral duties are unlikely to be recognised formally (cf. Wells 2002, 124) and might lead to females being given more time-onerous modules to teach such as core first year modules where student numbers are highest and students can be the most demanding.

In terms of class disruption, the best way to deal with it is to adopt a firm stance and stick to it: if students are not listening, refuse to speak until they are. Do not be afraid to wait – most students will begin to 'shush' others. You can warn disruptive students in the break or at the end, privately and non-confrontationally, that if their behaviour carries on they will be asked to leave future classes, but be prepared to follow through. Check your student conduct policy and ask your line manager for support should you need to resort to asking students to leave. If you are being constantly questioned by a student (as a form of disruption) in a large group lecture, one way to deal with it is to make it clear you have a lot of material to get through and you will take questions at the end. In small seminar groups you can ask a problematic student difficult questions. It is crucial to always remember that you know more than they do. Although it might feel counterintuitive, do not be too friendly and do not divulge personal information – in short, do nothing that might make you appear a 'soft touch'. Try to maintain a professional detachment. It is unfortunately necessary to mention appearance. We judge others by their appearance. The business suit carries a presumption of authority, particularly on men. Whilst wearing a suit or other professional dress will not change anything you say, it can influence how what you say is received (cf Farley 1996, 343–347). Pay attention to how other female academics and senior female managers in your department dress. All these constraints will ease as your career progresses, as you become more established you will gain in confidence and authority.

Many women will internalise and personalise any less than positive feedback. If the feedback is gendered and you recognise it as such, you can de-personalise it. If you talk to other women, both in your peer group and of more senior status, you will find that you are not alone and most will have experienced similar feedback; it will be patterned.

A good way to manage time and workload is to keep strict office hours for students and make it clear that students must email for an appointment and not just drop by. If the issue is not academic but personal then refer them on to your wellbeing services, it is not your job to provide this type of care. This advice may seem harsh but is crucial for self-preservation, particularly as all academics in all institutions are facing increasing demands on their time.

You may also encounter difficult situations where gender issues manifest in class between students: it is not uncommon for male students to try to dominate discussion and sometimes to talk over female students or belittle them. You can ensure an equal environment by enforcing a 'respect and listen to all' rule and foster an understanding that students cannot expect that their opinions are the only ones to be heard. You can also encourage women to speak more in small groups where they may speak less. Recent student surveys also reveal high levels of sexual harassment in universities: be aware of your institution's policy and reporting strategy.

Another area that is potentially problematic is teaching issues about gender. That women are perceived as lacking objectivity, having an agenda and are criticised for over-emphasising feminist issues (even when they do not) (Farley 1996), makes teaching gender issues perhaps doubly problematic for women. Women law teachers are likely to face hostility and/or resistance to any teaching remotely identifiable with feminism, gender equality and patriarchy as male students are likely to perceive it as antagonistic and blaming of men (Fenton et al. 2014). This is less likely to be a problem where you teach a specialist module that students choose to do in the knowledge that gender is critically explored, but may well be problematic if you seek to teach, for example, a feminist analysis in large group teaching on core modules. Research and focus groups with students conducted in preparing the Intervention Initiative revealed that gender issues need to be dealt with 'softly', without using feminist language, by reassuring male students that they are not being blamed, by encouraging empathy and by taking an inclusive approach that empowers and engages men to think about changing gender issues (Fenton et al. 2014). It is a good idea to prepare answers to difficult questions that you anticipate. If you are talking about particularly sensitive issues such as sexual offences or domestic abuse then be aware that you might be disclosed to and check your institutional policies in advance.

The key messages for Meg and other academics reflecting on gender issues in the classroom:

1. Be firm and stand your ground in class and look for support from colleagues and your managers.
2. Do not take on unrecognised pastoral care and be strict about time managing pastoral duties.
3. Think very carefully about how you structure and deliver teaching about gender issues in order to counter resistance and hostility.

FURTHER READING

JOURNALS

Farley, C. H. (1996) Confronting Expectations: Women in the Legal Academy, *Yale J. L. & Feminism*, 8, 333–358.

Wells, C. (2001) Working Out Women in Law Schools, *L. S.*, 21(1), 116–136.

WEBSITE

Fenton, R. A., Mott, H. L., McCartan, K. and Rumney, P. (2014) *The Intervention Initiative*, Bristol: UWE and Public Health England. www.uwe.ac.uk/bl/research/InterventionInitiative in particular, see the Theoretical Rationale.

CHAPTER 5

Research and Scholarship

RICHARD MULLENDER

> Meg is expected to carry out scholarship and research and has a time allocation for both. She is therefore trying to understand what exactly the differences are so that she can meet expectations.

Scholarship and research involve the use and refinement of skills that academic lawyers acquire and develop as students. Scholars and researchers seek to acquire knowledge: for example, knowledge of a particular area of law. Likewise, they engage in analysis of the knowledge they acquire and, in this way, seek to advance understanding. This might involve, for example, identifying a pattern of development in the law. While scholars and researchers often use the same skills, they do so with different aims. Scholars seek to demonstrate a clear grasp of the field they are surveying. This may lead them to describe relevant law (e.g., a statute or a decision of the Supreme Court) in fine-grained detail. This emphasis on detail may reflect the scholar's desire to provide others with guidance on the law. Researchers generally have more particular aims. For example, they may be seeking to bring a problem, in a particular legal field, into focus. This might be a feature of the law that is giving rise to injustice. Where a researcher succeeds in alerting others to such a problem, he or she may also seek to propose a solution. This may result in the researcher making a contribution to debate that is original and that could, if acted on by law-makers, have significant social impact.

While scholarship and research have different aims, the second of these activities often grows spontaneously out of the first. A legal academic who is surveying a particular field with the aim of identifying its main features is undertaking a scholarly task. But it may, very rapidly, turn into a research project. Consider a legal academic who is seeking to offer a clear account of the protections that English law provides against harassment or bullying in the workplace. This will involve description of the protected characteristics (including race, religion, sex and sexual orientation) on which an individual may seek legal redress. So far, this looks like a straightforward instance of scholarship. But our imagined academic may reflect on the way in which protected characteristics limit the scope of the law relating to harassment or bullying in the workplace. While recognising that each of these characteristics picks out a ground on which people suffer invidious discrimination, the academic may think that the existing law offers inadequate protection against harassment or bullying. At this point an issue – differential treatment of the victims of harassment or bullying – comes into view. And issues (e.g., matters of pressing practical concern) are the stuff of research projects. Moreover, issues often prompt those who research them to make responses built around a clear theme: an organising idea that focuses a researcher's efforts. This theme might be the relevance of particular concepts to the process of law reform in a particular context. This is something that our imagined academic could do by arguing that harassment or bullying on grounds other than existing protected characteristics is often harmful and, as such, a threat to personal autonomy. Such behaviour could, for example, make it extremely difficult for the victim to pursue his or her freely chosen career and in this way undercut autonomy. From here it is a short step to the conclusion that the law is unduly narrow and, as such, a source of injustice.

The researcher who pursues a particular theme may (having brought his or her research project to completion) continue to reflect on its implications in ways that lead on to more work in the same field. The career of the legal philosopher Ronald Dworkin shows just this sort of thing happening. Early in his career, Dworkin pursued the theme that a legal system is not simply a body of rules. He argued that principles (general guides to morally sound action) are also a prominent feature of legal systems such as those in the USA and the UK (Dworkin 1977). Having worked up a highly influential argument in support of this view, Dworkin went on to pursue a number of related themes. He argued judges who seek to act in accordance with principle must render decisions that show equal respect and concern for all people affected by the law's operations. Dworkin later argued that this approach to judging shows the law (as it operates in the USA) to be an expression of 'community' (Guest 2013). These later contributions to debate illustrate how a well-chosen theme may give a researcher's career a definite trajectory (with later projects growing out of earlier ones). In Dworkin's case, this happened because he made a sustained effort to think through the implications of his original argument concerning principles.

Dworkin's contributions to debate throw light on another consideration relevant to scholarship and research. This is the range of perspectives that scholars and researchers may adopt when doing their work. When working up his account of principles, Dworkin analysed law from the internal point of view. People who take this view of law treat it as a legitimate institution. However, they also adopt a critical, reflective attitude towards the obligations it imposes and claims concerning its nature (Hart 2012). This internal point of view is the one that legal scholars typically adopt. Likewise, it is standpoint adopted by many legal researchers: for example, academic tort lawyers who seek to explain the incremental development of this branch of private law. However, many legal researchers make use of standpoints outside the law. A researcher might, for example, analyse the law from an economic standpoint and draw the conclusion that it operates inefficiently. Moreover, he or she might also conclude that the law's inefficiencies arise from its commitment to the pursuit of justice. Here, we can see how interdisciplinary research (legal and economic in this case) may enable a researcher to gain understanding of tensions within the law.

Examination of the law from a range of standpoints brings into focus the intensity of research as an activity. The same sort of intensity is apparent when researchers seek to make thematic responses to the issues that they identify as important. While intensity is a prominent aspect of research, it is usually a less obvious feature of scholarship. This reflects the fact that the set of tasks performed by researchers is broader than that undertaken by scholars. Accurate description and illuminating analysis feature prominently in the work of scholars. While researchers have to describe and analyse law and other relevant considerations, their work also involves a great deal of criticism and argument (for example, a proposal for reform of the law). This means that researchers must make difficult editorial decisions. Extended description, for example, may deflect a researcher's attention from those activities (criticism and argument) that could yield an original and/or socially impactful contribution to debate.

Because of its intensity, research may give rise to a danger that is less acute for scholars. In their efforts to bring an issue into focus or to pursue a powerful theme, researchers may lose sight of considerations relevant to their work: for example, an analysis that casts doubt on their own work. When this happens, the researcher may have fallen prey to the problem of confirmation bias: the tendency to filter out any information that contradicts the view he or she holds (Dobelli 2013). This is a danger to which the overlap between research and scholarship is relevant. Like the scholar, the researcher wants to get things right: most obviously an accurate account of the law and comment on it. This means that he or she must pay close attention to the legal sources and analyses relevant to his or her work. As a result of this attention to relevant detail, the researcher may have to stake out a more modest or tentative position than he or she had in mind when beginning the project. Researchers who go about their business in this measured way demonstrate a commitment to accuracy and honesty that they share with scholars.

Finally, it is worth considering not just the aims and activities that shape scholarship and research but also the mental abilities that they involve. Scholars and researchers spend a great deal of time interpreting particular objects: for example, cases, legal practices and academic contributions to debate. Here, they make use of the human brain's ability to deliver a highly focused beam of attention that enables them to invest the objects they examine with meaning. Alongside, this ability we should set a less-well understood but important capacity that features in the work of scholars and researchers. This capacity is apparent in what a number of commentators call 'aha!' moments (Irvine 2015; McGilchrist 2009). In such a moment, a person may grasp how to impose order on considerations that had seemed to be in a state of disarray. Likewise, he or she may see the outlines of a solution to a practical problem. Legal scholars experience 'aha!' moments when, for example, they identify ways in which to offer a clear explanation of an area of law that is apt to cause confusion. Legal researchers have the same sensation when, for example, they identify a discipline other than law as relevant to a reform agenda. Breakthroughs such as these typically take scholars and researchers by surprise. As a result, the insights that race through their minds may slip rapidly from view. For this reason, many scholars and researchers make a note of new – and often not fully formed – insights as soon as they come into possession of them. This makes it possible for them to bring them into focus and to explore their implications. This is worth doing. The results may take a variety of forms: for example, a more sophisticated analysis of the relevant field, a crisper account of the issue under scrutiny, or the pursuit of a novel theme.

> The key messages for Meg and other academics thinking about research and scholarship:
>
> 1. Research and scholarship are not entirely distinct activities and one may lead to the other.
> 2. Scholarship provides an overview of an existing area whereas research offers new insights.
> 3. It is OK to note down ideas which are not yet fully formed and it is also not uncommon for academics to develop their ideas and argument on an issue over their entire career.

FURTHER READING

BOOKS

Dobelli, R. (2013) *The Art of Thinking Clearly*, London: Hodder & Stoughton, 23–25.

Dworkin, R. (1977) *Taking Rights Seriously*, London: Duckworth, 180–183 and 272–278.

Guest, S. (2013) *Ronald Dworkin*, Stanford, CA: Stanford University Press, chapters 1 and 6.

Hart, H. L. A. (2012) *The Concept of Law*, Oxford: Clarendon Press, 3rd edn, 56–57 and 88–90.

Irvine, W. B. (2015) *Aha! The Moments of Insight that Shape the World*, New York: Oxford University Press.

McGilchrist, I. (2009) *The Master and His Emissary: The Divided Brain and the Making of the Western World*, New Haven, CT: Yale University Press, chapter 2.

CHAPTER 6

Designing Research

MATTHEW WEAIT

> Meg now has an idea of what she would like to do in research terms, and is designing her first research project.

There are many different sources of inspiration for designing a research project; but among them a passionate and enduring interest in the subject matter is the most important. Without this, designing the project and completing it will be harder work than it needs to be. A good place to begin, then, is to reflect on your interests – not just your area(s) of legal expertise (though these will be important as a foundation), but your ethical, political, social and other interests. What really matters to you? What provokes you, or makes you angry? Where do you see injustice and a need for legal change or reform? Are there things you have read where you think: 'That can't be right', 'I really don't agree', or 'it's just not like that'? Such responses may arise from a political, or moral stance, or from professional experience; but each is a potential trigger for a research project that will be exciting both to design and to do, and to which you are more likely to be committed and find time for among your other obligations. Having identified an area for a potential research project, it is useful to summarise the central question(s) that you think need answering, the issues that need clarifying, and any deficiencies/errors that you perceive existing based on your experience or in what you have read. At this stage, these can be very general – they will be refined later when you come to the nitty gritty of design.

The next stage is to conduct a more in-depth literature survey. The literature review is critical. As an academic researcher you are a member of a scholarly and research community, and although it's possible that the questions you feel need addressing have never been engaged with before, the chances of this are slim. It is far more likely that your project will contribute to and complement an existing body of research. As you go through the literature, using online research databases and other reliable resources and concentrating where possible on research published in peer-reviewed publications, do not just note the findings and conclusions: make a note of the formulation of the research question (how does it differ from the way you would frame it and why?), the methods that the researcher has used to answer it (are they quantitative or qualitative or both?), the jurisdiction(s) in which the research has been undertaken and the literature to which the author refers. Each of these will be a valuable resource when it comes to finalising your design and making it as robust (and potentially fundable) as possible. As you make notes on what has already been explored and discussed by others, refer back regularly to your own general questions and, if necessary, refine, adapt (or, sometimes, abandon) them. This will ensure that what you propose to do will add constructively and/or critically to the literature rather than merely repeat what has been well established. Identify, too, research skills that you may already have, and ones which you may need to gain or develop.

Once you have completed your literature survey, you are in a position to formulate your design proper. At this stage you need to answer the following question before going further: is my research project a 'what' project or a 'why' one? In other words, is your focus on providing an account of a problem or a situation, or on explaining why the problem exists? An empirical research example of the former might be 'Do former legal practitioners find research more difficult?', and of the latter, 'Why do former legal practitioners find research more difficult?'. Doctrinal examples could be 'Does case law protect academics who are asylum seekers more than non-academics?' and 'Why does case law … (etc.)'. It should be obvious that the latter question can only be asked if the former is answered in the affirmative, and that 'what' research is often just as important as 'why'. Indeed, as a first research project, a 'what' one has the significant advantage of enabling you to explore an area of interest and to generate questions and hypotheses which you can test subsequently in 'why' research. (If you are only interested in pursuing a 'why' project, you will have to be very sure, based on your literature review, that the question you are asking is warranted.) A second advantage of a 'what' project is that it enables you to mark out your distinctive research territory. In a crowded research arena, one of the most valuable things you can do is to identify a new and original area (and/or a new approach to studying it), and to begin to develop a unique expertise. This will not only improve the chances of publication, but of external funding. (Funding for 'why' research is far more likely if you have a track record of publication and expertise in the 'what' of your subject.) Whichever kind of project you propose to do, it is important that you identify its significance and potential impact. Why is it important to engage with this issue/these questions? What will my research contribute (to scholarship, to policy, to teaching and training, etc.)? Many funders, whether your institution or an external grant-making body, will expect clear engagement with, and critical reflection on, the 'value' of your research to stakeholders and potential users – and the impact element of the Research Excellence Framework is making this more important than ever.

Now that you have decided on your topic and whether it is a 'what' or a 'why' one, you need to identify the research methods you will employ. If your project is empirical or socio-legal you should not decide on these unless and until you have studied relevant literature and practical 'how to' guides. The subject matter of your project, and the question(s) you hope to answer, will determine whether you use qualitative or quantitative methods (or a mixture) and the wrong choice, or thinking that you know what you are doing when you don't, will be disastrous. It is also advisable to check out what training your institution provides (often this will be for postgraduate students, and often in faculties of social science). If it is offered, try to negotiate time with your line manager to undertake such training. Even if your project is primarily or wholly doctrinal (using case law, legislation, reports, etc.), you will need to give thought to the theoretical or analytical perspective you will be adopting (for example, you may be proposing a feminist, critical race theory, intersectional, or interdisciplinary approach; if so, you will need to ensure that core texts from exploring these perspectives form part of your initial literature review). Finally, be realistic about timeframes. How long do you have? Is there a deadline? What is your timetable like? What are your other responsibilities? Can you limit your teaching obligations so as to leave you with one day free for research? You will probably be overly ambitious about what you can achieve, and it is vital to be as realistic as possible, even if this means limiting the scope of the project. It is far better to complete a small project with a narrow focus, than not to complete a larger one.

Lastly, if your project involves live human subjects you will need to consider ethics; not only because this is important for its own sake but because you will not get funding without getting ethics approval from your home institution (and/or, for some research, from the institution in which you propose to conduct your research). Essentially, the approval process requires reflection on such matters as the potential risks to participants (including you) and how these will be avoided or minimised, the benefits of the research to those being researched, and how you will secure and maintain confidentiality. It is wise to think about the ethical implications of your project from the outset, and to anticipate any concerns which may be levelled against it. As much as your project must be practically doable, it must be ethically defensible.

The key messages for Meg and other academics considering research design (including ethics)

1. Choose a research topic about which you are passionately interested.
2. Ensure that you feel secure in the existing literature and have the requisite research skills before embarking on the design of the project.
3. Be realistic about what you can achieve given the time and resources available to you.

FURTHER READING

BOOKS

Association of Law Teachers Research Ethics Statement. www.lawteacher.ac.uk/ethics.asp

Banakar, R. and Travers, M. (eds) (2005) *Theory and Method in Socio-Legal Research*, Oxford and Portland, OR: Hart Publishing.

Creswell, J. R. (2014) *Research Design: Qualitative, Quantitative, and Mixed Methods Approaches*, Thousand Oaks, CA: Sage Publications.

Van Hoeke, M. (ed.) (2011) *Methodologies of Legal Research: Which Kind of Method for What Kind of Discipline?*, Oxford and Portland, OR: Hart Publishing.

WEBSITES

Genn, H., Partington, M. and Wheeler, S. (2006) *Law in the Real World: Improving Our Understanding of How Law Works*, London: The Nuffield Foundation. www.nuffieldfoundation. org/sites/default/files/Law%20in%20the%20Real%20World%20full%20report.pdf

Socio-Legal Studies Association (2009) Statement of Principles of Ethical Research Practice (January 2009). www.slsa.ac.uk/images/slsadownloads/ethicalstatement/slsa%20ethics%20 statement%20_final_%5B1%5D.pdf

CHAPTER 7

Reference Writing

GARY WATT

> Meg has received several requests for references from her current students.

Even as a quite junior academic you might be called upon to write a great many references, especially if you teach lots of students in small-group contexts and if you are perceived to be friendly and approachable. When you become a more senior academic, especially if you have some impressive sounding official title, you can expect to be approached to write references on that account alone – and for colleagues as well as for students.

The first point I want to make is that writing references can be an exercise of great power. The quality of a reference can be the difference between the candidate securing or failing to secure opportunities for employment and further education. To exercise this power positively in favour of a good student is a real pleasure and privilege. But with great power comes great responsibility. (I think it was Spiderman who taught us that!) Once you have been asked to write a reference it is your responsibility to say promptly whether or not you will consent to write it. If you consent to write the reference it is then your responsibility to write it in a timely fashion and to write a reference that is appropriate. This begs two important questions. First, when will you agree to write a reference? Second, what amounts to an appropriate reference?

The question of your duty to write a reference and your freedom to decline may be determined by your contract of employment. Academics in my department have a small number of students, known as our personal duties, who are entitled to receive a reference from us. In addition to that group of students any other student is free to request a reference from any of us. If I do not have an official duty to write a reference for a student I might still consent to do so if I feel that I know the student well enough and if I believe that I can write positively in their favour. If I do not know the student very well I will sometimes advise them that my reference might be rather bland and factual. I might even advise them to seek a more appropriate referee. I have to say that in more than 20 years as a full-time academic I have only very rarely declined to write a reference when asked.

The question of appropriate content can be vexed. I think the best advice is to consider that any written reference is potentially a public document. At the very least it is a document that might have to be disclosed to a court in the event of, say, a complaint that the reference was negligent or defamatory. It is important that your reference makes clear when you are expressing a fact and when you are expressing an opinion. I have seen something like the following wording used by a firm of solicitors: 'it is our usual practice to give references on a factual basis only and so may not be able to answer all the questions you have asked. This should not reflect on the individual concerned.' I have never taken such a blunt approach, which seems to me to be excessively legalistic, but it makes the point that you should be cautious. The same law firm added a lengthy disclaimer to their reference, including the line 'this reference is given in the strictest confidence and for your use only, in line with the Data Protection Act 1998'. Again, this seems to me to be over-the-top, but it would perhaps be prudent to add a short line to say that the reference is relied upon at the recipient's own risk.

You should not disclose any factual information to a third party unless you are quite sure that the student in question has consented to the disclosure. Of course most students will inform the referee in advance that the third party will be seeking a reference. Whatever facts are disclosed, they must be accurate. For example, the student's academic grades should only be included if they have been checked against the official record. It is also a good idea to check the student file for any indication that the student has special issues or has been in trouble. You owe a duty of care to the recipient of the reference as well as to the student. Another basic element of care is to adhere to the formal demands of the person asking for the reference. If they require the reference by a particular date, you should meet that deadline or inform all parties that you will be unable to do so. If they require certain questions to be answered, you should answer them all or explain why you have been unable to give an answer.

I have developed a practical technique for supplying appropriate references in a timely manner. In brief, it is to enlist the student as a co-writer of the factual elements of their own reference. As soon as a reference has been requested I ask the student to send me a word document addressed to the full name and address of the person requesting the reference and including the deadline for receipt of the reference. I ask the student to include a list of all factual points that they would like me to and personal achievements they would wish me to refer to.

Having received the student's word document with its factual contents it is then down to me to check the facts as far as I can and to express the reference in my own words. If I know the student well and wish to communicate the high regard I have for him or her I will make sure that the document conveys real warm mention, including their complete set of university grades to date. I also ask them to include any personal factors and not just mere facts. I might even sign off with something along the lines of 'I commend Jo to you warmly'. Some issues require an especially sensitive response. Student's medical circumstances or factors of personal hardship should not be disclosed unless the student has expressly authorised their inclusion. This is another good reason for asking the student to send through a draft of the matters that they would expect and want to be covered within the reference. Sometimes the person requesting the reference will ask you to comment upon personal strengths and weaknesses of the candidates, or upon such matters as their reliability and honesty. In response to such questions one should be as factually accurate as one can be, and, within that constraint, as positive as one can be.

Perhaps my advice has seemed a little too cautious or defensive. I would therefore like to conclude by emphasising what a positive experience it can be to write a good reference. The golden rule in reference writing, as in most things, is to do for others as you would have them do for you. After all, each of us is in employment because some kind soul wrote a reference to support us.

> The key messages for Meg and other academics considering reference writing:
>
> 1. To write a reference is a great power that entails a great responsibility.
> 2. To write a reference can be very positive and rewarding for all parties.
> 3. There is a practical burden to reference writing but there are ways to lighten the load.

FURTHER READING

WEBSITES

Pinsent Masons LLP guidance on the law of reference writing out-law.com/en/topics/employment/recruitment/references-how-to-write-them/

University of Dundee guide 'Guidance on Writing References' dundee.ac.uk/hr/policiesprocedures/references/

CHAPTER 8

PhD by Publication

TIM CONNOR

> Meg's institution is keen for all its academic staff to have PhDs. Meg has heard about the possibility of doing a PhD by publication and is thinking about whether this might be a good route for her.

The award of the PhD by publication offers an alternative to the more traditional way of PhD study through a defined programme of research for those who are already published researchers and who can therefore draw on their existing work to satisfy the learning outcomes of a PhD programme.

Many institutions offer a PhD by publication route, some as a general alternative to more traditional PhD programmes, some as a route open to their own employees only. The regulations governing the award of a PhD by publication can vary substantially so it is important that anyone considering this route checks them carefully. In all cases though the published work has to be independent and original and the published pieces taken together must make a distinct contribution to knowledge.

A common first step is the requirement for submission of a thesis title to a research or PhD committee for approval. Once this hurdle is cleared, the published pieces which will form the basis of the submission must be collated. If there are already sufficient published pieces then this is a fairly straightforward task, if not, you need to think carefully about what additional pieces you may need to prepare for publication. Most institutions have detailed guidelines on the material which can be included in a submission but selecting your publications from peer-reviewed journal articles, book chapters or even longer case notes should help ensure that you choose quality publications as the foundation of your submission.

In addition to the published work, the submission must include a submission statement, or linking piece. This typically sets out how the published articles are thematic; its purpose is to uncover a common and recognisable thread which forms the basis of an advancement in knowledge in relation to the particular area under consideration. Again, the requirements for this document vary in length and in style but whatever the requirements are at your particular institution, do not underestimate the time required to write this. The document has to bring the published pieces together, explain how and why they are coherent and/or how one builds on another or how your thinking and arguments have developed. Remember that your examiners will not be as familiar with your work or your area of research as you are and things that may seem obvious to you will need spelling out. A strong linking piece can make your final viva voce examination a much more pleasant experience.

An important part in the process is the appointment of a mentor or supervisor. The mentor fulfils a very similar role to that of a traditional PhD supervisor and offers advice and guidance with respect both to the composition of the submission statement or linking piece and also to the interpretation of the university's regulations as to submission. While a supervisor of a more traditional PhD would help introduce the student to the field and recommend literature as well as guide the student on a research question and methodology, the mentors role here is more that of a critical friend. You are already familiar with the field and aware of the literature and do not need that introduction. Your mentor can and should, however, provide you with guidance on the linking piece and with advice on how best to highlight the strengths of your work. They should also help you navigate the formal process of submission.

In the process of submission for the Degree of Doctor of Philosophy by Published Work a number of other useful documents can often be submitted but it is always worth checking the regulations and seeking guidance as to what is required and what is allowed. The appendices to the submission could for example contain a list of journals/text books which had cited the articles under consideration in order to highlight impact and credibility.

The final stage in the process for the PhD by Publication is the viva voce examination. Normally two examiners are appointed, one internal to the university and the other an external examiner from outside the university. The viva voce examination is conducted on the basis of the candidate's submission statement and the published articles. You should expect the examiners to have read your work carefully and to ask you questions about the work. The format of the viva voce can vary and there is no fixed minimum or maximum time. Questions are likely to be based on the linking piece as the quality of your articles is not usually an issue as they have already undergone scrutiny by peers prior to publication. Questions may also focus on your future research plans and how you will develop your thinking further.

The key points for consideration for Meg or other academics proposing to follow the route of PhD by Publication:

1. The specific regulations of each university with respect to this award may vary. Check the requirements of your university before you start this process.
2. This route to PhD is about you. You must show how your publications contribute and advance further the knowledge and understanding of the area.
3. It is important to remember that the articles under consideration have already been published and are in the public domain. That they are of publishable quality is therefore not an issue – they have already been subject to external review. The examiners' role in this process is therefore different from the traditional PhD. They need to establish that the applicant is author of the articles under review and is fully conversant with the concepts and the arguments contained therein.

FURTHER READING

BOOK

Powell, S. (2004) *The Award of the PhD by Published Work*, Lichfield: UK Council for Graduate Education.

JOURNALS

Park, C. (2005) New Variant PhD: The Changing Nature of the Doctorate in the UK, *Journal of Higher Education Policy and Management*, 27(2), 189–207.

Robins, L. and Kanowski, P. (2008) PhD by Publication: A Student's Perspective, *Journal of Research Practice*, 4(2), Article M3. http://jrp.icaap.org/index.php/jrp/article/view/136/154

CHAPTER 9

Work–Life Balance

RICHARD COLLIER

> Meg has a relatively high teaching load but is expected to deliver research outputs. She is struggling to fully understand and meet the many demands the institution is placing on her. She has one young child at home and is planning for another.

Over the past two decades the idea of work–life balance or reconciliation has moved from being a largely fringe topic, often couched in terms of family-friendly policies, to a position where it is a central feature of political debate about economic productivity, social wellbeing, equality and inclusion. 'Work–life' is commonly seen as referring to any connection between the work and personal domains of an individual, and not just matters of family responsibilities, care and dependency (although these are central to the discussion about the gendered dimensions of debates in the area). Work–life balance involves both structural (e.g. time commitment, geographical location, family size) and psychological dimensions (job/life satisfaction, stress, general health and wellbeing: see elsewhere, this volume). Work–life balance is about people having a measure of control over when, where and how they work, with the underlying assumption being that creating such a balance is what many people, including many legal academics, are looking for.

In the case of the legal profession problems in this area are well documented and work–life balance is now widely seen as a core business issue within legal practice. Addressing the work–life problem in law involves questions, variously, of meeting externally imposed gender equality and diversity agendas; tackling the well-documented 'drift' of women from the law post-qualification; maximising the organisational efficiency of law firms; winning the 'war for talent' and maintaining competiveness. Across national legislation at the interface of work and family and a wide range of EU directives and treaties, meanwhile, the importance of this right to reconcile family and professional life is explicitly recognised in ways that are embedded with the promotion of gender equality. What has all this, however, to do with legal academics?

Mapping directly to the concerns and debates around wellbeing and the changing nature of academic life discussed elsewhere in this book, there would appear to be a growing sense that the marketisation of higher education in the UK has redrawn debates about work–life balance within universities. Noting the traditionally 'open-ended' nature of academic work in terms of working hours, for example, new kinds of organisational commitment have been identified on the part of legal academics, not least amongst early career scholars seeking to establish themselves. Increasingly, it would seem, there is a sense that 'being an academic' is a 24-hour job and at issue in the debates about work–life balance in universities, and with it their law schools, are broader concerns about the increasing pressures many academics at all stages of their careers now face from diverse sources; the demands arising from students, as the consumer/customer of university education; the implications of 24-hour technology and the sense of never being 'away' from work; and, in particular, the intensification of what is now required of legal academics in relation to workloads around research productivity, funding, audit and administration. Each has been seen in the literature as having potential consequences for the work–life balance of contemporary legal academics (see e.g. Collier 2013; Cownie 2004; Thornton 2012).

Yet is the picture more complex? Does academic life not still provide, as Anthony Bradney has put it (2003), possibilities for autonomy and a unity of 'vocation and avocation' unlike many other fields of employment? Set in a wider social context, job security and salary levels for legal academics could be viewed as relatively secure and advantageous. In talking of poor work–life balance in law schools should academics 'get real' and recognise their relative autonomy at work and how fortunate they are, notwithstanding what are undoubtedly the increasing demands placed on them?

One thing seems clear. Across UK universities, as equal opportunities employers wishing to be seen at the forefront of 'best practice', diverse work–life policies and related initiatives have now been established seeking to make the university a more positive working environment (the details of which usually available via websites and/or human resource/equal opportunity offices). It is widely accepted in the HEI sector, for example that work–life balance is desirable not just for individuals and families but also for universities themselves. Many legal academics will be conscious of the need to obtain a good work–life balance (and many may struggle to do so). A more difficult question is what can be done?

In terms of the development of practical policies, the umbrella term work–life balance has come to embrace a wide range of issues; the provision of opportunities for flexible working, including part-time working, staggered and compressed hours; parental, maternal and paternity leave; the establishment of guidelines for home working; career breaks; adoptive leave; better support for working parents and those with caring responsibilities, including leave provision for emergencies; job-sharing and flexible retirement; various other staff benefits (e.g. child-care vouchers) and, in some instances, bereavement leave.

At a personal level, meanwhile, whilst recognising there is no 'one' solution as perceptions of work–life balance will vary between individuals, there are also things the person who feels they may be working too hard, too much or for too long can do; reflect on and try to find your own personal 'balance', prioritising tasks and making adjustments if necessary; take breaks, try and keep a weekend (if not all weekends) free, connect with others and remember that working long hours is not necessarily productive in itself – there is no such thing as 'perfect' and the 'good enough' may be sufficient in many cases; try and draw a line between home and work and establish boundaries between work and non-work; book breaks and holidays; ask for help if difficulties arise and if a formal change in working arrangements is needed consider what may be available in terms of the specific workplace policies outlined above.

In 2008 the Careers Research and Advisory Centre (CRAC) produced a booklet *The Balanced Researcher* (Kearns and Gardiner 2008) detailing a range of practical strategies for busy academics, just one of a plethora of texts now available offering advice on achieving a good work–life balance. Certainly, notwithstanding well-documented challenges and frustrations, it is important to not lose sight of the pleasures and rewards of life as a legal academic. At the same time, a body of work suggests changes in universities are throwing up new questions about the boundaries between work and life. In such a context it is likely that this debate around work–life balance in universities may be of increasing significance in years to come.

The key messages for Meg and other academics considering work–life balance issues:

1. Maintain boundaries between work and life, whether through establishing clear divisions between work and home or else seeking to integrate work with other activities in the course of the day.
2. Take control of technology and '24-hour' communication, which can mean we are never truly 'away' from work.
3. There is more to life than work; do things that make you happy (and, of course, just take holidays where available).

FURTHER READING

BOOKS

Bradney, A. (2003) *Conversations, Choices and Chances: The Liberal Law School in the Twenty-First Century*, Oxford: Hart Publishing.

Cownie, F. (2004) *Legal Academics: Culture and Identities*, Oxford: Hart Publishing.

Kearns, H. and Gardiner, G. (2008) *The Balanced Researcher*, CRAC/Vitae. https://www.vitae.ac.uk/vitae-publications/guides-briefings-and-information/balanced-researcher-vitae-june-2008.pdf

Thornton, M. (2012) *Privatizing the Public University: The Case of Law*, Abingdon: Glass-House Press.

JOURNAL

Collier, R. (2013) Privatizing the University and the New Political Economy of Socio-Legal Studies: Remaking the (Legal) Academic Subject, *Journal of Law and Society*, 40(3), 450–467.

CHAPTER 10

Wellbeing

RICHARD COLLIER

> Meg is feeling increasingly stressed due to the many, growing, and competing demands upon her time.

Wellbeing has become the subject of increasing interest and concern in recent years both in the media and on the part of politicians, employers and health care professionals alike. Notwithstanding that the meaning of the term is often ill-defined, the legal profession and higher education institutions (HEIs) have also begun to pay attention to wellbeing. In the case of legal practice, there is a pressing background to this. A rich body of international research suggests significant problems can exist in this area for many legal professionals (e.g. Kelk et al. 2009; Law Society 2012), with some evidence, for example, of the high propensity of legal professionals, and City workers especially, to use alcohol or other drugs to reduce or manage symptomatology associated with poor wellbeing. In a now rich international literature concerned with the 'unhappy lawyer' (Seligman et al. 2005) the argument, importantly, is not that lawyers are somehow genetically predisposed to poor wellbeing, whatever the cohort attributes of those who enter the law. Rather, there may be something *about* the cultures of law and professional practice – including 'what goes on' in university law schools and legal education – that, for some at least, can exacerbate problems in this area.

What has all this to do with legal academics? The wellbeing agenda is more advanced in legal practice than the legal academy precisely because problems in the former are resonant and well documented. This does not mean, however, that questions about wellbeing in the workplace relating to physical and psychological health (including issues of, for example, managing stress, anxiety and depression) are not of considerable concern to legal academics at all stages of their careers. Within universities generally some studies point to high levels of poor subjective wellbeing in UK HEIs. There has, certainly, been an explosion of discussion around wellbeing recently within academic Blogs, articles and at a wide range of academic events (see further Collier 2014). If its self-selecting methodology should be treated with caution, the 2014 *Guardian Academic Health Survey* suggests negative stress in working lives is common in universities, with around one third of academics having taken time off over the previous 12 months due to ill-health, and 17% reporting 'severe' or 'extreme' levels of stress at work (Shaw 2014). Other accounts suggest there are social and psychological

risks and stresses associated with the rise of 'new academia' and the growing marketisation of universities (Anonymous 2014; Gill 2009; Sparkes 2007; Thornton 2012).

In this work, two themes tend to recur. First, structural and cultural changes transforming the landscape of higher education are seen to have resulted in new pressures
and demands, not just on the part of law students (positioned as customers/consum-
ers of the law degree) but also university legal academics. Related issues concern poor
work–life balance (see further this book) and long hours in academia; the need to
perpetually 'perform' to a requisite level, whether in terms of research outputs, securing funding, teaching satisfaction levels and so forth; the impact at a personal level of
a myriad of processes of audit and 'metrication' (Burrows 2012) and the highly competitive nature of universities, the demise of collegiality and, more generally, a growing
individualisation.

Second, and turning to the discipline of law itself, studies have focused on the
connections between particular aspects of conventional legal education and practical
training programs in law and poor wellbeing (with, in some accounts, levels of psychological distress identified in the law school cohort from point of entry). This is seen
as raising questions about how law students are (or are not) encouraged in personal
and interpersonal skills in their legal education around, for example, self-reflexivity,
communication and self-awareness. The very traditions of legal education and cognitive skills of 'thinking like a lawyer' have been seen to have a personal impact, sitting
uneasily with the everyday demands of work for those who enter professional legal
practice.

Caution is needed in approaching this topic. Features associated with poor wellbeing,
such as experiences of low mood, anxiety disorders, insomnia and other depressive-
associated symptoms, are the product not of one unitary factor but of complex, and
often unpredictable, interplay of the personal and structural: of, for example, life course
events, illness, genetic disposition and lifestyle. Each can potentially 'come together' at
moments in life to foster problems for individuals. Poor wellbeing, in the sense of an
association with emotional and mental health broadly defined, is itself, like depression,
a trans-historical and cross-cultural phenomenon. Further, far from depicting universities and their law schools as beset with insecurities and anxieties, a case can be made
not only that the discipline of law has fared and will fare well with any new academic
marketplace, but also that workplace contentment in law itself remains generally high
(Bradney 2003).

Nonetheless, it is clear that wellbeing, at a time of rapid change and uncertainty in
universities, is now receiving increasing attention. There are reasons why legal academics should also remain vigilant to issues relating to wellbeing as the demands of their
work change and the contexts in which legal academic labour takes place are reshaped.
Poor academic wellbeing has significant consequences, most obviously, for the individuals concerned. It is also a matter for university law schools in terms of human
resources and retaining talent. Wellbeing, in the way these discussions raise questions
about the cultures and practices of the academic workplace, is also a topic central to, if
often unspoken of in, wider debates around work-life balance and equality and diversity in legal academia discussed elsewhere in this book.

Causes of stress amongst law students are well documented; the balance of study
with other commitments, the amount of study required, finding a job on graduation,
personal financial situation and, of course, just trying to get good marks. Universities

take these issues profoundly seriously, with extensive networks of dedicated welfare support in place. Importantly, there are signs also of a 'ratcheting up' of provision and support for academic staff around these questions of wellbeing, and across the HEI sector there appears a concern to tackle problems in this area and promote wellbeing and mental/physical health awareness amongst staff as well as students. Universities are seeing, for example, a growing focus on the potential of 'mindfulness', seeking to foster and encourage better mental and physical health in the academic workplace (e.g. via 'stress awareness weeks', staff development and management workshops on stress and mental health awareness and a range of workplace health related initiatives).

These should not be seen as 'side issues' for legal academics. The overworked, unhappy, but financially successful lawyer is a familiar image. Yet as academia changes in far reaching ways, and as the cultures of the university increasingly resemble those of the business world, it is important to consider what these questions of wellbeing in law can tell us about the contexts in which academic labour is undertaken and the various pressures legal academics experience at different stages of their career and life course. The recent greater focus on wellbeing both in the legal profession and legal education is to be welcomed in helping academics at all stages of their career better understand and cope with these pressures.

> The key messages for Meg and other academics considering their wellbeing and that of their colleagues and students:
>
> 1. Seek support and advice if you feel you are experiencing difficulty; do not struggle in silence.
> 2. Difficulties relating to poor wellbeing in universities are more common than they may appear (you are not alone).
> 3. Remember – there is more to life than work (see elsewhere this volume).

FURTHER READING

BOOKS

Bradney, A. (2003) *Conversations, Choices and Chances: The Liberal Law School in the Twenty-First Century*, Oxford: Hart Publishing.

Gill, R. (2009) Breaking the Silence: The Hidden Injuries of the Neoliberal University, in R. Flood and R. Gill (eds) *Secrecy and Silence in the Research Process: Feminist Reflections*, Abingdon: Routledge.

Kelk, N. et al. (2009) *Courting the Blues: Attitudes towards Depression in Australian Law Students and Lawyers*, Brain and Mind Research Institute/University of Sydney.

Law Society (2012) *Health and Wellbeing: The Law Society's PC Holder Survey*, Law Society.

Thornton, M. (2012) *Privatizing the Public University: The Case of Law*, GlassHouse Press, Abingdon: Routledge.

JOURNALS

Burrows, R. (2012) Living with the H-index: Metric Assemblages in the Contemporary Academy, *Sociological Review*, 60(2), 355, 358.

Collier, R. (2014) 'Love Law, Love Life': Neoliberalism, Wellbeing and Gender in the Legal Profession – The Case of Law School, *Legal Ethics*, 17(2), 202–230.

Seligman. M, PR Verkuil, TH Kang (2005) Why Lawyers are Unhappy, *Deakin Law Review*, 10(1), 49.

Sparkes, A. (2007) Embodiment, Academics and the Audit Culture: A Story Seeking Consideration, *Qualitative Research*, 7(4), 521–550.

WEBSITES

Anonymous Academic (2014) There is a Culture of Acceptance Around Mental Health Issues in Academia, *The Guardian Higher Education Network*. http://www.theguardian.com/higher-education-network/blog/2014/mar/01/mental-health-issue-phd-research-university

Lawcare, lawcare.org.uk/

Shaw, A. (2014) Overworked and Isolated – Work Pressure Fuels Mental Illness in Academia, *TheGuardian*, 8 May 2014. http://www.theguardian.com/higher-education-network/blog/2014/may/08/work-pressure-fuels-academic-mental-illness-guardian-study-health

Wellness for law. wellnessforlaw.com/

CHAPTER 11

Managing Maternity, Paternity and Parental Leave

HELEN STALFORD

> Meg is pregnant and is looking for advice on maternity and parental leave.

Legal academics' entitlement to maternity, paternity and parental leave is supported by a fairly robust legal framework, derived largely from the UK's obligations under EU equality legislation (JSWFL 2015). In addition, it is fair to say that legal academia is more accommodating than many academic disciplines (and certainly the sciences) of periods of leave connected to parenting. But that does not mean it is not without its challenges.

The legal and policy framework governing the rights of pregnant women and new parents comprises a blend of paid and unpaid maternity, paternity, parental and shared parental leave, all subject to minimum eligibility requirements which may differ again from one HEI to another. By way of summary: all pregnant employees have the right to a maximum period of 52 weeks maternity leave (comprised of 26 weeks ordinary maternity leave plus 26 weeks of additional maternity leave). Pregnant employees can also request reasonable time off with full pay for antenatal care. Maternity leave is paid through a mixture of contractual maternity pay, maternity allowance or statutory maternity pay for at least 39 weeks (depending on the individual circumstances of the woman so you should check this carefully) and individuals can claim up to ten keeping in touch days (at full pay or time off in lieu) during the period of leave. The translation of this entitlement into university policy differs between HEIs; some are more generous than the statutory minimum, but most pay full salary for at least the first eight weeks of maternity leave.

Paternity leave is rather less generous. It is available to employees who have or expect to have responsibility for the child's upbringing, are the biological father of the child or the mother's husband or partner (including same sex relationships). It is generally limited to those who have worked continuously for their employer for 26 weeks ending with the 15th week before the baby is due although some universities do not impose such restrictions. Staff may take up to a minimum of two working weeks ordinary paternity leave (OPL) at full pay. Additional paternity leave is also available for a maximum period of 26 weeks to men whose partner returns to work before the end of their maternity (or adoption) leave or pay period (but no earlier than 20 weeks after the child's birth or adoption). There are few HEIs that offer more generous entitlement than the minimum two-week OPL, but that is all set to change since the introduction of Shared Parental Leave (The Shared Parental Leave and Leave Curtailment (Amendment) Regulations 2015). This is aimed at facilitating a more equal distribution of care responsibilities (and opportunities) between men and women and should offset the limitations of the restrictive paternity leave entitlement.

Shared Parental Leave came into force on 5 April 2015 to enable eligible mothers, fathers, partners and adopters to choose how to share time off work in the first year following the birth or adoption of their child. This right applies specifically to parents whose baby is due to be born or placed for adoption on or after 5 April 2015. A parent will only qualify to take Shared Parental Leave if the other parent meets basic work and earnings criteria and the parent taking the leave meets the individual eligibility criteria (such as having 26 weeks' continuous service at the 15th week before the due date and remaining in the same employment). In terms of pay, aside from an initial compulsory two weeks of maternity leave for the mother, up to 50 weeks of leave and 37 weeks of pay can be shared between parents. Significantly, Shared Parental Leave can be taken in one block, or split into blocks with periods of work in between, and, unlike other schemes, parents can take leave simultaneously.

Importantly, for both mothers and fathers, all contractual benefits with the exception of pay will continue to accrue during the whole period of parental, maternity, paternity and shared parental leave (including annual leave entitlement and employers' pension contributions).

The maternity and paternity leave provisions are also complemented by parental leave and flexible working entitlement which are available for parents with children up until they reach the age of 18. Parental leave (not to be confused with Shared Parental Leave) entitles all employees who have completed one year's service with an employer to 18 weeks unpaid parental leave for each child born or adopted. The leave can start once the child is born or placed for adoption, or as soon as the employee has completed a year's service, whichever is later. Employees can take it at any time up to the child's 18th birthday. In the same vein, extensions to the right to request flexible working came into force on 30 June 2014. Initially, this was restricted to employees who had parental responsibility for a child under six years old (or under 18 if the child had a disability – Part 8A Employment Rights Act 1996). Since then, the right has been extended to include a wider circle of carers who are responsible for any child under the age of 18 (Work and Families Act 2006, s.12). The right enables those who have worked continuously for their employer for at least six months to request a change in their hours of work, times of work or place of work (Atkinson 2014).

Of course, legal entitlement is one thing; the reality of legal academics' experiences of maternity, paternity and parental leave is another thing altogether. The relatively high degree of autonomy that academics generally enjoy, coupled with the broad and fluctuating nature of academic work, often mean that it is neither favourable nor particularly practical to conform to conventional patterns of leave. Pregnant academics commonly prefer to work up to the bitter end, finalising that article or book chapter that you promised, offering one last supervision session to your PhD student to tide them over, easing your replacement into the various aspects of your administrative role, or offering last-minute advice to anxious students preparing for assessment. Even the most legally informed academics are also notoriously uneasy about completely switching off *during* maternity leave, even during the two weeks' supposed compulsory leave immediately following childbirth. The temptation to dip into emails, read colleagues' and students' work-in-progress in between (and even during!) breast-feeding is constantly there, aided in no small part by the accessibility of our university email accounts. The standard out-of-office notices are now so ubiquitous (even for people going on a day's leave to attend a conference) that they barely register with or deter their recipients (perhaps we should learn from some of the global private companies that have a policy of blocking all incoming email to employees on leave?). Indeed, it is not all that uncommon for legal academics to regard maternity, paternity or parental leave as a much needed opportunity to catch up on research rather than a legally endorsed and essential period to recover from childbirth and adapting to the life-changing events brought about by having a new baby.

Arguably, these are autonomous choices rather than routine expectations, but recent research by The Education Guardian Unit has revealed a worrying downward trend in the number of women in academia taking maternity leave compared to other sectors, as well as a significant reduction in the length of maternity leave:

> Women in academia take less time off to have a baby than those in other careers … figures from the Department for Work and Pensions suggests the typical length of maternity leave is 273 days. Out of the top 10 institutions in the Guardian league table, six were able to provide data on the length of maternity leave taken by academics. The average was 191 days. (The Guardian 2014)

Rather than attributing this to the enhanced flexibility of the academic contract that enables women to combine work and family life more successfully, the findings suggests that it is more symptomatic of the fragile (lower-paid, part-time and temporary) contracts that female academics typically occupy.

And then there's the period leading up to and following your return to work after a period of leave. This can be the most stressful, anxious time of all. Even short periods of leave can have a dramatic impact on a person's confidence as a teacher, researcher and manager/administrator. We forget that our lives and responsibilities have shifted dramatically in a relatively short period of time, necessitating equally dramatic changes in how we juggle our work and domestic commitments. This is compounded by the fact that all too often little or no concessions are made to our teaching, administrative or research responsibilities as we negotiate these tricky and highly unpredictable transitions, physically, emotionally and practically. The relatively minor but essential measures that might facilitate effective reconciliation of work and family life before and after maternity/parental leave might include priority car-parking (a sore point in nearly every university at the best of times); phased returns, flexible timetabling arrangements; and an administrative role that accommodates, positively and constructively your change in personal circumstances. There should also be a greater willingness on the part of managers to adjust expectations relating to international conference travel, attendance at weekend recruitment events, or participation in evening or breakfast management meetings, all of which are likely to impact disproportionality on new parents' domestic commitments. Achieving this in a way that does not adversely impact upon progression prospects (implicitly if not explicitly) or generate resentment among colleagues who feel they have to absorb new roles to accommodate such commitments, is no easy task. It requires strong and unequivocal support from above and a high level of transparency, with more open acknowledgement of the fact that it is generally the parent academic him or herself that makes the most dramatic and even painful sacrifices in their ongoing endeavour to keep all the plates spinning.

Some universities are tackling these issues at institutional level, implementing returning carers' schemes, allowing a gradual increase in hours, or cash awards to support all parents on their return. Others are competing openly for the Gender Equality Charter Mark (GEM), an extension of the Athena Swan initiative, which evaluates, among other things, how pregnancy, maternity leave and women's return to work are managed in the humanities departments.

When all is said and done, the flexibility of legal academic work can be relatively accommodating of our family commitments long after maternity and paternity entitlement has expired. But that flexibility can be a double-edged sword: our working day is never really defined, and often lasts well into the night as we catch up on time lost through the unpredictability of children's illnesses, visits to the GP, to nursery and school events, and the sheer exhaustion that suspends any meaningful work until we have had chance to catch up on some sleep. But it also teaches us a heighted level of resourcefulness and pragmatism – to squeeze every last drop out of the hours or minutes that we can snatch; to make considered choices about what we can and cannot commit to outside of our core contractual commitments; to challenge presumptions and conventions about the format and environment for meetings or research events; where they should take place, how long they should be, and, indeed, whether they need to take place at all. In mainland Europe, it is not uncommon to see women breastfeeding their babies at conferences and meetings; and there are significant technological resources at our disposal now to enable us to conduct the occasional meeting virtually (over Skype, for instance) without compromising on the quality or effectiveness of that encounter. Of course, none of this should undermine the importance of being available in person to our colleagues and students for those more organic, spontaneous discussions that are so important for our intellectual, personal and professional development and, indeed, for sustaining a thriving university community. But rather than viewing our parenting role as competing with our role as academics, we should regard it more positively as enhancing our professional currency, enabling us to nurture sensibilities, skills and a resourcefulness that can be life-enhancing for us, our students, our colleagues and, indeed, our children.

The key messages for Meg and other academics considering maternity, paternity and parental leave:

1. Be clear about your leave entitlement.
2. Engage openly with colleagues and line managers about your plans, needs and anxieties in the period prior to taking leave and returning to work.
3. Focus on the way in which parenting enriches your professional life rather than solely on the challenges it presents.

FURTHER READING

JOURNALS

(2015) Reconciliation of Work and Family Life in the European Union, Special Issue *Journal of Social Welfare and Family Law*, 38(3).

Bawden, A. (2014) Academia for Women: Short Maternity Leave, Few Part-time Roles and Lower-pay, *The Guardian* (Higher Education section), 18 November 2014.

WEBSITES

Atkinson, J. (2014) Extending the Right to Request Flexible Working: Could it Initiate a Culture Change for British Fathers? *October Blog, Families and Work Network*. http://blogs.reading.ac.uk/fawn-news/

Equality Challenge Unit, a registered charity funded by the UK HE Bodies to Promote Equality and Diversity for Staff and Students in Higher Education Institutions Across the UK. http://www.ecu.ac.uk/

http://www.ecu.ac.uk/equality-charters/charter-marks-explained/gender-charter-marks-consultation-response/

CHAPTER 12

From Module Leadership to Course Leadership

DONNA WHITEHEAD

> Meg has returned from her recent maternity leave. She has now been asked to take over the programme leadership of one of the law school's programmes.

At the outset, it is worth clarifying some of the terms used throughout this chapter. Someone who leads a course – that is someone who takes academic responsibility for a BA Accounting degree or an MSc Anthropology course, for example, is referred to as a course leader. An academic who takes responsibility for a particular module on a course – a marketing module on a BA Business Studies course, for example, is referred to as a module leader.

Acting as a course leader is an essential component of personal development and career progression. It is also one of the most important student-facing roles in a university. Most early-career academics will start as lecturers, hourly paid/visiting lecturer staff or research assistants; and in terms of opportunities to progress to more senior positions, institutions tend to look for experience of course leadership. It is common for academics to begin a student-facing role as a module leader where they will be responsible for designing teaching, learning and assessment strategies for their modules. After a period of module leadership, academics are often asked to become course leaders; most new course leaders would say that they found the prospect a little daunting at first. Something that would be really helpful but is in fact rare in higher education is a role profile/description for a course leader. This lack of a role profile perhaps reflects the changeable nature of the role. Paterson (2006) has stated that course-leader tasks are varied, fragmented and often unrelated in nature; similarly, Murphy and Curtis (2013) suggest that the role is ambiguous and complex; and one that uncomfortablly straddles academic and manager profiles. This inevitably means that course leader roles are challenging but also varied and interesting.

As a course leader you will develop your listening, influencing, advising and supporting skills. It will also help you to view things from a student perspective. You are likely to find that when module leaders suggest changes to teaching, learning or assessment strategies in their module or when a change to a particular process or procedure is proposed, you see the change as part of the bigger course picture. This is very

43

different to being a module leader where the focus is naturally on one particular module. This sometimes can be frustrating for course leaders and so having good relationships with module leaders is vital.

When starting as a course leader, a good idea is to work closely with the outgoing course leader if at all possible. Ideally there will be a transition period where you take over the course leadership under his or her supervision. If this isn't possible, then it is advisable to work closely with course leaders for other courses. This will aid a comfortable transition from one course leader to the next.

You may find that your experience and the skills you will have developed in leading your own module are transferable. As a module leader you will have thought about teaching, learning and assessment strategies for your module(s) and how these link to the learning outcomes of your module; you will probably have dealt with student issues in relation to your particular module; you will also have assisted students who are finding a subject difficult. All of these experiences and skills will prepare you well for a course leader role. It is quite normal to feel overwhelmed, particularly at the demanding times of induction and enrolment, assessment hand in weeks, assessment board time and graduation, but with forward planning, these periods can be managed. Some institutions have level or year leaders in addition to an overall course leader; staff in these roles will look after the first, second or third year students on a course. If your institution has level leaders as well as course leaders then ask those individuals for support.

One of the key responsibilities of a course leader is to design an effective student induction programme. This is a challenging task as you will need to balance the pressures from the institution of ensuring as many students as possible are retained, with the pressure from the course team of setting out their expectations of the cohort. Preparation and planning for the induction are essential. Rather than seeing induction as solely your responsibility, encourage the course team (and level leaders if there are any) to get involved. Plan an induction schedule with the different exercises and topics to cover, and finalise this no later than the last school/team meeting of the preceding academic year. This will mean that you are not asking for help from other academics at the last minute.

Another challenge is your role in validations and revalidations. As a module leader you will have designed module assessment and teaching activities. You may even have designed a new module. As a course leader you are likely to take a lead role in the validation or revalidation of your courses. This means that you will be involved in designing the *overall* teaching, learning and assessment strategies; you will need to ensure that the module learning outcomes meet the course outcomes and that there is a sufficient spread of assessment methods. This can sometimes be difficult particularly if module teams do not understand why you are asking them to teach, assess or deliver in new ways. At the revalidation event, you will be expected to know the detail about the course and you will find that colleagues on the panel defer to your judgment. This can be an exciting time as it will allow you to develop your leadership skills. If quality assurance and enhancement is something of a blind spot for you, ensure you work closely with your administrative team or ask for a mentor.

As a course leader it is important that you don't feel under pressure to be the fountain of all knowledge. You will undoubtedly experience some unusual requests or queries from students; feel confident in pointing them in the right direction rather than trying to deal with everything. This is important for two reasons: first, you are probably setting yourself up to fail if you try to get to know absolutely everything – it really is not possible; and second, there is an expectation at university level that students should be able to undertake a degree of problem solving for themselves. This is a difficult balance.

A key skill that you will develop as a course leader is influencing change. It will soon become apparent to you what students would like to be changed or what needs to be changed as a result of National Student Survey (NSS) results, changes in staffing, student feedback or a range of external factors. Students may, for example, want more innovative teaching methods. Here, rather than asking the team to change their methods, you could set up a demonstration of Prezi or a piece of lecture capture software. If a professional body changes its regulations then the team will look to you for support in changing the course outcomes or content. Supporting your colleagues is important here and by doing this, you will play a key role in influencing change.

Being a course leader will certainly offer you a new challenge. It should also help you to think about your career progression. Throughout a period of course leadership you will have developed leadership and management skills and you will have influenced change in the curriculum. You will also have a clear understanding of the impact of league tables and of course the National Student Survey. These are important experiences and skills that are transferable to future management roles.

The key messages for Meg and other academics considering progressing from module leadership to course leadership:

1. Work alongside other course leaders who will guide you and support you in your new role.
2. Plan all activities for the academic year in advance. Focus particularly on those challenging times of year: induction and enrolment; assessment submission weeks; assessment boards; and graduation.
3. Work closely with the quality team and become familiar with the quality assurance (internal and external requirements) for course review and revalidation. Your role in this is crucial.

FURTHER READING

JOURNALS

Lieff, S. J. (2009) Evolving Curriculum Design: A Novel Framework for Continuous, Timely, and Relevant Curriculum Adaptation in Faculty Development, *Academic Medicine*, 84(1), 127–134.

Murphy, M. and Curtis, W. (2013) The Micro-politics of Micro-leadership: Exploring the Role of Programme Leader in English Universities, *Journal of Higher Education, Policy and Management*, 35(1), 34–44.

Paterson, H. (2006) The Changing Role of the Course Leader Within a Higher Education/ Further Education Context, *Research in Post-compulsory Education*, 4(1), 97–114.

WEBSITE

Quality Assurance Agency (2008) Framework for Higher Education Qualifications for England, Wales and Northern Ireland. www.qaa.ac.uk/publications/information-and-guidance/publication/?PubID=2718

CHAPTER 13

Quality Assurance Agency and Validation

GRAEME BROADBENT

> Meg has recently become a programme leader. She must now revalidate the programme, and validate a new proposed programme.

QAA is just one of the many acronyms you will encounter during your career. It stands for the Quality Assurance Agency, which is the body charged with the oversight of standards in higher education. You may ask why universities are not able to decide and monitor their own standards: after all, what about academic freedom? This is, however, part of a wider question of regulation of the public sector. While public sector organisations used to self-regulate, there has, since the 1980s, been a government-driven move to ensure that there is some external scrutiny of their activities, as public sector organisations are no longer trusted to regulate themselves and that they should be accountable to the public for the expenditure of taxpayers' money: institutions and individuals are not only expected to do a good job, they need to produce evidence to demonstrate that they are doing so (O'Neill 2002). As a result, a number of regulatory bodies have appeared across the public sector. QAA is one of a complex matrix of regulatory bodies covering higher education, which also includes HEFCE, OFFA and the OIA in addition to BIS, the government department with overall control of universities; other organisations, such as the OFT (now replaced by CMA) and ASA, have also become involved in examining higher education provision from their particular perspective. The regulatory requirements of these bodies are, of course, in addition to the quality assurance procedures of individual universities. The specific remit of QAA relates to standards: its website provides the official version of its role and functions, whilst Roger Brown (Brown 2004) provides a historical and more critical perspective.

QAA performs a number of functions designed to ensure the establishment and maintenance of standards at higher education institutions. It also sees itself as having a role to encourage universities to improve the quality of their provision and to disseminate good practice. It acts not only through its own staff, but also through a system of reviewers drawn from staff and students of other higher education institutions who are approved for the purpose by QAA: you might ask why their judgement is any more valid than that of staff and students at the university in question. The answer would appear to lie in the idea of the desirability of external, independent scrutiny of public sector organisations.

A key feature of the work of QAA is the promulgation of the Quality Code, which is essentially a set of expectations that universities have to achieve in their provision. It is a lengthy document in three parts. Part A deals with academic standards and includes requirements about qualification frameworks for higher education, setting standards appropriate to the level of study and the design of programmes and modules. It also includes the subject of benchmarks, of which there is one for law, which provides in detail what a law graduate is expected to be able to do. Part B relates to academic quality and outlines the mechanisms for ensuring that the standards outlined in Part A are met. It deals with matters such as programme design and review, external examiners and student appeals and complaints. Part C deals with the information provided by universities to the various stakeholders such as current or prospective students, employers and other users. You are unlikely to have to read the Quality Code in detail unless you have a responsibility that includes quality assurance. QAA sends teams of QAA-approved academics and students to conduct reviews in individual institutions as a further way of ensuring that not only are the expectations of QAA, as set out in the Quality Code, met, but also that the university does what it says it does in terms of its provision. The nature and frequency of QAA reviews will vary so that those longer established institutions that have a good track record of upholding standards will be treated with a lighter touch than newer institutions or those that have caused concern in the past. The outcomes of reviews are published by QAA and are public documents. You will probably only come into contact with QAA indirectly through your quality committee which will deal with changes to existing programmes or modules, or the creation of new modules. You may also be involved in the validation of new programmes, which tends to be conducted at university level, or in the periodic review of subject provision, both of which may involve you as a member of a subject team. Both of these typically involve an event with members of the validation panel drawn from outside the law school and will involve a great deal of work for those actively involved in preparing for it.

The system of quality assurance is the subject of regular debate. Academics are not naturally wedded to administrative requirements, as this is not what motivated them to work in higher education: a regular complaint is that the requirements of quality assurance detract from the core activities of research and teaching. A further, frequently expressed, reservation about the whole process is that it is largely concerned with quality assurance procedures rather than substantive quality. A former head of QAA, John Randall, (Randall 2002) argues, however, that QAA is necessary to provide the public with confidence in the standards of universities and their graduates. Writing from a different perspective, Anthony Bradney (Bradney 2001) sees the quality agenda as a vehicle for the implementation of government policy designed to change the nature of universities and academic life. The educational sociologist Louise Morley (Morley 2003) locates the quality agenda in debates about power and gender. She argues that it gives management additional levers of power, by providing enforceable regulation in teaching, research and administration, and so strengthens their hold over staff. Whilst it also provides career opportunities, she argues that this becomes a gendered issue as quality assurance is something that women, who are seen as 'housekeepers', can be steered into. While this may provide short-term promotion or enhancement, it does not carry the kudos and ultimate promotion prospects provided by research, which is the traditional route to the higher posts in universities and which tends to be dominated by men, though it might be countered that this may not be true in all universities, as, in some of the post-1992 universities, administrative roles are more highly valued than in the more research-orientated institutions. Externally, as we have seen, QAA employs reviewers from higher education institutions to carry out its various functions and other universities seek external members for validation panels or to act as external examiners for courses or PhDs, so these may be attractive functions to become involved in, not least as a way of finding out what happens elsewhere and playing a part in ensuring credibility and comparability across the sector. While there are opportunities for career advancement in quality assurance, you need to think carefully where your ultimate career aspirations lie and whether involvement in quality assurance will take you there in the longer term.

The key messages for Meg and other academics considering QAA and validation:

1. As with other public services, universities are subject to external scrutiny as a facet of accountability to the public. One of the bodies charged with this function is the QAA whose particular remit relates to standards.
2. Universities have internal mechanisms for ensuring quality of provision which will affect you in some way in relation to your teaching and any changes to teaching and courses.
3. Quality assurance has created career opportunities for both academics and administrators, but may be a cul-de-sac.

FURTHER READING

BOOK

Brown, R. (2004) *Quality Assurance in Higher Education*, London: RoutledgeFalmer.

Morley, L. (2003) *Quality and Power in Higher Education*, Maidenhead: SRHE/OU.

O'Neill, O. (2002) *A Question of Trust*, Cambridge: Cambridge University Press.

JOURNAL

Bradney, A. (2001) The Quality Assurance Agency and the Politics of Audit, *Journal of Law and Society*, 28(3), 430–442.

Randall, J. (2002) Quality Assurance: Meeting the Needs of the User, *Higher Education Quarterly*, 56(2), 188–203.

WEBSITE

Quality Assurance Agency (QAA) www.qaa.ac.uk/Pages/default.aspx

CHAPTER 14

Navigating University Management Committees and the Meeting Structures

ANNABELLE JAMES

> Meg has recently become a programme leader and in that role has been invited to attend many more meetings. She is trying to understand how her role fits into the general structure of roles and how to negotiate the committee and meeting structures.

While every university will have different names for the numerous meetings held at all levels, their composition and remit are likely to be essentially the same across the higher education sector. It is probably the case for most that, on starting one's first appointment at a university as a member of academic staff, you think that all your time will be taken up with teaching, teaching preparation, dealing with students, various bits of admin and research, the balance of all of these activities varying depending on what time of year it is and what the focus of the role you have been appointed to is (for example teaching or research focused). What goes on behind the scenes at universities, structurally and strategically, may not need to cross the mind of a newly appointed lecturer at the outset and may seem somewhat of a mystery – however the more senior you get on even a very academically focused career path, the more dealings you will have with meetings on all kinds of topics at all kinds of levels.

Whatever level you enter a career in higher education at, you will be expected to attend different types of meeting. You are unlikely at the outset to be involved in anything at university or probably even faculty/school level; however an understanding of the overall structure is useful as university meeting structures across the sector operate on a feedback and reporting structure, both horizontally and vertically. Thus decisions made at the highest level by for example the university governors regarding the setting of fees, by the vice chancellor, the vice chancellor's executive or the university academic board/senate will be fed down through various committees, sometimes for consultation, the results of which will then be fed back up through the committee structure or sometimes just for the purpose of giving information. Take for example a decision made at university level as to recruitment targets for each different area of the university. This will be fed down to the more discrete areas at faculty/school level where discussion as to allocation amongst specific subject areas will take place and may further go to each individual area's marketing group for action planning and reporting back as to outcomes. Similarly a proposal may be made at programme level to introduce a new programme – this would usually then be considered in meetings at school/faculty level before proposals for new titles are put forward at university level.

For an individual just entering academic life, the most common encounters with meetings are likely to take place at subject and discipline level. Modules will generally be delivered by module teams and meetings will usually take place involving all staff delivering that module to discuss delivery, future plans for the module, changes to content and/or assessment and of course moderation and second marking of assignments and exams! Similarly at programme level, that is, degree or group of awards level meetings are likely to be held on a regular basis to discuss the degree programmes as a whole, potential changes and additions to the programmes and reapproval events. These may be attended by all staff or each subject area may be represented by a module leader. You will also generally be required to attend regular staff meetings involving everyone in your subject area. This will be chaired by the head of department/subject area and generally serve a variety of functions. The head will represent the subject area on a number of committees as may a number of other senior members of staff. The head for example will attend senior management/leadership meetings and will report back on decisions made in that forum. He/she and other members of staff are likely to attend meetings that discuss school/faculty policies, academic standards and quality matters, international and national recruitment and research and enterprise. Members of staff should be given the opportunity to give feedback on any issues raised – meetings like this should operate on a two-way basis but often, due to time pressures, turn into information dissemination sessions instead.

At school/faculty level, as already mentioned, groups will exist to discuss discrete areas of academic and procedural university life. There will be meetings held to discuss policy changes and implementation, academic standards where proposed changes to modules and courses will be discussed and external examiners approved. If your university works with other partners at college level there is likely to be a partnership committee as well and there will inevitably be at least one set of meetings that deal with research, ethics and research-funding-based issues. Branching off from these will be sub committees – for example those set up to consider programme reapprovals and working groups, working towards a specific aim. These committees and meetings will be comprised of representatives from individual subject areas and when vacancies arise represent a good opportunity not only to become more familiar with how things operate in your university but also has the advantage of getting you known outside of your subject area and department which can only be to your advantage when seeking promotion later in your career!

Similarly at university level, whilst most meetings will be attended by people at head of department level or higher, there are often opportunities for academic staff to act as staff representatives on academic boards or even as staff representatives on the board of governors. Again this gives insight as to how the university operates and into its decision making processes and also serves as putting down a marker that you are interested and engaged. Beware however of volunteering to serve on every committee going – you will be expected not only to read through numerous sets of minutes and sets of paperwork prior to the meeting but also be prepared to discuss your views on them!

The key messages for Meg and other academics thinking about university committee and meeting structures:

1. University committee and meeting structures are complex; there is no need to figure it all out initially.
2. Make sure you know what meetings you are expected to attend and what the terms of reference for those meetings are.
3. Do not overcommit yourself.

FURTHER READING

JOURNAL

Thody, A. (1989) University Management Observed – A Method of Studying Its Unique Nature? *Studies in Higher Education*, 14(3), 279–296.

CHAPTER 15

Undertaking Peer Review

NIGEL DUNCAN

> Meg's career is developing as she settles into her new job with its major management responsibilities. She recognises, however, that she needs to maintain her engagement and output in scholarly work and seeks advice as to how to develop a role undertaking peer review for academic publications.

One of the tricky aspects of editing an academic journal is finding a wide group of peers who are willing to undertake the demanding job of peer review in an objective, thoughtful and constructive way. So approaches from academic colleagues who express an interest in doing so will almost certainly be welcome. Likewise, should an editor invite you to carry out peer review, your agreement will be very welcome. However, to be sure that the process is mutually beneficial, you should establish some clear parameters and understand what is required to ensure that your engagement is effective.

The principle of peer review is to maintain and improve the quality of what is published in academic journals. Typically, articles submitted will be anonymised and sent out to two (or more) referees for their views. The process is generally double-blind and this mutual anonymity will be preserved carefully by the editor. Often, authors are self-referential, and their identity is clear. This should not deter you from acting as a referee, as anonymity is available for the author if they wish, and not a formal problem if they choose to abandon it.

Typically you will be sent a pro-forma along with the article to be reviewed. This will ask for your view as to whether the article is publishable as it stands; with minor amendment; only with major amendment or revision; or not publishable. There may be other categories. It will generally ask if you are willing to look at a revised copy if you have recommended that this is necessary. Finally it will ask you for comments that can be sent to the author to assist them in their revision. In order to make this judgment, it should be clear that you should only agree to review articles in a field with which you have sufficient familiarity, both with the issues being raised and the related literature. Even if you do this you may find analyses that stretch you. For example, I have reviewed articles which included technical statistical arguments designed to validate conclusions being drawn from quantitative data. My review addressed the article and the arguments, but I warned the editor that I was not a reliable referee on the statistical validity of the claims and that another referee should be sought in respect of that. This seems to me a perfectly correct approach to adopt.

The comments are even more useful than the overall evaluation. Please be polite, concise and constructive. Your approach should be a combination of how you would provide feedback to a student (particularly as a dissertation supervisor) and how you would act as an external examiner. In effect, you should be a critical friend. You should not pull your punches if there are serious errors in the draft article. But you should not criticise without explaining your criticism and suggesting ways of remedying the problem. It may be, for example, that the author has ignored (or missed) a line of articles which would support their argument, or which challenges it and ought to be addressed. It may be that you have identified problems with a line of logic or overconfident conclusions drawn from limited methodology. You should state your concern with clarity and suggest what might be done about it, which might be to propose a line of reading, a different approach to analysing data or further research. Such is the pressure to publish that authors may be tempted to write articles at various stages of a research project. I have sometimes argued that an article based on a pilot project was, frankly, premature, and that the full research should be completed before it is worth publishing. There may, of course, be value in publishing the results of a pilot project, particularly if it is likely to stimulate others to research and test out the area or to assist the researcher in broadening their research population.

Many reviewers return an annotated copy of the draft article with their review, and this is very helpful. It is easiest to engage Track Changes in Word and add comments in boxes at the side of the text. Note that, in order to ensure anonymity you should set your computer so that your name does not appear on the comments.

Please make sure that you always moderate your language. It is an irritating job for an editor to have to moderate the tone of a referee's comments and it is unnecessary if you recall your 'critical friend' role. You may wish to express a view which is not to go to the author. Some pro-formas provide for this. If they do not, you may include them in a covering email.

The request to act as a referee will give you a deadline. I generally give reviewers a month unless there is a need for greater speed. Please observe this and get your review back in time. If you are not going to be able to achieve that, contact the editor and either negotiate a later date or give her early notice of the need to find another referee.

You do not need to undertake proofreading or copy-editing. If the quality of the English language is poor you do not need to correct it, although you should say that it needs improvement (and perhaps give a couple of examples). This might include style issues, particularly where they impact upon legibility. Thus, identifying over-long sentences which would be better broken up can be very useful. You don't need to do the re-writing. Try to exercise a degree of self-restraint here. Many of us have our own personal style dogmas and a perfectly well-written article may not comply with them.

You do not need to correct the numbering of the footnotes. It is very common for this to go wrong. As authors add more footnotes early in the text the numbers of later footnotes change and references back to them become inaccurate. Draw attention to the fact, but do not do it yourself.

You do not need to express simple disagreement with an argument. Academic discourse thrives on disagreement and opposing views should not be stifled. However, if you disagree with a view expressed it will probably be because you perceive a flaw in the premise, the argument or the evidence base. Your explanation of these concerns will be helpful.

Mutual anonymity lies at the heart of conventional peer review and it is important in that it should enable a critical approach without fear of personalities skewing decision-making. However, the élite nature of many groups of 'peers' has been criticised for stifling innovation by commentators such as Higgs (see further reading). The process itself has been criticised for allowing rubbish to be published. The famous Sokal hoax involved submitting an article entitled *Transgressing the Boundaries: Towards a Transformative Hermeneutics of Quantum Gravity* to the journal *Social Text*. It was published in 1996. It was nonsense. Sokal argues that he achieved this by writing in the sort of language that appealed to the journal's editors and by flattering their ideological preconceptions. This editor's view is that the more authors can use accessible language comprehensible to a wide educated audience the less likely it is that nonsense will slip through.

Other approaches to peer review have been developed to attempt to address some of these concerns. On several occasions the *Law Teacher* has used collective peer review, where the authors of a group of papers (typically initially presented at a conference and honed by the debate at that conference) act as peer reviewers for each other and debate (in a virtual environment) each article over a specific period of time. This can be challenging, as anonymity is lost, but the group will generally observe the principles of constructive critique with, in my experience, excellent results.

You will learn a lot, both in terms of the analytical work of doctrinal research and the results of empirical and socio-legal work. The process will help you to improve your own academic writing. However, you should recognise that anonymity means that you will not receive much recognition other than amongst the editors of the journals concerned. Bear in mind, however, that it is perfectly legitimate to refer to your work as a reviewer in promotion and job applications. What is more, editorial boards may be looking for serious committed scholars who are willing to put in the necessary work when filling their vacancies. Membership of the editorial board of an academic journal with a good reputation is good for the career.

Another side of it is the satisfaction of a job well done when you read the finished article, improved by the author in the light of your review. Look down at the bottom of the first page. Just occasionally a thoughtful author will include thanks to the anonymous reviewers who commented on the draft article. A private pleasure, but a pleasure nonetheless.

The key messages for Meg and other academics thinking about peer review:

1. It can give you an insight into the latest research in your specialist area.
2. Find out exactly what the expectations are including what the timescales for the review are.
3. Undertaking peer review can improve your own research and writing.

FURTHER READING

JOURNALS

Hutchinson, T. and Duncan, N. (2012) Defining and Describing What We Do: Doctrinal Legal Research, *Deakin Law Review*, 17(1), 83.

Maharg, P. and Duncan, N. (2007) Black Box, Pandora's Box or Virtual Toolbox? An Experiment in a Journal's Transparent Peer Review on the Web, *Int Rev Law, Computers & Technology*, 21, 109.

Sokal, A. (1996) A Physicist Experiments with Cultural Studies, *Lingua Franca*, May/June 1996.

WEBSITE

Higgs, R. (2007) Peer Review, Publication in Top Journals, Scientific Consensus, and So Forth, *The Independent Institute*. http://www.independent.org/newsroom/article. asp?id=1963 (accessed 16 July 2014).

CHAPTER 16

Open Access Publishing

LAURA J. WILKINSON

> Meg has finished writing a research output, and is considering Open Access publishing.

As part of their university employment, academics read each other's scholarly writings and produce research outputs of their own. In this chapter, I will often refer to articles, but the principles apply to a range of formats. Commercial publishers provide an editorial process, and then make journals and books available to read for payment: typically a one-off cost for books, or a subscription for journals. The commercial publisher does not pay the academics for their outputs or peer review services.

This traditional (or legacy) model of academic publishing is currently being challenged:

1. Falling costs of production as publishing moves online.
2. Costs of library subscriptions to academic journals rising well above the rate of inflation (*serials crisis*).
3. Academics usually sign over their intellectual property rights to the commercial publisher, so they no longer own the copyright in their work.
4. Pressure to include re-usable datasets in scientific papers, allowing the methodology to be scrutinised and tested.
5. No single university library collection can provide access to all academic content; and researchers in developing economies, UK researchers without a university affiliation, retired academics, staff and students in schools and/or further education, and other interested lay persons are further disenfranchised.
6. Increasing demand for the products of publicly-funded research to be freely available to be read by taxpayers.

The open access (OA) movement challenges this traditional academic publishing model, which relies on denying access to knowledge. At the heart of OA is the idea that research outputs should be available to read online without payment (gratis OA) and that the outputs are licensed to share and re-use, with attribution (libre OA). Gratis OA removes barriers of cost and libre OA removes barriers of permission. Libre OA means that the intellectual property rights of the document remain with the author (rather than being signed away to the commercial publisher); that the work can be indexed by computers (such as internet search engines); and that users can legally link to, download and share the document.

OA is possible via two routes: gold, in which the OA-published edition of a work is available from the publisher's website; and green, in which the final copy of the published work is available under OA licence from a repository. A repository is a database of research outputs, typically organised by institution (e.g. a university), or by subject (e.g. bepress Legal Repository).

The difference between the gold and green routes is whether OA is provided by the journal itself, or by a repository. It is not a measure of quality. OA journals may or may not be peer-reviewed, just as traditional journals.

As the model of academic publishing changes, new funding streams are being explored, including:

a)   institutional support
b)   research centre & society partnerships
c)   research funding subsidy
d)   library expenditure
e)   direct publication charges such as article processing charges (APCs)

Some of these also challenge the for-profit business model of commercial publishers.

The main driver for open access is the 2012 Finch Report, which mandated that all UK publicly-funded research outputs be free to access, with gold OA as the preferred route. Post-REF2014, research outputs submitted to the research assessments process must be accessible from the author's institutional repository. Furthermore, universities are increasingly developing their own OA policies.

Commercial publishers are starting to offer OA options, however, the Finch Report did not specify that OA had to be libre as well as gratis. The Finch Panel (which included a number of representatives from the world of commercial publishing) favoured gold over green as the preferred route to OA, and recommended that this would be funded by APCs.

Unlike born-OA journals, commercial publishers seek to maintain their subscription revenue (e.g. Elsevier reported 36% profit on $3.2 billion revenue in 2010), so they charge high APCs for OA. Commercial publishers typically provide gratis OA, but not libre OA, as the author still signs away their copyright and the article isn't licensed for sharing and re-use. Some commercial publishers allow green OA after an embargo period, thus achieving the letter rather than the spirit of gratis OA; as current access to the article is only for those with subscriptions, leaving others to wait until the embargo has passed.

It is foreseen that there will be a transitional period as traditional publishers move from subscriptions revenue to an APC-funded model. During this time, university libraries will have to pay journal subscriptions as well as APCs, putting yet more pressure on already-squeezed budgets. Commercial publishers will benefit from income from both subscriptions and APCs. Some have promised to reduce subscriptions in proportion to APC revenue, but nonetheless it seems likely that a 'double-dipping' dual revenue will develop during the transitional period.

Additional APC funding is being provided to research-intensive institutions from central public funds, reinforcing a cycle of research success and making it even harder to develop new research nuclei (at newer universities, for example).

The value of a journal is often measured by impact factor (IF), which is a measure of a journal's readership and frequency of citation of its articles. IF is coming under increasing criticism for its reliability, susceptibility to manipulation; and competition from alternatives such as article-level metrics (ALMs). Some academics perceive being published in a journal with a high IF as necessary to gain tenure or REF status, and this is a powerful factor keeping academics tied into commercial publishers.

There are also positive reasons for authors to embrace OA:

- OA allows you a broader readership, which is particularly useful in an interdisciplinary subject such as law.
- Making your research OA maximises the impact of your work, and gives you a citation advantage, as no-one is prevented by a paywall from reading it, and therefore citing it.
- Reader interaction – libre OA allows you to track sharing of and commenting on your work by others, and the opportunity to respond and engage.
- Born-OA journal platforms allow you greater use of web technology in your writing, such as embedding multimedia and links to other articles, statistics and reports.
- You can easily re-use and cite the OA work of others.
- Libre OA allows you to retain the intellectual property rights in your own work.
- OA brings the linking and indexing power of the internet to your research.

Find out what (if any) are your obligations to your institution and your funding body; and your involvement in next REF (2020, at the time of writing).

Most UK HE institutions now have a repository. Find out who manages yours – they will be an excellent source of information and advice.

Once your obligations have been met, other decisions about OA publication are yours. Academics' decisions about where to publish their work is the strongest driver in determining access to, licensing of and funding for scholarly research and its outputs.

The key messages for Meg and other academics considering Open Access:

1. OA is about access to scholarly research outputs and has two main elements: gratis and libre.
2. OA can be achieved via journal (gold) or repository (green) routes.
3. OA maintains your copyright in your outputs, increases your readership and gives citation advantage to your work.

FURTHER READING

WEBSITES

Sherpa, Juliet. www.sherpa.ac.uk/juliet/index.php – information on research funders' archiving mandates and guidelines.

Sherpa, Romeo. www.sherpa.ac.uk/romeo – information on publishers' copyright & archiving policies.

OTHER

bepress Legal Repository law.bepress.com – a subject-specific OA platform.

Budapest Open Access Initiative www.budapestopenaccessinitiative.org/read – definition of OA, and its aims.

Open Access, by Peter Suber mitpress.mit.edu/books/open-access – Suber's concise and accessible book is available OA in a variety of formats.

CHAPTER 17

Taking on a Management Role

MARK O'BRIEN

> Meg has seen a management role advertised at another institution and is considering applying.

Elsewhere in this book, Jessica Guth has written about promotions in higher education, arguing that it is easier to be promoted externally than internally, and discussing additional factors that appear to impact upon this process, such as gender. Taking on a management role at a different institution could come about as a consequence of an external promotion, or even via assumption of a management role for the first time at an existing grade.

As higher education has developed over the last five decades, debate over the exact rationale for universities has taken place alongside what Tribe viewed as an 'unparalleled' period of change in higher education, with a concomitant impact upon the understanding and articulation of institutional goals and, importantly for this chapter, university roles.

Established notions of a 'liberal education' – described by Bradney as the advancement of a particular view of life, and the acquisition of knowledge but also a particular 'habit of mind', have been joined by perspectives emphasising 'positive attitudes' to work; for the training of students; and an increased focus upon considerations such as the student experience.

This culture of change, together with an increasing need to manage and measure (for financial and league table reasons) the success or otherwise of change, has meant that the nature and ambit of academic management roles have changed significantly over recent decades. Moreover, there is the further complication of diverging cultures between institutions, depending upon differing priorities and strategies: in many cases, university management is far removed from the world of university management typified by Professor Alan Marvin, the head of department in Malcolm Bradbury's *The History Man*, or satirised by Lawrie Taylor in the form of Professor Lapping, the hapless Head of Media Studies at the University of Poppleton.

Whereas historically heads of departments, vice-chancellors and similar may have been the only people unambiguously labelled a 'manager' in a university (and even then, in the case of heads of department, perhaps only for a three-year term before a grateful return to a bookish existence), nowadays roles with an explicit management focus are much more prevalent, for the reasons outlined above. A university management role might consist of specific tasks, such as examinations or admissions tutor, the wider responsibility of degree programme management (often carried out at senior-lecturer level in post-1992 institutions, and by lecturers or senior lecturers in pre-1992 universities), or a more senior role (possibly at principal lecturer in the 'new' universities, and senior lecturer in the 'old' universities) with a responsibility for a strategic portfolio within a department – student experience, or quality assurance, or enterprise, or international development, as part of cultures of change within institutions, and often reflecting particular institutional priorities at given times. Similarly, there is an increasing trend towards research management roles, via research directors and champions, in addition to traditional research centre head roles, as research funding, impact, and resourcing considerations require increased support and strategising.

Higher management roles include the traditional head of department position, often with an array of other senior roles evolving in recent years: executive deans of faculty (replacing 'ceremonial' deans and fixed-term sub-deans), associate deans (again with strategic portfolios), and associate heads, culminating in an increasingly diverse and stratified array of assistant vice-chancellor, associate pro vice-chancellor, pro vice-chancellor, and deputy vice-chancellor posts before reaching the top job.

For someone taking on a management role at a different university, a key factor that they may underestimate beforehand is the 'culture shock' caused by differences between their old and new institutions – in terms of prevailing cultures of management, ethos, practices, and even at the most arcane level, a bewildering array of (completely different) acronyms for the otherwise familiar procedures and processes. Becher and Trowler have discussed the phenomenon of approaches derived from academics' subject discipline impacting upon aspects of academic behaviour, but Trowler also highlights the added complexity of other 'conditioning factors' upon academics, including prevailing organisational cultures – the 'conditioning structures' in universities, which would be particularly relevant to an incoming manager unversed in their new institutional culture.

Key to taking on a new management role, therefore, before a candidate even applies, is to try to find out as much as possible about the ethos and 'positioning' of the university: is it one where someone can be an academic who is a researcher as well as a manager? Is it an institution where divergent career paths have been developed so that 'management' and other, academic, pathways are separate? Is it an institution where a head of department is an academic who manages, or a manager who now dabbles in academia? Being clear about this is important, whether someone is in the business of adapting to fit with it, or setting out with a view to shape and change practices or cultures. It is also worth bearing in mind that, over time, as more senior management moves on and is replaced, these institutional goals may alter, and as such what a person does (and thus where they choose to work) may well change over time.

Once in a new management post, it is advisable to invest a great deal of time in getting to know the institutional structures, and most importantly, the academic and administrative staff – finding out who officially does x, who *really* does y – and absorbing the culture, which will provide the insight into the how and why of the university's operations. In this regard, aligning with an experienced member of staff is incredibly useful – someone who genuinely understands how everything works, and who knows how and where the theory and reality of the institutional practices diverge. At whatever level a university manager assumes responsibility within an institution, they will usually be assigned a mentor who is experienced in the area of responsibility that the new manager is assuming, so it is wise to make full use of this resource, and also cultivate relationships more widely.

In addition to the mentoring process, a useful source of information to the incoming university manager will be their new peers: many institutions will hold regular faculty or institutional meetings between programme managers, admissions tutors, heads of department, research centre heads or whatever is the relevant peer group; again, these are invaluable for understanding the culture of the new institution. Vital to all of the above is listening and absorbing information in this learning cycle – over time, the new manager will be able to form judgments about the value or otherwise of the information that they receive. Furthermore, human resources departments will also provide a range of optional management training and refresher courses over and above any of the 'required' courses – taking a carefully-picked selection of these would be useful. As well as internal networks, external support networks, such as subject- or function-based networks may be able to provide support, as will more general, higher education organisations such as the Leadership Foundation for Higher Education.

The key messages for Meg and other academics considering becoming a manager at another institution:

1. Finding out at the earliest stage if the culture and ethos of the place is right for them, and considering the changes to which they may need to adapt.
2. Being aware that the complex reality of 'conditioning structures' could exacerbate the culture shock of moving to a new institution.
3. Build networks within the organisation, gather experienced peers' views and engage with mentoring and training opportunities.

FURTHER READING

BOOKS

Bradney, A. (2003) *Conversations, Choices and Chances: The Liberal Law School in the Twenty-First Century*, Oxford: Hart Publishing.

Collini, S. (2012) *What are Universities for?*, London: Penguin.

Cownie, F. (2004) *Legal Academics: Cultures and Identities*, Oxford: Hart Publishing.

Trowler, P. (2008) *Cultures and Change in Higher Education: Theories and Practices (Universities into the 21st Century)*, London: Palgrave Macmillan.

Trowler, P. (ed.) (2012) *Tribes and Territories in the 21st Century: Rethinking the Significance of Disciplines in Higher Education (International Studies in Higher Education)*, Abingdon: Routledge.

CHAPTER 18

Gender Issues in HE Management

ROSEMARY AUCHMUTY

> Meg has recently been appointed to a management position at a different institution. She is now facing a number of management issues relating to gender.

In seeking a management role, even if you tick every box on the job description, you need to be aware that gender will play a role in whether you are appointed, and how you experience the job if you are appointed. There are no two ways about it: in higher education (HE) management, women are at a disadvantage. However egalitarian the law school – and many do now take equality and diversity seriously, and are pleasant places for women to work in – you will find that attitudes are less reconstructed at the top. HE management remains wedded to a masculine culture and models of competence and merit that women somehow fail to fit. As one head of school said to me, 'The default position is male'. You need to recognise that prejudice, sometimes amounting to misogyny, characterises the management style and actual personnel in many universities, both pre- and post-1992; and you need to talk to as many people as possible who have experience of HE management before committing yourself to applying.

In researching this entry, I canvassed friends of both sexes who have had experience of management at school, faculty or university level. Here are some of their observations. In meetings where no woman is present, the atmosphere quickly turns to that of a roomful of teenage, or even pre-adolescent, boys. One woman told me she had sat through meeting after meeting where male colleagues engaged in a 'mine is bigger than yours' debate about research groups, grants or publications. A man said it was worse than that: he sensed a general view of 'Girls – yuck!'. Women managers spoke of being judged by their appearance, clothes and domestic situation, of being the butt of sexual jokes and objects of sexualised gawping. Those who had children were thought to be bad mothers if they put their careers first, and uncommitted to the job if they didn't; but childlessness, for a woman, was also a problem: this unnatural state appeared to render them unsuitable for management.

Women spoke of being allocated the service roles, whether organising the coffee or overseeing pastoral care – work which, like their equivalents in the home and society, is valued less than other roles in management. A gay male manager told me that, since his university's executive team is all male, he is allocated these duties, an 'honorary woman' by virtue of his sexuality. 'It is still thought negative to have emotions', a woman remarked. Women described being unable to get a word in in meetings, and of being ignored when they did. The older they got, the more invisible they became. Decisions always seemed to be made in venues where they were not present. If the job required representing the institution abroad, which is becoming more common with HE's greater reliance on international students, a woman manager might be seen as inappropriate because *other countries* do not take women seriously.

'The language used to describe one's style is deeply gendered,' a former head of school told me. A quiet woman, she was surprised to find herself described as 'aggressive': 'this can only mean that decisiveness – and heads do have to make decisions – is thought to be *aggressive* in a woman'. Yet using a more typically feminine collegial style, as someone else told me – trying to bring people with you, rather than imposing a top-down rule – is often viewed as weak. 'Decision-making by a woman head of school is always more likely to be challenged,' declared a third. No wonder Margaret Thornton concluded that there is no acceptable position for women in authority (2012, 157).

Equal pay does not exist in HE management. A man appointed to the same job as a woman will almost invariably be paid more; it is well established that men set a higher value on themselves when negotiating their starting salary, but the differential will be justified on other, generally spurious grounds. The Equality Challenge Unit's Report on Equality in Higher Education (2011) found 'rampant gender inequalities' among HE staff, with women earning 20% less than their male equivalents (David 2014, 40).

Should you decide to go ahead with your management ambitions, you need to realise that seeking promotion in your own institution may be harder than going elsewhere. Competent, reliable older women are the mainstay of university departments whose managers do not want to lose them in their current teaching/admin/pastoral role. You will probably be judged to be *not ready yet* by senior colleagues who still see you as a beginner after 20 years or feel you lack the essential drive or spark of the bright young male competitor for the post. Applying to a different institution, however problematic for those with family obligations if far from home, at least means that the appointments panel sees you with fresh eyes and judges you on the basis of your CV, not what they think they know about you. Of course there is always the danger that they, too, have in mind a man in their own image or a bright young lad, or find it impossible to see management qualities in a woman. You should research the institution thoroughly beforehand and speak to everyone you know who has experience of the way it functions.

If you are appointed, you need to decide whether it is worth playing the sexist game. Some women feel better going along with the dressing up (or down), spending money on make-up, childcare, or whatever their institution expects (face-lift, breast-reduction or enhancement), being charming to (even flirting with) male colleagues, and producing a 'partner' from somewhere. Others succeed by *just being themselves,* usually because they command such respect in other areas, like research excellence or bringing in external funding, that they cannot be challenged. Others still call the men out on their sexism, and risk failure and stigma. 'She's *difficult*' is a description that is hard to live down.

What helps women to progress more than anything else is to have mentors, the more powerful the better, who can write glowing references and, if possible, sit on the appointments panel. The presence of even one other woman on committees can make a huge difference, while a female vice-chancellor or a sizeable body of women in senior management can completely transform the institutional atmosphere. A leadership programme like Aurora may be helpful, since many women lack confidence and are too ready either to believe that management roles are beyond their capabilities or to retain a realistic modesty in an environment where blowing your trumpet is expected. They may fear failure or, as one dean expressed it, that they will be 'found out' as incompetent. They may feel awkward having to manage former peers, who may in turn resent what they see as a betrayal of their friendship.

Once in post, the challenge will be setting and, if necessary, transforming the management style. My informants spoke of being facilitative and enabling rather than controlling; nurturing junior colleagues; being prepared to admit to uncertainty and mistakes; not making favourites, and not promising the world. They advised *choosing your battles* and *making allies among other women and sympathetic men*. Some have set up support groups among other women managers in their institution or across the sector to share experiences and determine joint strategies, for example around equal pay.

Progress in HE management has been much slower than the most pessimistic feminist could have imagined 40 years ago. It seems astonishing to most women that only 8% of vice-chancellors and 20% of heads of law schools are women (O'Connor 2014, 69); that many HE managements still think it is acceptable to have no women, or only one, on their executive teams; and that 72% of senior management in HE are men, while women make up 56% of our students (David 2014, 36, 40). O'Connor found, however, that male managers are generally unaware that there is a gender problem, and only realise it after they experience the difference that working with women makes (2014, 160). Universities may promote their equality and diversity policies and leadership schemes as much as they like but, until male managers are forced to go on 'working with women' or 'taking women seriously' courses, and/or have affirmative action plans imposed on them, little will change; and you may decide it is not worth the effort.

The key messages for Meg and other academics considering gender issues in HE management:

1. Get the best mentors you can and use them for advice, references and so on.
2. Do your research on the institution you are applying to, including (if possible) meeting with women who work there, so that you know what to expect.
3. Be strategic as a manager: choose your issues and form alliances with other women and sympathetic men.

FURTHER READING

BOOKS

Brooks, A. and Mackinnon, A. (eds) (2001) *Gender and the Restructured University*, Buckingham: Society for Research into Higher Education and the Open University.

David, M. (2014) *Feminism, Gender and Universities: Politics, Passion and Pedagogies*, Farnham: Ashgate.

O'Connor, P. (2014) *Management and Gender in Higher Education*, Manchester: Manchester University Press.

Thornton, M. (2012) *Privatising the Public University: The Case of Law*, Abingdon: Routledge.

JOURNAL

Collier, R. (2002) The Changing University and the [Legal] Academic Career, *Legal Studies*, 22, 1–32.

CHAPTER 19

Performance Review

CHRIS GALE

> Meg is now line-managing a team.

A performance review, performance appraisal, performance developmental review (or one of a number of names given to an annual discussion with a more senior colleague in the institution) is a process for individual employees and those concerned with their performance, particularly line and senior managers, to engage in a dialogue about their performance and development and the support they need in the role. It is commonly used to both assess recent performance and to focus on future objectives, opportunities and resources needed. It is an important part of performance management but, in itself, it is not performance management. Rather, it is one of a range of tools that can be used to manage performance. (CIPD Factsheet updated June 2014, accessed at www.cipd.co.uk). Whatever the name, the processes and outcomes are usually similar.

To my certain knowledge, very few HEI's in England and Wales had a developed or, in many cases, any, form of performance review in the mid 1990s. Attempts to bring such measures from the business world at local level were often seen as attempts to thwart academic independence and introduce a system of 'weeding out' unsatisfactory performers. As HEI's clumsily linked performance review to attempts to introduce performance related pay, they were opposed by the unions and were largely not implemented or ineffectual. Following the publication of the Dearing Report in 1997 (Dearing Report, formally known as the reports of the National Committee of Inquiry into Higher Education), an acceptance of some sort of performance review, as part of an agenda of 'professionalisation' of HEIs grew and I underwent my first 'appraisal' in 1999. Subsequently they were renamed 'performance review' in my then institution as the word 'appraisal' was deemed too judgemental and the memories of the earlier moribund systems were still in the collective memory. A lot of 'tiptoeing' around meant they were largely information gathering exercises for a number of years.

By this point in time, it is anticipated that some system or other of performance review operates in each HEI. As with most things in this life, it is dominated by forms. Reviews are usually conducted every 12 months, but sometimes more frequently, especially in relation to a new employee undergoing a period of probation or where a previous review has been deemed unsatisfactory. Each HEI has developed its own, but the common theme is for a reviewee to prepare details of what they consider to have been the highlights and lowlights of the previous year. Pleas for resources, from conference funding to requests for research time, through less teaching to more sympathetic timetabling go into the paperwork which is then reviewed by the reviewer, typically the reviewee's line manager, before a meeting of an hour or so in length at which the reviewee's form is discussed, agreed (or not) and targets for the following year built. The line manager will usually complete their run of reviews and report upwards any underlying themes for training or resource. They often, in relation to more senior staff, make judgements about performance which can then feed in to increases in salary – a modest form of performance related pay. The forms then often disappear from sight, never to be seen or commented upon again until the following year's round of reviews.

In order to avoid this being a meaningless exercise, all parties can at least try to make the forms meaningful. Genuine needs can be logged, discussed and debated and it is in everyone's interests for the outcomes, the objectives for the following year, to be expressed in S.M.A.R.T. term (specific measurable, achievable, relevant and time-bound. This occurs in the November 1981 issue of *Management Review* by George T. Doran).

terms, so that it genuinely can be evaluated whether they have been met or not.

It could be thought having read the above, that performance reviews are merely a clumsy managerial tick-box exercise with little point and no teeth – and that is what, at worst they can become. Given that sometimes it is a member of staff's only opportunity in a year to have some 'quality time' with their line manager, they deserve to be prepared for with a little more cunning. Notwithstanding that the more savvy members of staff will have made sure that their line manager knows all about their achievements by dint of telling them by email, bumping into them regularly with a cup of tea or at the water cooler, the reviewee's form can sometimes come as quite a surprise to the reviewer – both in terms of the richness of content and also the obvious pleas for help which can come through. It behoves everyone to give this exercise the time it deserves and to ensure that maximum benefit can be derived from it. Despite the managerial nature of the exercise, petty irritations can be aired, trumpets can be blown, markers can be put down for the future, and a valuable opportunity for a structured discussion with a line manager can be enjoyed. These are the people who will write references for new posts, make recommendations on promotion and hold (or have access to) funding streams within the HEI and have a heavy say in deployment, so they must be given the full picture of what an individual is, wants and sees themselves becoming.

The key messages for Meg and other academics embarking on doing performance reviews:

1. Encourage staff to get the full story across in their review form – they should not shrink from putting a positive spin on what they have achieved. Their aspirations can be considered even to the point of mutual acknowledgement that a move to another institution may be for the best.

2. Make sure that staff can get more information about the research requirements and other managerial expectations on them.
3. Take the opportunities to talk about future aspirations.

FURTHER READING

WEBSITES

www.cipd.co.uk
Own HEI Human Resource and Review policies.

PART II

Anton

Anton has worked as a solicitor for ten years in a national and later a city firm. He also previously worked in quality assurance for a European legal services regulator. He's now joined a private-sector legal-education provider following a number of years of requests to join from his new employer. They are rapidly expanding and want to draw upon experienced practitioners with major city connections. Anton is an accomplished practitioner but is new to education. He believes passionately in training the next generation of lawyers through a practical and employment-focused approach to their education. He holds little interest in academia and what he believes are antiquated methods of working and an inherent inability to appropriately respond to a fast changing marketplace.

CHAPTER 20

Being a Private University

CHRIS MAGUIRE

> Anton, a successful solicitor, is considering his future employment options and is
> considering working for a private university to teach the next generation of lawyers.

Identity and difference are complex and uncertain notions. The differences between
the public and private university sectors are decreasing and their identities converging;
but this is taking place at a time when the public university sector is diversifying and
its cohesiveness, even within the 'self-selecting "gangs"' of its mission groups, (Watson
2014), is contested.

The term 'public university' is a short-hand for publically funded university; all of
which are, confusingly, self-governing and part of the private sector, as defined by HM
Treasury. Private higher education institutions are also commonly referred to as 'alternative providers'. I shall follow Middlehurst and Fielden in using 'traditional' to refer
to the public university sector, alternative providers to refer to the wider private higher
education sector and within this shall refer to private universities separately.

The distinction between traditional and alternative providers is shrinking: 'since
most not-for-profit higher education institutions now operate in a business-like manner and seek to generate surpluses from many of their activities' (Middlehurst and
Fielden 2011). In addition, alternative providers may now access public funds through
HEFCE's course designation process. Students may then use their Student Finance
England loans to pay the fees; albeit to a maximum of £6,000 rather than the £9,000
available to the traditional sector. The end of the block teaching grant for all but
STEM subjects and funding from the Research Excellence Framework (REF) creates significant funding variations (Collini 2012) between traditional universities and
increases the convergence between those traditional universities that do not receive
such funds and their alternative provider counterparts. The funding of expensive and
high employment STEM programmes also raises issues within the traditional sector
itself about public, private and positional goods which ironically is often used as an
argument against alternative providers. Further convergence is likely in 2015/16 when
the student numbers cap is (also) removed for the private sector.

If it is increasingly difficult to define the traditional sector it is impossible to do
so for the alternative provider sector. To do so it is important to separate private universities and those with degree-awarding powers from the alternative provider group
as a whole. The latter is comprised of almost 700 institutions, widely diverse in size,

nature and mission. A third are non-specialist, a third specialise in business and management, 10% had religious foundations, 10% offer arts subjects, 5% engineering and 2% alternative medicine. 54% are for-profit, 39% not-for-profit and 6% 'other'. Over two-thirds are located in London and the South East. It serves approximately 160,000 students (out of a total student population of 2.5 million). 30% have fewer than 100 students; the average is 200; only 30 have over a thousand, only five of those have over 5,000 students. The student population varies across institutions but overall 49% are from the UK, 10% are from the EU and 41% non-EU. It is diverse ethnically and socially with a preponderance of students over the age of 25. Students' levels of satisfaction equalled or exceeded those of National Student Survey responses from students at traditional universities (Hughes et al. 2013).

There are five private universities: BPP, Buckingham, IFS, Regents and the University of Law, which represent fewer than 25% of the private-sector student population. It is questionable whether students at the private universities are aware of the distinction between them and traditional universities. It may be argued that the private universities are simply the latest iteration in the evolution of the university sector, following the 'Godless' University of London and other civics from 1826, the Robbins universities of the early 1960s, and the 1992 FHEA, post-binary, new universities.

Private universities are thought to have more regulatory freedom than their traditional counterparts; this is untrue. They are subject to the prescriptions of the QAA, HEFCE, HESA, the OIA and the UKVI. Degree awarding powers are renewed on a six-yearly cycle, while for traditional universities they are granted in perpetuity. Both sectors are subject to accreditation visits from relevant professional bodies; however, it is likely that, given their origins, private universities would have more such provision and thus more frequent regulatory oversight. Private universities are perceived to be agile in reacting to opportunities and developments. However, this is more likely to arise from the lean-management structures, sensitivity to the market, the avoidance of Gormenghastian processes and the absence of a public-sector financial safety net.

What, then, might be distinctive for a tutor joining a private university like BPP?

The working environment will be unashamedly corporate: service desks will open early and close late to accommodate the variety of programme modes delivered throughout the day; reception areas will be as busy in the evening as first thing in the morning. Professional dress is required for staff and expected of students.

The university delivers programmes through a multi-site, multi-start, multi-mode, environment, which makes the concept of an academic year less relevant than in the traditional sector. Tutors frequently deliver to multiple cohorts in a number of dispersed locations geographically and virtually. They will report to a number of team leaders who have responsibility for different programme modes and university centres, and liaise with module team colleagues who may be in a different city. Tutors will frequently communicate through and meet using technology such as Skype and webinars, and they will be aficionados in train timetables and hotel chains. The majority of tutors will be professionally qualified and have extensive experience of practice; an increasing proportion will have taught at other universities and hold doctorates. Their focus is on preparing independently minded, adaptable future practitioners with the intellectual skills to succeed in their chosen profession or to pursue further academic study.

Consequently, the university is research-informed, practice-facing but teaching-led. Teaching is paramount. Success and financial sustainability depends on students choosing the university and succeeding within it. While a high proportion of staff will be on full-time permanent contracts, planning models take account of the potential variation in market demand and build flexibility in to the staffing base.

Effectiveness in teaching is closely monitored, and tutors are expected to achieve a minimum student feedback score of 3 out of 5 in their first year and 4 thereafter and to achieve positive reviews in lesson observations. Teaching skills will be enhanced through individual learning plans, peer review, training director support and engagement in the university's PgCHE. Tutors will be also be supported through engagement in module teams, which meet weekly or fortnightly to review teaching from the previous week and preview teaching for the forthcoming week. Each session will be supported by a detailed set of tutor notes setting out the objectives, intended learning outcomes, syllabus, reading lists, resources, approach and variants for each class. Consistency of delivery is critical to ensure that students are afforded a fair and appropriate opportunity to achieve the learning outcomes of the module in relation to both the FHEQ and to relevant professional bodies' criteria. Students report that delivery is highly structured, expectations are clear, knowledge and skills acquisition is immediate and systematic and it is evident why the intended learning outcomes matter.

The importance of teaching and its relationship to student learning is reflected in the importance attached to programme design and the centrality of tutors in the design and approval processes. It is here that a new tutor will see the principles of programme construction – the alignment of intended learning outcomes, valid assessment instruments and effective delivery methods – played out in practice.

A significant difference between private and traditional universities is the emphasis on, and interpretation of, scholarship and research. Research, traditionally, has been accorded higher prestige than teaching and is regarded as the route to promotion (Becher and Trowler 2001). The definition of research is confined to what is recognised and financially rewarded by HEFCE's Research Excellence Framework (REF). The culture and paradigms of scholarship and research are less constrained, if also less developed, in the private universities. Scholarship is fundamental to currency in the discipline and changes in practice. Practice updating is a key aspect of staff development. Practitioners have commented that they developed a closer understanding of their subject when they were required to teach it, and that their teaching benefitted from refreshed practice experience. This cycle is invaluable in fostering greater integration of the academic and practice elements of programmes. Research in a private university will be closely related to teaching and practice matters; such as the implications of the Francis Report for Nursing, or the effects of advances in mobile phone technology on criminal evidence. The private university is similar to the traditional sector in that scholarship is a requisite and fundamental activity: it differs in that research, while encouraged is secondary to the quality of teaching and the student experience. The language of commerce has intruded into the traditional as much as in to the private universities (Collini 2012). There is now a fear that students are regarded as customers purchasing products. That is not the case in the private universities any more than it is in the traditional universities; our relationship with our students is much more sophisticated than that: like an intellectual health club we provide the environment, equipment, programmes, mentors, even the inspiration, but students must lift the weights themselves.

The sector will continue to converge as the unkempt meadow of current regulation evolves into a level playing field, and institutions will continue to evolve and diverge as Darwinian logic dictates. However, the differences within the sector will remain less important than what drives us:

the quality and standards of what we offer ... opportunities for learners across the life-course, ... the goals and conditions of membership of our rather peculiar institutions. (Watson 2014)

The key messages for Anton and other academics considering working at a private university:

1. More corporate, practice-facing and teaching-led than traditional universities. More engaged and responsive to the professions and practice.
2. More agile, with quicker decision-making processes of necessity than traditional universities.
3. Teaching is valued more than research but scholarship is essential.
4. The sectors are evolving and both converging as governance and regulation are made consistent and diverging as individual institutions respond to pressures and opportunities.

FURTHER READING

BOOKS

Becher, T. and Trowler, P. (October 2001) *Academic Tribes and Territories: Intellectual Enquiry and the Cultures of Disciplines*. London: Society for Research into Higher Education.

Collini, S. (2012) *What are Universities for?* London: Penguin.

Crossck, G. (2010) *The Growth of Private and for-Profit Higher Education Providers in the UK*, London: Universities UK.

WEBSITES

HESA (April (2011) Press release 159: *Survey of Private and For-Profit Providers of Higher Education in the UK* 2009/10. www.hesa.ac.uk/index.php?option=com_content&task=view&id=2086&Itemid=310

Middlehurst, R. and Fielden, J. (May 2011) *Private Providers in UK Higher Education: Some Policy Options*, 5. http://www.hepi.ac.uk/455-1969/Private-Providers-in-UK-Higher-Education-Some-Policy-Options.html

OTHERS

Hughes, T., Porter, A., Jones, S. and Sheen, J. (June 2013) Department of Business Innovation & Skills (BIS) Research Paper No. 111: *Privately Funded Providers of Higher Education in the UK*.

Watson, D. (2014) *'Only Connect': Is there Still a Higher Education Sector?* Higher Education Policy Unit Occasional Paper No. 8.

CHAPTER 21

Academic Dress

JESSICA GUTH

> Having moved to the private sector legal education provider Anton is unsure about the correct approach to his dress/appearance.

What do academics wear to work? Does it matter? Elsewhere in this volume Rachel Fenton highlights that women in particular may have to dress in a certain way in order to be taken seriously. That is of course something to remember but it is also worth remembering that as academics we do different things in one day: we might teach, attend meetings, carry out research and spend time behind a desk doing paperwork. Comfort is important.

There is no universal dress code in academia. It is interesting to walk around different institutions and different departments within institutions and observe how academics are dressed. There are the stereotypical slightly scruffy sociologists or philosophers and the equally stereotypical lawyers in suits and every level of formal in between. How you fit into that is mostly up to you. Of course it is difficult to be the one in jeans when everyone else is in a suit or vice versa but how you choose to dress depends on what you want.

Whether we like it or not, how we dress does say something about us and dress can be used to send a message or make a statement. Partly therefore we all conform to expectations to a greater or lesser extent. In some institutions, often those which offer the vocational courses or are more vocationally focused, it is not unusual for the majority of lecturers to be in suits or other smart office wear. In other institutions it is normal for most people to be dressed in a very casual way. My advice, however, would be to choose what feels right and this might mean wearing different sorts of things on different occasions depending on what your day involves. Cownie's work with Legal Academics for example suggests that for some dress is an important consideration and that some at least dress more formally when they are teaching.

My own experience suggests that I do dress differently depending on the work I am doing and on how confident I am feeling. I have noticed for example that my style of clothes for work has become more casual as I have settled into my role as a legal academic. When I first started I would dress more formally. While often wearing jeans I would wear quite formal shirts or blouses with them, or if wearing a slightly more casual top I would wear smarter trousers. Mostly now comfort is my first (and often only) consideration and if I consider clothes at all I use them for a purpose. For example, I almost never wear high heels of any description but I often wear a slight heel for my first teaching session of the academic year because they make me feel a little taller and more confident. I will dress smartly when carrying out empirical research with professionals or other stakeholders but will 'dress down' when speaking to other groups of research participants; I deliberately wear jeans for open days and other activities with prospective students because I do not want to create barriers by dressing really formally and I do the same in teaching. I do wear a suit when assessing moot or presentations because I expect the students to dress smartly during those assessments and because it adds formality to the occasion.

Other activities such as conference presentations also throw up questions of what to wear and again this is about what you are comfortable with. I have some clothes (both smart and casual) that I associate with 'getting in the game' and 'performing' and they help me prepare myself for whatever it is I am doing – be it teaching a new class or presenting my research or going to a meeting I suspect will be a little tense. Clothes are about confidence and if you feel confident you can do those performative elements of our job so much better.

There are one or two anecdotes about dress which I think are worth sharing because they were shared with me and are probably also the stuff of academics' nightmares. The first was shared with me on my first day of teaching in higher education. I was wearing a skirt, not something I have done when teaching since, and my colleague told me about one of her first ever lectures that, it turns out, she delivered with her skirt tucked in the back of her underwear. That story was quickly followed with another anecdote from another colleague who was giving a lecture during which a student kept trying to get his attention. He asked all students to keep their questions until the end but the student in question was persistent. Eventually my colleague was handed a note by the student which pointed out that my colleague's flies were undone. There are others of buttons popping on shirts, wearing things inside out or back to front (this I have done!). If this happens to you nothing can get you away from that initial sense of total embarrassment but a sense of humour will get you through!

There are other things about what (not) to wear which I have learned over the years. The first relates to graduation ceremonies. If you take part in them and wear the traditional academic dress of gown and hood, wear a shirt with buttons so you have something to hook the hood onto but make sure it is a well-fitting shirt otherwise the hood just pulls your shirt up. Wearing a tie can help with that too. Also wear comfortable trousers that are not tight anywhere because most graduation ceremonies involve a lot of sitting down – if you are uncomfortable you might see yourself on the graduation video fidgeting!

I keep a cardigan or jumper in the office because heating in teaching rooms and other areas in my institution can vary hugely. It can also be sensible to keep a spare top if like me you are prone to throwing coffee down yourself and would rather not teach or go to meetings with coffee stains on a white shirt. For those of you who like wearing high heels or other smart shoes which look good and make you feel confident but perhaps are not as comfortable as you would like, keep comfy shoes in the office to change into and remember – on those precious working-at-home days – nobody will ever know if you never get round to changing out of your pyjamas!

> The key messages for Anton and other academics considering academics dress:
>
> 1. What you wear is up to you!
> 2. Focus on comfort and confidence.
> 3. Different institutions have different cultures so how you dress while working there might be different to how you would dress when working somewhere else.

FURTHER READING

BOOK

Cownie, F. (2004) *Legal Academics: Culture and Identities*, Oxford: Hart.
http://thisishowacademicsdress.tumblr.com/

CHAPTER 22

The Standardised Client and Clinic

RORY O'BOYLE

Anton is keen to develop the use of Standard Client as part of the learning and teaching strategy for the law clinic.

This chapter describes a method of teaching and assessing students' client interviewing and communication skills using a type of simulated legal encounter involving what are known as standardised clients. The method is a form of clinical legal education, a broad-ranging concept defined as learning through participation in real or realistic interactions coupled with reflections on that experience. At one end of the clinical spectrum are in-house advice and representation clinics, often seen as the 'gold standard' of law clinics as they seek to replicate in the law school the type of services clients could expect if they went to a firm of solicitors. At the other end of the clinical spectrum are simulated legal encounters. Such simulated encounters can be extremely valuable from an educational perspective as they can be used either as a bridge to prepare students for participation in a live client clinic, or, alternatively, as a more low-cost and low-risk form of clinical legal education. Such forms of 'clinic light' can be particularly useful for law schools which are new to, but interested in becoming involved in, clinical methods.

In summary, standardised clients are lay people who are trained to perform in a simulated legal encounter such that they assume the same profile, know the same facts, and respond to students' questions and techniques so that the experience of each student is as close as possible to that of all other students. However, the innovative and interesting aspect of the method is that the standardised clients are also trained to complete a formal assessment of the students' communication skills in accordance with a strict set of criteria (see below). Given that the process involves using lay persons to assess students' communication skills, it is in some respects radical. However, the method has potentially positive cost implications, which from a practical perspective can be extremely important because skills-based teaching and assessment is generally extremely resource intensive. Furthermore, from a research perspective, the method presents great scope for adaptation in how it is applied, which in turn opens up the possibility of rich opportunities for pedagogical-based research. All these issues are explored in greater depth below, but firstly it is worthwhile briefly considering the broader context within which interviewing and communication skills are taught, traditional methods of teaching and assessing such skills and the case for implementing changes.

Research indicates that when in practice our students will be to a large extent judged by their clients' *experience* of them as service provides, but that the required communication skills will not necessarily be gained 'on-the-job', there being little or no correlation between years in practice and the quality of legal service providers' communication skills (Cunningham 2006; Sherr 2000). In fact, it is worth noting that the 2013 Legal Education and Training Review has identified teaching and assessing communication skills as a core concern for those involved in the provision of legal services education and training.

Traditional methods of teaching interviewing and communications skills have generally combined large-scale lectures, followed by small group work. Assessing students' abilities, if it is done at all, usually involves individual videotaped role-play sessions whereby actors pose as clients and are interviewed by students. Each recording is subsequently reviewed and assessed by a law teacher, a cumbersome process that is expensive when dealing with large numbers of students. The validity of the assessment process may also be questioned because of the possible variation in how each actor presents the particular legal scenario to students and, when dealing with large numbers of students, the risk of variation in the assessment criteria applied by each individual law teacher. The issue for legal educators therefore is to devise methods of skills-based assessment that are reliable and cost effective. Barton et al. (2006) conducted a large-scale project to test the validity of using standardised clients for assessment purposes. In doing so, the authors were drawing heavily on an analogous method of teaching and assessing communication skills used in medical education involving the use of 'standardised patients' (see Grosberg 2001). As part of Barton et al.'s study, 265 student interviews with standardised clients (who were intensively trained for the process – see below) were conducted and all student performances were assessed on two separate occasions; firstly by a standardised client and then independently by a law teacher, with responses compared. All aspects of the assessment showed significant levels of correlation between the standardised client and law teacher responses, leading to the conclusion that the use of standardised clients was at least as reliable as and more cost effective than law-teacher assessment. As such, the Glasgow Graduate School of Law (where the study was conducted) now relies on standardised clients for assessment purposes. In 2009, graduates from the Franklin Pierce Law Centre became the first group of law students in the USA to take part in a high-stakes interviewing assessment using the standardised-client approach. In the UK in 2010, the Solicitors Regulation Authority adopted the standardised-client method as part of its Qualifying Lawyers Transfer Scheme assessment process. In 2012 the Law Society of Ireland adopted the method when assessing communication skills on postgraduate professional diploma courses.

It is worthwhile summarising some of the key issues that you will need to be aware of if implementing the standardised client method at your law school. The limitations of this chapter do not permit a detailed analysis of the process. However, Barton et al.'s 2006 paper provides very useful resources for those interested in replicating the approach, including for example the assessment forms and assessment criteria used to evaluate the students' performances and guidelines for the training of the standardised clients. Additional excellent resources are also available from the '*Standardised Client Initiative*' website, details of which are also provided below.

The overall validity and reliability of the assessment process conducted by the standardised clients is to a large extent determined by the quality of the training provided. The first task is to draft a believable scenario that will form the basis of the simulated interview. This is a job for the law teacher, who must be able to clearly distinguish for the standardised clients between facts that must be consistently provided in each student interview, or otherwise the legal meaning of the scenario is altered, and those issues that the standardised clients are free to improvise. You must also be mindful of the importance of selecting your standardised clients, as they must have an ability to perform the chosen scenario consistently and not be prejudiced in their assessment of students, for example due to racial or sex bias. The challenge then is to train each standardised client so that the experience of each student in the interview is as close as possible to that of all other students. Furthermore, the standardised clients must then be trained to evaluate the students' performance in a consistent, accurate and fair manner, the goal being to achieve a standardisation in both performance and assessment. Such training is intensive and is usually conducted over a number of days involving numerous simulated role-plays and group marking of performances to ensure that common understandings of assessment standards emerge within the group of standardised clients.

It is important to emphasise that the method, in the first instance at any rate, is primarily used in the assessment of students' communication and interviewing skills, not legal knowledge, which of course is consistent with the fact the assessment is conducted by non-law teachers. The assessment form asks the standardised clients to evaluate specific aspects of the students' interviewing abilities, for example, their listening skills, their questioning technique and their ability to summarise the client's problems. However, to ensure that the assessment is not merely a subjective analysis of the standardised clients' impressions of the interview, each question in the assessment form is based on a much more detailed set of assessment criteria which analysis in clear specific objective terms the skills under review. Again, if you are seeking to apply the method in your law school some of the resources listed below provide excellent guidance on practical considerations including examples of the assessment forms and assessment criteria used.

The key messages for Anton and other academics considering using standardised clients:

1. Standardised clients can be a reliable and cost-effective method of teaching and assessing client interviewing and communication skills, particularly when dealing with large groups of students.

2. The method presents opportunities for innovation in your approach to teaching and assessment of particular legal skills, which in turn presents interesting opportunities for pedagogical-based research.

3. As a form of clinical legal education 'light', the use of standardised clients is particularly useful for those organisations wishing to engage with clinical methods but without having to commit to, initially at any rate, full in-house advice and representation clinics.

FURTHER READING

JOURNAL

Barton, K., Cunningham, C., Jones, G. and Maharg, P. (2006) Valuing What Clients Think: Standardized Clients and Assessment of Communicative Competence, *Clinical Law Review*, 13(1), 1–65.

Grosberg, L. (2001) Medical Education Again Provides a Model for Law Schools: The Standardized Patient Becomes the Standardized Client, *Journal of Legal Education*, 51(2), 212–234.

Sherr, A. (2000) The Value of Experience in Legal Competence, *International Journal of the Legal Profession*, 7(2), 95–124.

WEBSITES

Cunningham, C. (2006) What Clients Want From Their Lawyers, Paper prepared for *The Society of Writers to Her Majesty's Signet*. http://clarkcunningham.org/

Standardised Client Initiative (2011). http://zeugma.typepad.com/sci/

CHAPTER 23

Developing Clinic

Victoria Murray

> Anton has been asked to develop a law clinic at his institution.

Clinical Legal Education (CLE), the pedagogy of students learning through doing in an authentic legal context, was historically the mainstay of US and modern UK universities, but is now embedded across higher education (HE) both in the UK and internationally. CLE takes many shapes and forms including law clinics, where students work on real legal problems on a pro bono basis under supervision. For the purpose of this chapter, the definition of clinic is restricted to live client activities; simulation, standardised client and Street Law are covered elsewhere in this handbook.

Law clinics exist in almost every corner of the globe. For example well-established clinics can be found at City University New York (USA), Monash University (Australia), Northumbria University (UK) and University of KwaZulu-Natal (South Africa). The prominence of law clinics continues to grow nationally, with over 60% of UK law schools engaged in pro bono work (LawWorks Student Pro Bono Report 2011). There is therefore an emerging clinical trend and it remains a fast developing area of legal HE.

Any readers contemplating setting up a clinic should recognise that this brings with it significant challenges and rewards, both pedagogically and professionally, outlined below.

Conventional research-focused universities have traditionally shunned CLE, believing the role of HE institutions is to educate rather than train students, but this attitude is fast becoming outdated. Red bricks are now just as likely to be engaged in some form of clinic, however limited. Notwithstanding, a hangover of this bygone view is that schools and intractable colleagues may need some concentrated persuasion when it comes to supporting and 'buying in' to the benefits of CLE.

There are many reasons to implement a clinical programme. Potential law students are alive to the need for relevant (legal) experience as a precursor to a training contract and expect their prospective institution will support their development of relevant skills and provide exposure to legal practice. Clinic can therefore be a strong contributor to student recruitment and greatly assist with employability statistics. From a teaching perspective, students tend to engage much more deeply with this methodology, often driven by the desire to achieve a positive outcome for their clients. Supervising students and clients can be extremely rewarding. CLE also provides rich research material and can generate numerous collaborative opportunities.

On the other hand, the challenges are wide reaching, but by no means insurmountable. Clinical activities must be appropriately resourced and one of the key tests for academics is balancing the time that must be devoted to supervising cases and students, which is intrinsically laborious owing to the professional obligations and potential consequences arising from the provision of legal services. This must be managed taking into account other demands including research outputs, traditional classroom-based teaching and administrative duties. Central to the success of any clinic is ensuring sufficient time is provided within the academic workload to support the project, and this is particularly important in the development stage.

Planning will, naturally, be crucial. *A Student Guide to Clinical Legal Education and Pro Bono*, edited by Kerrigan and Murray (2011), contains a detailed chapter outlining a wide range of pedagogical and practical considerations which should be fully addressed in any development and implementation phases. Some of the key issues are covered briefly below.

All legal work must be properly supervised. This can be done by an academic within the institution who is also a practising lawyer, or where this is not possible, by using an adjunct legal professional from a partner law firm. This available supervision may dictate or limit the scope of work and types of cases a clinic can offer. Common service areas include housing, welfare benefits, immigration, crime (often through an Innocence Project), employment and civil disputes. Small business clinics can be useful to equip students with specialist commercial experience, particularly if they are seeking a training contract with large firms.

Carrying out legal activities will necessitate appropriate insurance cover. The clinic's institution may cover the legal activities under its own insurance or through an appropriate scheme, available through LawWorks. Other resource issues to consider will include premises, equipment and administrative support.

A fundamental point to contemplate is which model to adopt. Clinics can be predicated on a variety of models ranging from providing basic referrals, advice only, to full representation services. Institutions which cannot accommodate in-house clinics may wish to provide opportunities via placements with law firms or advice agencies, such as the Citizens Advice Bureau (CAB).

Consideration should be given to how, or indeed whether, the clinic will be integrated within the curriculum. This may depend on the resources available and aims of the project's activities. Whilst law clinics typically serve undergraduate students, they also increasingly feature in postgraduate programmes. Very few clinical offerings are compulsory and there is a variance in approach between clinics which are optional, credit bearing and extracurricular.

Devising a clear set of objectives and learning outcomes is also crucial. There is a longstanding and ongoing debate about the purpose of law clinics, with some academics believing in the social justice agenda with others asserting the function is to develop legal and transferable skills.

In conclusion, developing a clinic requires dedication and careful planning. Once established, the impact on students, the institution and community is almost immediate and for supervisors it is often one of the most rewarding aspects of the academic role.

The key messages for Anton and other academics considering developing a clinic:

1. Make sure colleagues are fully informed of clinical plans as it is important that the clinic is properly supported across the institution's department/school/faculty.
2. The clinical community is very welcoming – develop contacts and networks at an early stage to draw on support to help develop the clinic. Reputable groups include GAJE, ENCLE and the UK arm of CLEO.
3. Engage with the legal and voluntary communities as they can be an excellent source of case referrals.
4. There is a wealth of free resources available online so don't waste time reinventing the wheel.
5. Build a clinical profile and that of your institution's clinic, by attending clinical specific conferences, entering awards such as the annual LawWorks and Attorney General Student Pro Bono Awards and participating in National Pro Bono Week.

FURTHER READING

BOOKS

Bloch, F. (2010) *The Global Clinical Movement: Educating Lawyers for Social Justice*, Oxford: Oxford University Press.

Kerrigan, K. and Murray, V. (co-eds) (2011) *A Student Guide to Clinical Legal Education and Pro Bono*, Basingstoke and New York: Palgrave Macmillan.

WEBSITES

Clinical Law Review. www.law.nyu.edu/journals/clinicallawreview

Clinical Legal Education Organisation (CLEO) – to join the mailing list contact francess. daly@york.ac.uk

European Network for Clinical Legal Education. www.encle.org/

Global Alliance for Justice Education. www.gaje.org/

International Journal of Clinical Legal Education. www.northumbriajournals.co.uk/index. php/ijcle

LawWorks. www.lawworks.org.uk/

National Pro Bono. Centre www.nationalprobonocentre.org.uk/

CHAPTER 24

Further Developing Street Law

SARAH MORSE AND PAUL MCKEOWN

> Following the success of the law clinic, the institution is also keen to develop a street law programme.

Street Law began in 1972 at Georgetown University Law Center when a group of students developed an experiential curriculum to teach high school students about law and the legal system (Street Law INC no date). It has been described as 'a powerful tool for social change, promoting greater awareness of civic rights and encouraging participation in the democratic process' (Grimes et al. 2011). Street Law is a form of public legal education that aims to educate the public on their legal rights and responsibilities. It involves students going into the community to provide information about the law and how it affects particular groups or individuals. Street Law programmes can be delivered to a variety of groups, including schools, prisons, tenant federations and other community organisations.

Grimes et al. (2011) identifies various models of Street Law that include:

- The credit-bearing or integrated model
- The nonclinical or pro bono model
- The law student organisations model

The differences between these models of Street Law generally relate to whether students gain academic credit for their participation and who takes responsibility for the organisation of the Street Law programme. Academics are usually involved in the credit-bearing or integrated model although they may also be responsible for organising a Street Law programme on an extra curricula basis.

A Street Law programme can involve students engaging in a one-off activity (such as delivering a presentation on welfare rights to a homeless charity) or alternatively require a more regular, sustained contribution (such as preparing and running a mock trial with high school students). The activity developed by students ought to be engaging and relevant to the group and can take any form such as a debate, case study, mock trial or workshop. There is a great deal of flexibility within a Street Law programme to allow students to work in a self-directed way or instead for it to form part of a more supported learning activity with greater academic involvement.

As an academic responsible for a Street Law programme, you are likely to engage with a number of stakeholder groups including students, third party partners (such as lawyers) and community groups. The programme will provide a number of benefits to each of these groups and to you and your institution.

The benefit of Street Law for students is that it allows them to connect their academic understanding of the law to the practise of law. Numerous lawyering skills are utilised throughout the course of preparing and delivering a Street Law activity including research, problem solving, and communication. Students also have the opportunity to develop and demonstrate a real understanding and knowledge of legal issues through the requirement to explain these in layman's terms to the community groups. As part of the programme, students will often also work in a group thus encouraging teamwork and collaboration.

Street Law also connects law students to social issues and engages them in aspects of society that they may not have previously experienced thus providing a valuable encounter with political, social and economic issues. MacDowell (2008) states that

> The Street Law program appealed to [her] because [she] thought it would provide a powerful reality check in terms of connecting as a law student with a community far from the law school classroom. It also fit with [her] conception of one of the meaningful things [she] could do as a lawyer: obtain important, specialized knowledge, associated with power, and make it available to people who otherwise lacked access.

Activities such as this provide opportunities for students to develop practise-based skills and therefore arguably better prepare them to enter the legal profession. Street Law programmes may also enhance the employability of students and facilitate the development of transferable skills. The importance of Law Schools advancing both theoretical and practical knowledge is highlighted by the Carnegie Report (concerning teaching in American and Canadian law schools) and the Legal Education and Training Review (a review of education and training in England and Wales).

For the university, a Street Law programme presents a valuable clinical experience but is lower risk and far less resource intensive than other forms of clinical legal education. It does not require any form of professional indemnity insurance as legal advice is not being provided to an individual client. Nor does it require a physical space within the law school to store files and for students to carry out casework. The level of academic supervision required is also far lower than a casework clinical model and indeed some models are solely student-led. Offering practical, clinical opportunities to students can be a valuable marketing tool to assist in the recruitment of prospective students.

There is also potential for third parties, such as lawyers and non-governmental organisations, to become involved in Street Law programmes. These partners can support the students and add their own knowledge and experience to the programme. Pinder (1998) states that 'Street Law allows lawyers and judges to connect with law students and the community with a much more flexible time commitment than many other pro bono service.' Many lawyers and organisations want to engage in pro bono work and recognise they have a responsibility to society. However, many pro bono opportunities can be demanding and therefore dissuade participation. These issues can be addressed in a Street Law programme, allowing flexibility in the commitment they give.

Street Law also has the potential to provide a valuable service to the community. Universities sit at the heart of the community with many adopting this notion as part of their mission statement or ethos. Whilst it is recognised by McQuoid-Mason (2008) that most of the evidence concerning the impact of Street Law programmes is quantitative and anecdotal, groups are empowered by knowledge. Grimes et al. (2011) highlights the example of South Africa and how Street Law helped to break down the apartheid racial barriers by enabling black and white school children to share their experiences and debate important societal issues. In many jurisdictions, where access to justice is restricted, increasing knowledge about legal rights and responsibilities is vital.

For all of these reasons, academics may wish to become involved in developing a Street Law programme. These programmes can be both innovative and rewarding. A successful programme can afford you networking opportunities (in the wider community and with third party partners), enhance career prospects through forward-thinking teaching methods and enhanced student satisfaction. It can also be an enjoyable experience for you.

The key messages for Anton and other academics considering developing a Street Law programme:

1. It provides an opportunity to engage in innovative teaching.
2. It is a flexible and less resource-intensive clinical teaching method.
3. It affords opportunities and benefits to you, your students the community and the university.

FURTHER READING

BOOKS

Arbetman, L. P. and O'Brien, E. L. (2009) *Street Law: A Course in Practical Law*, 8th edn, McGraw-Hill/Glencoe: Columbus, Ohio.

Grimes, R., Mcquoid-Mason, D., O'Brien, E. and Zimmer, J. (2011) Street Law and Social Justice Education, in F. S. Bloch (ed.) *The Global Clinical Movement: Educating Lawyers for Social Justice*. DOI10.1093/acprof:oso/9780195381146.001.0001

JOURNALS

MacDowell, E. L. (2008) Law on the Street: Legal Narrative and the Street Law Classroom, *Rutgers Race & Law Review*, 9, 285–333.

Mcquoid-Mason, D. (2008) Street Law as a Clinical Program – The South African Experience with Particular Reference to the University of KwaZulu-Natal, *Griffith Law Review*, 17, 27–51.

Pinder, K. A. (1998) Street Law: Twenty-Five Years and Counting, *Journal of Law & Education*, 27, 211–233.

WEBSITE

Street Law INC (no date) www.streetlaw.org/en/home (home page).

CHAPTER 25

Writing for a Professional Audience

John Hodgson

Anton would like to disseminate his research and expertise to practitioners.

One thing to bear in mind is that, while a legal professional audience has different characteristics to an academic or student one, the differences are one of degree. Indeed there are a number of publications which seek to appeal to a mixed audience, particularly those focusing on specific subject areas. Even here, there will be distinctions. Some publications are aimed primarily at practitioners, and only incidentally academics with an interest in the field; some are the reverse and others appeal equally to both audiences. In all cases authors are likely to be drawn from practitioners as well as academics, and it is the audience which differs. It must also be remembered that there is no hard and fast dividing line between practitioners and academics. Lady Hale is only the most eminent of a number of judges who have at some time held academic positions, and there are many visiting academics with a professional background, and some academics also practice or sit judicially. The point of this introduction is to stress that there is in many respects no hard and fast dividing line between writing for a professional audience and writing for an academic one. There are a number of distinguishing features, but it is largely the emphasis which varies rather than the fundamentals of the process.

We need to consider a little more closely the type of material which is in demand. This will include material in a range of types of journal, but also other forms of publication.

The first point to note is that professionals, whether legal or otherwise, are practitioners. They are therefore primarily concerned with accessing material which is of utility in the conduct of their practice. But this does not mean that they are simply concerned with the nuts and bolts of techniques and practicalities. Effective practitioners take an active interest in the theoretical underpinnings of their discipline and are as concerned to understand why they are adopting a particular procedure or course of action as with the detail of the steps being taken. However, they will typically be less concerned with what one might call abstract theory. To take an example, any legal practitioner currently concerned with civil dispute resolution will be well aware of the

Jackson reforms to civil procedure, and the way in which these have been interpreted in cases such as those on relief from sanctions: Mitchell v News Group Newspapers Ltd [2013] EWCA Civ 1537 and Denton v TH White Ltd and another, Decadent Vapours Ltd v Bevan and others and Utilise TDS Ltd v Davies and another [2014] EWCA Civ 906. Information and comment on the implications of these cases is of vital importance. Failure to comply with the requirements of the rules is not only costly, but also damaging in professional terms. A discussion of the rationale of the decisions is valuable in order to perform a view as to how practice is going to develop, and whether judges will maintain the very strict approach to non-compliance or become more generous in granting relief from sanctions. What is not seen as helpful is discussion explicitly in the light of any theoretical socio-legal or even socio-economic approach. Unless and until it can be demonstrated that the judges are acting in accordance with the dictates of such theories, they will not be helpful in predicting the actual course of events. Practitioners perceive themselves as extremely busy, and do not consider themselves to have time to devote to what they would see, rightly or wrongly, as a distraction from the main objective of ascertaining the direction of travel of judicial thinking in relation to the type of problem which they are likely to meet in practice.

Successful writing for this audience will reflect this. If the target audience is looking for an intelligent commentary which focuses on practical implications, it makes sense to provide this. There is in principle no reason why such articles, if of the appropriate standard, should not contribute fully to the REF or similar research evaluation exercises.

There is, however, a wider professional audience also available. A whole range of professional activity has legal implications, and practitioners are interested in the commentary and discussion in this area. There are many professional journals which cater to a range of audiences, including the medical profession, and allied professions such as nursing, the range of professions associated with the construction industry, as well as those associated with banking, insurance and other aspects of commerce. The majority of their contents will be on substantive issues relevant to the particular profession, and contributed by a specialist in the field, whether practitioner or academic. However, the editors of these publications recognise the relevance of the legal aspect outlined above, and commonly look for a legal perspective. Often, they look primarily to legal practitioners to provide this, but there is scope for an academic to contribute. However, very often the material that is being sought is more in the nature of current awareness, or commentary on current developments, rather than anything more challenging. These are normally commercial journals, and they do pay a fee, although this is hardly generous. It should be noted that the nature of this work is highly unlikely to count directly towards any research evaluation exercise, although it may be valuable in terms of engagement with the profession in question, and may help to raise the profile of a research cluster or otherwise demonstrate relevance. There is of course the possibility of doing more advanced work, and a legal contribution of a medico-legal nature, albeit in a medical journal, would be a suitable example.

The important point to remember in relation to these types of publication is that the primary audience is a non-legal one. Although some will have had some formal legal education, many will not, and the extent to which they have been exposed to legal concepts and terminology is very variable. It is therefore important to ensure that your writing in this context is as accessible as possible. It may be necessary to explain specific legal technical terms in a way that would be wholly unnecessary when writing for a legal audience. It is always helpful to look at previous legal contributions to this journal. This will give you a good idea of the level of explanation which is appropriate.

This piece has tended to focus on contributions to journals and other periodicals. This is because the vast majority of material will take this form. There are however opportunities in the field of the writing of textbooks and other similar material. Essentially, the same advice holds good. When writing for a non-legal audience, aim for maximum simplicity and clarity of language and ensure that all technical legal terms and concepts are properly explained, either in the text or as a glossary for similar appendix.

The key messages for Anton and other academics considering writing for a professional audience:

1. Be aware of the audience you are writing for.
2. Focus on the practical implications and application in practice of the area you are discussing.
3. If writing for a non-legal audience, make sure you are writing accessibly.

FURTHER READING

BOOK

Orwell, G. (2004) *Why I Write*, London: Penguin Books.

WEBSITE

The Plain English Campaign. http://www.plainenglish.co.uk

Chapter 26

Simulation and Legal Education

Karen Barton

> As part of Anton's broader approach to learning and teaching he is looking to integrate simulation into the law curricula.

In 2007, a Harvard Law School study of practicing lawyers found that a large majority of them perceive critical gaps between what they were taught in law schools and the skills they needed in the workplace (Koo 2007). Unfortunately this perception (perhaps even the reality) has not altered greatly in the intervening years and yet there are effective ways in which the education of the future generation of lawyers can be made more relevant, practical and experiential.

Many legal academics and tutors already employ case-study or scenario-based approaches to learning; and debates, moots and other types of role-play activities are generally embedded throughout most legal curricula. In general these types of situational, constructivist, problem-based learning approaches help bring the curriculum to life and develop essential legal skills and reasoning. Simulation is a further development of the same underlying philosophies to educational design and is defined for the purposes of this commentary as a representation of aspects of legal reality in which a student can, to a greater or lesser extent, create and manipulate data and/or artefacts in order to learn legal procedures, concepts and values. Though there are many different definitions of the term *simulation* (see for example Sauvé et al. 2007) in this context, and for simplicity, the term is used to mean a realistic representation of a legal 'transaction' or process which takes place in meaningful contexts rather than in a more formal, instructional setting.

Learning through simulation provides an environment where law students can learn by doing and, if designed correctly, can help enhance their legal knowledge as well as their legal skills. It allows them to practice non-linear, client-centred and ethical decision making, close to real-world legal transactions. Most importantly it prepares them for the workplace and should therefore appeal to educators who are interested in a practical and employment-focused approach to law students' education.

Since the world of simulations is large and complex, rather than providing a form of 'how-to' guide, this commentary will focus instead on the three most important questions that need to be considered when moving to this form of learning: the what, why and how of using simulations in legal education.

By its nature, a simulation represents some aspect of reality, but since reality can never be truly replicated, the design of a simulation involves extrapolating certain aspects of reality relevant to the educational task. Essentially this produces an overlap of three distinct elements: the disciplinary content, in this case legal reality (what should the simulation simulate?); the educational intention and design (why should it do so, and which criteria will be applied?); and finally the simulation implementation within the legal curriculum (how will it do so?). Each of these is highly complex in its own right. When overlaid, the complexity can easily spiral out of control if all three are not understood and managed within a design environment that takes account of the relationships between the three elements.

At a very basic, procedural level, the shape and function of a simulation is determined by the shape and function of the legal process it represents. Therefore legal reality, as well as the educational design and intention, affects the form and content of a simulation. Barton and Maharg (2007) characterised legal educational simulations as existing across a broad spectrum with 'bounded field' simulations at one extreme representing the more linear type of predictable, operational legal processes such as conveyancing or probate where chains of documentation are produced in some form of sequential pattern; to the more varied, diffuse or 'open field' domains such as negotiation-based transactions which are more fluid with variable (and equally correct) outcomes, no specific pre-defined sequence, and less of a requirement to follow specific actions or procedures or produce a set of pre-defined documents. A simulation characterised by one of the extremes at either end of the spectrum may not exist in practical terms in reality, but the concept helps to define the nature and clarify the processes of simulation learning. For example, using this metaphor, it is possible to characterise and place the study of other subject areas (e.g. civil court procedure) somewhere between these two poles.

Just as simulations represents reality across a broad spectrum of transaction types so too can they be applied across a broad range of educational intentions. It is possible, for example, within the construct of an educational simulation to assess sets of pre-defined learning outcomes which can be demonstrated by achievement of task or delivery of a specific output; or to shape the simulation around the production of 'bodies of evidence' to benchmark standards, with less emphasis on pre-specified outcomes themselves. Put another way, simulations are useful educational tools for learning complex concepts and values as well as procedural tasks and knowledge. This is highly important in the study of law and especially as it applies in professional life where, even the merest of operational tasks, are always based on embedded concepts. It is difficult to think of any legal process, for example, which does not contain concepts or principles which are an essential, if sometimes hidden, part of the process. Simulation may help raise awareness of those hidden concepts and make them, at least, more consequential.

Finally, the way in which simulations are embedded within the curriculum is also informed by this notion of closed or open field types. Simulations may be highly model driven and designed so that the simulation tasks and outcomes are tightly aligned with the teaching and academic structure (e.g. the lectures and tutorials) and so that learning resources are also tied in closely. The learning is effectively heavily 'pushed' by the curriculum structure. At the other end of the spectrum, teaching is provided where needed according to learners' needs, often according to a professional, just-in-time learning structure (e.g. Q&A sessions, seminars, discussion forums). Simulation resources are not linked directly to tasks and the learner needs to structure the trans-action themselves through interactive querying of resources in a highly learner-driven model. In other words, learning is 'pulled' by learners.

In summary, if proper consideration of the purpose, applicability and feasibility of using simulation in legal education is undertaken then it can be one of the most rewarding and effective forms of learning for both students and teachers.

The key messages for Anton and other academics considering simulation and legal education:

1. Design the form of the simulation based on WHAT the purpose of the simulation will be in terms of the disciplinary content to be learned.
2. Ensure you understand WHY simulation is the best educational design for this purpose and WHICH educational outcomes will be assessed.
3. Consider and plan HOW the simulation will be implemented in the broader curriculum design.

FURTHER READING

BOOKS

Barton, K. and Maharg, P. (2007) E-simulations in the Wild: Interdisciplinary Research, Design and Implementation of Simulation Environments in Legal Education, in D. Gibson, C. Aldrich and M. Prensky (eds) *Games and Simulations in Online Learning: Research and Development Frameworks*, London: Information Science Publishing.

Barton, K. and McKellar, P. (2010) From Master to Games-master: Disequilibrium and Scaffolding in Simulation-based Learning, in Maharg, P and de Freitas, S (eds) *Learning Through Play*, London: Continuum International Publishing Group.

Maharg, P. (2004) Virtual Communities on the Web: Transactional Learning and Teaching, in A. Vedder (ed.) *Aan het Werk met ICT in het Academisch Onderwijs – RechtenOnline*, Rotterdam: Wolf Legal Publishers.

Maharg, P. (2007) *Transforming Legal Education: Learning and Teaching the Law in the Early Twenty-first Century*, Hampshire, UK: Ashgate.

JOURNAL

Sauvé, L., Renaud, L., Kaufman, D. and Marquis, J. S. (2007) Distinguishing Between Games and Simulations: A Systematic Review, *Educational Technology & Society*, 10(3), 247–256.

WEBSITES

Koo, G. (2007) New Skills, New Learning: Legal Education and the Promise of New Technology, Berkman Center Research Publication No. 2007-4. SSRN: http://ssrn.com/abstract=976646 or http://dx.doi.org/10.2139/ssrn.976646

CHAPTER 27

Large Group Teaching

KAREN DEVINE

> Alongside Anton's work with the law clinic he is teaching mainly large groups of students.

Since the mid-1990s, legal education has witnessed a proliferation of students entering higher education institutions (HEIs) with universities accepting far more women, ethnic minorities and those from widened participation schemes in ever-increasing numbers. This influx of diversity amongst students and an increase in class sizes has led universities to implement teaching styles best suited to reach large groups comprised of students from a wide variety of intellectual vantage points. Moreover, research carried out in the late 1990s (Boyle and Dunn 1998) highlighted that there are four distinct forms of 'learners' amongst law students: Auditory, Visual, Tactual and Kinaesthetic; all of which should be catered for within the delivery of legal education. For large-group teaching this can be particularly challenging; however, it is possible to combine a number of instructional methods and ones that are likely to reach a broad spectrum of legal learners when used interchangeably.

Traditionally, large group teaching has been conducted via lectures delivered in sizeable auditoriums where the lecturer imparts key information and expert knowledge in a predominantly auditory and passive fashion. Whilst this style is conducive to the auditory learner, less than 30% of a typical cohort respond to this style of teaching, leaving the majority of the group in a state of disconnect with the lecture content. Modern lecture styles attempt to address this issue by keeping the student more involved and invested in the lecture. One example can be seen in the 'mobile lecturer' – those who pace the auditorium platform or wander freely into the audience, stimulating engagement by frequent changes of pace combined with the use of accessible language. Such 'inclusive' tactics can engage the audience for longer periods; and in a physical sense, the mobile lecturer 'reaches' a wider number of students within the group.

It would appear from student feedback that the 'enthusiastic lecturer' fares far better than those who lecture in a dry, monotone way, with little thought to how they or the content are perceived. This has led to a greater desire to 'entertain' students and to take them on a journey of active rather than passive engagement. Active-learning can be achieved via a number of methods, many of which appeal to the needs of the visual learner. Visual aids such as PowerPoint slides, YouTube clips, Prezi and the use of the more traditional visuals – whiteboards and handouts – all contribute to effective study for those who learn by remembering what they see rather than hear. Simple PowerPoint slides can be enhanced with visuals such as google images, banners, photographs – or even legal cartoons to appeal to the comedic senses. YouTube clips and news reels are also an excellent way of imparting information in an innovative manner, as are certain film trailers, which can be used to stimulate debate and contextualise relevant legal points across a wide audience. However, it has been argued that the use of overtly textual slides can be a precursor for passive learning where the student becomes either fixated on the text itself, assuming that further reading and analysis are unnecessary, or becomes overwhelmed by the sheer volume of text. Scaled-down information that is limited to key words and phrases helps to address this issue and encourages students to think about the presented information in its wider context rather than relying on the slides as a summarised form of the entire picture.

In addition to the visual methods deployed above, tactual learners respond to more enhanced illustrative modes of delivery. Students with tactual responses have the ability to recall information that is presented to them in an analytical manner. They respond well to the use of mapping systems and flow charts, which are particularly effective in communicating legal hierarchies such as the court system, devolution of power within government or tiered levels of responsibility within local authorities. Flow diagrams are also an effective tool to teach the application of legal structures in problem questions and can be used to communicate the processes required in navigating problem scenarios to large groups, encouraging them to present legal arguments in a logical, cohesive manner. Deploying the use of acronyms and mnemonics – the creation of a word, phrase or image that in itself triggers the recall of subsequent primary and secondary information – is also an effective mental recall method, which stimulates associations between the mnemonic and its related material by utilising the brain's multi-sensory memory. Prompting cognitive recognition within the tactual learner can provide the mental stimulus to satisfy the need for familiarity and order when digesting dense pieces of information.

In the quest to engage students in an interactive manner, lecturers typically request a 'show of hands' in response to a question directed at the group before engaging in a dialogue with a chosen student in a Socratic fashion. Large class sizes, however, problematise this form of pedagogy – research has shown that by focusing on one individual, the rest of the group risk becoming alienated from the discussion and may lose concentration. Furthermore, students who lack confidence in public speaking may be reluctant to voluntarily participate in this methodology, especially within a large group. A simple way to circumvent this problem is to divide the group into smaller groups, carving out time for each group to consider their collective response before speaking as a whole to the question at hand. This method stimulates an investment in the task, whilst allowing each member to participate in the activity but in a supportive and inclusive manner. This type of active group-learning appeals to the kinaesthetic learner. Research has shown that there is a high proportion of kinaesthetic learners within law schools – those that academically thrive in an atmosphere of active participation, often cementing their own learning by assisting their peers and who flourish when performing an integral role to the lesson. Advancements in the use of lecture technology have enabled law schools to tap into the psyche of the kinaesthetic learner by the use of 'clicker technology' – a hand-held response system that allows students to respond electronically to the 'question and answer' method. Research has revealed that students have found clicker technology to be non-intrusive, inclusive, provided instant feedback, and when incorporated as a regular mode of teaching, gave lecturers the opportunity to track individual student performance.

Kinaesthetic learners tend to thrive on activities such as role-play. This author's law school has capitalised on student-centric learning by teaching case method as 'stories', inviting students to personally 'step into' the studied case law. Seminal cases are presented in large groups and students are encouraged to view the legal actors as 'characters' in the same way as they would a storybook, film or popular soap or drama. This characterisation allows the legal action to be personalised and humanised, making it easier to grasp the idea of relationships between the parties and the public and private law obligations they may generate. The doctrine of precedent is also taught via this method by locating the 'story' within a timeframe of past and future case law. In our experience, storytelling in the teaching of cases to large groups has shown great pedagogical benefit: students appear more engaged with case reading and appear less reticence (or perhaps better equipped) to map cases within a timeline and demonstrate a better understanding of how precedent works in practice.

In conclusion, lecturers who are responsive to the needs of a diverse range of learners within large group teaching will enable effective learning outcomes for the entire group.

The key messages for Anton and other academics considering large group teaching:

1. Adopt a degree of interaction with the group to foster interest and investment in the lecture material.
2. Adopt lecture styles that appeal to visual, auditory, tactual and kinaesthetic learners interchangeably and change the pace of the class periodically.
3. Adopt active-learning as opposed to passive-learning as this is of pedagogical benefit.

FURTHER READING

JOURNALS

Boyle, R. and Dunn, R. (1998) Teaching Law Students Through Individual Learning Styles, *Albany Law Review*, 62, 213–247.

Caron, P. L. and Gely, R. (2004) Taking Back the Law School Classroom: Using Technology to Foster Active Student Learning, *Journal of Legal Education*, 54(4), 551–569.

Dey, E. L. Burn, H. E. and Gerdes, D. (2009) Bringing the Classroom to the Web: Effects of Using New Technologies to Capture and Deliver Lectures, *Research in Higher Education*, 50, 377–393.

Various Authors (2009) Clickers in College Classrooms: Fostering Learning with Questioning Methods in Large Lecture Classes, *Contemporary Educational Psychology*, 34, 51–57.

WEBSITE

Dalrymple, R. and Eaglesfield, S. (Undated) Teaching Large Groups – Toolkit, *The Higher Education Academy*. http://www.heacademy.ac.uk/reources/detail/new-to-teaching/large-group-teaching/introduction

CHAPTER 28

Designing Out Plagiarism

ALISON BONE

> Anton is confident about his subject matter but rather bemused about the assessments he is supposed to set. Examinations are necessary and he is able to write those but his colleagues keep warning him that plagiarism can be a real problem and that he should think carefully about any coursework he sets his students.

Although it is common knowledge that students' efforts are driven by the assessments attached to their learning many academics pay relatively little attention to how those assessments are designed. Plagiarism has been a problem since before computers were invented but undoubtedly their widespread use has made plagiarism easier. Plagiarism is a negative term and the modern approach is to promote academic integrity, but the desired outcome is the same: students producing their own work, properly referenced so that assessment grades given by the lecturer reflect their own learning achievements.

It is helpful to have some understanding of why students plagiarise as this can inform strategies for preventing it. There are of course as many reasons as there are students but when starting a new course at whatever level many students are unsure of what is expected of them. At school, teachers have explicit instructions to scaffold learning – see www.edutopia.org/blog/scaffolding-lessons-six-strategies-rebecca-alber for some examples – but there is relatively little of this in the modern higher education institution. Academics tend to assume that students understand technical terms such as 'learning outcomes' and 'assessment criteria' and the good ones do. It is the others that are more likely to plagiarise so it is important that lecturers spend time clarifying the nature of the assessment, what it is designed to assess and how students can maximise their opportunities for gaining a good grade. Timing and method is important. Giving out the assignment well in advance which is usually considered good practice can cause problems for students who are absent on that particular day or who are concentrating on work that is due in next week rather than next term. Clear instructions should be available online including any tips presented in class and these should be emphasised at appropriate intervals before hand-in.

The amount of support offered to students will often vary according to the level involved but ideally all students at whatever level should be given the opportunity to practise the learning outcomes being assessed by being given formative assessment. The feedback given should enhance their confidence and this in turn will help their motivation. It is also possible to devise a marking scheme that builds draft(s) into it so that students develop their thinking and learning. This does not require huge amounts of tutor time – peer review can be done in class to cover basic aspects.

Another reason why students plagiarise is because they can, that is, the assessment is requiring them to do something that has been done before by someone else. Students are asked to write essays at school and may be quite adept by the time they reach university so it is best to try and give them a task which will help them develop other talents. Setting a complex problem is one way of avoiding 'cut-and-paste' copying but it is also possible to devise assessments that require students to present information in a format that is not normally available in books or on the internet and at the same time assess skills that are far more useful to a future employer than essay-writing.

Risk-taking is a common feature of life in the real world but students learn to play safe while studying, a habit they usually learn from their tutors. An assignment that allows students to select their own evolving company/product to investigate potential intellectual property issues will challenge students but also engage them; getting them to write a monthly newsletter for clients on topical issues in any-area-of-law-that-is-changing with practical tips will be of benefit whatever career they eventually pursue. Even legal history or Roman law can be transformed if students are required to work the material into a modern format (a Skype duologue, a PowerPoint presentation for slave-owners). Whatever the format it is crucial that students are suitably rewarded for their research, for example that it is stressed that although in reality lawyers may not quote sources for their clients' digital newsletters, in academia quoting sources correctly not only gives credit to the work of others but demonstrates the student's ability to seek out sources. Try telling students that the first thing that will be looked at when the work is marked will be the references and that this may well define the grade boundaries. As anyone who has written a dissertation or thesis will know, cutting down really useful quality information into a narrow word count is intellectually challenging: get students to think big and present small by using the references to do the talking.

These are very practical tips for designing out plagiarism. The author's guide (Bone 2005) gives further context to how and why students plagiarise and also contains a link to the Plagiarism Awareness Pack (Bone and Ridley 2004), a resource developed for staff and students at the University of Brighton to explain the importance of clear referencing and how poor practice can cross the line into plagiarism with the penalties associated with academic misconduct. Unfortunately many academics assume it is not their job to ensure students understand what poor referencing is and a small percentage cannot face the challenge of having to deal with even the most blatant examples, which leads full circle back to risk-taking. If a student develops poor referencing habits which are not challenged it is possible that in their final year they may face a plagiarism allegation and state that they did not know they were doing anything wrong.

Computer software has been developed since the resources referred to above were written. Turnitin is used most widely in the UK and elsewhere as a dedicated tool enabling tutors to check for material that has been submitted elsewhere by producing an originality report. This does not in itself identify plagiarism as the student may have correctly referenced all quoted sources, but is useful especially when used by students to promote good referencing habits as well as showing them how easy it is to spot copied work.

There is no way to guarantee students will not cheat in written assignments. Essay mills pay students to submit their coursework and charge more for others to download them (with a few tweaks to avoid software detection) or it is possible to pay for a bespoke assignment which is 'guaranteed' not to be picked up as anything other than the student's original work. Occasional grammatical and spelling errors built in to lend authenticity!

Lecturers should act as role models for their students – always clearly quote their own sources in class, lecture notes and on presentations. Being human is appreciated too: a confident lecturer can admit a mistake, recognise that students have problems and may need to seek an extension, be aware of the university procedures regarding mitigating circumstances for students with ongoing unforeseen difficulties and be willing to listen. A confident student is unlikely to attempt to plagiarise.

The key messages for Anton and other academics who are worried about plagiarism:

1. If someone has written about a topic before there is a possibility of plagiarism.
2. Enthuse and engage students by setting them a different task to manipulate the material.
3. Build their confidence by giving them the opportunity to practise and receive feedback.

FURTHER READING

WEBSITES

Author unknown (2006) Top Ten Reasons Students Plagiarise and What You Can Do. http://offices.depaul.edu/oaa/faculty-resources/teaching/academic-integrity/Documents/Top10.pdf

Alber, R. (2014) Six Scaffolding Techniques to Use with Your Students. http://www.edutopia.org/blog/scaffolding-lessons-six-strategies-rebecca-alber

Bone, A. (2005) Plagiarism: A Guide for Law Lecturers. http://www.ukcle.ac.uk/resources/assessment-and-feedback/plagiarism/ (this also has a useful list of resources at the end)

Bone, A. and Ridley, P. (2004) All My Own Work? Plagiarism and How to Avoid it. http://www.ukcle.ac.uk/resources/assessment-and-feedback/plagiarism/guide/

Carleton University, Canada (2006) Academic Integrity an Instructor's Guide. http://carleton.ca/studentaffairs/wp-content/uploads/integrity_full_document.pdf

CHAPTER 29

Student Feedback

VERA BERMINGHAM

Anton is reviewing his approach to feedback/feedforward.

In her section on Promotions in Higher Education Guth notes that: 'generally speaking, institutions will look for competence in teaching, research and administration and external activities but the emphasis on these can vary considerably …'. Traditionally, the main route to promotion in the older universities was through research and publication; this route has been followed by post-1992 universities where the need to demonstrate 'research output' is now a key factor in career progression. However, even in the research-orientated institutions, teaching is becoming increasingly important for the purposes of promotion and 'excellence' in teaching needs to be demonstrated.

The increased emphasis on teaching skills also means that those currently embarking on an academic career are likely to be required to undertake a teaching qualification in the early stages of their teaching role. Obtaining this qualification at a time when you are preparing for your subject teaching and keeping on track with your research can create additional pressures of work. This discussion will focus on one aspect of an academic's teaching role 'assessment and feedback' and having outlined the reasons why this aspect of teaching has become more prominent, some thoughts on how the time you spend on your teaching and research might be balanced to enable you to achieve your targets in both areas will be offered.

As part of its role in ensuring that public money is used to deliver the greatest benefit to students in higher education, the Higher Education Funding Council for England monitors courses for quality and undertakes a National Student Survey (NSS) of nearly all final-year undergraduates in higher education institutions. The aim of the NSS is to help inform the choices of prospective students about universities and to provide data that assists universities in enhancing the student experience. The results from each year's NSS are summarised into charts reflecting question scales: teaching and learning, assessment and feedback, academic support, organisation and management, learning resources, personal development. The charts, which are made available through the Unistats website (the official website for comparing UK higher education course data) allow for comparisons with the sector average. This readily available information about student views on the quality of their learning experience may explain why the NSS results are seen by institutions as very influential in terms of recruitment to courses and to universities.

Since the NSS was set up in 2005 one of the areas about which students have consistently expressed the lowest level of satisfaction is 'assessment and feedback'. Although the NSS results from the 2014 survey show that 86% of students are satisfied with teaching, academic support and learning resources, assessment and feedback was again rated the lowest by students. Only 72% of students expressed satisfaction with assessment and feedback. The NSS results have led many universities to identify feedback on assessment as an area of priority in their learning and teaching strategies. The improvement of 2% in assessment and feedback reported in the NSS 2012 report may have resulted from institutional efforts to improve the student experience in these areas. However, the level of student satisfaction has not increased in the 2014 survey so assessment and feedback is likely to remain a priority for institutional learning and teaching strategies. It should also be noted that, at programme and at module level, feedback on assessment is seen as a factor in student progression, an indicator of quality of teaching and of the overall students' academic experience. Meanwhile, larger classes, greater student diversity and diminishing resources mean that the provision of feedback is a significant workload factor. Nevertheless, it is generally recognised that good feedback on assessment can accelerate learning and enable students to achieve higher-quality learning outcomes than they might have otherwise attained or by enabling them to attain these outcomes sooner or more rapidly.

> Assessment is a crucial part of the learning process. It enables students to gauge their progress, tutors to judge the effectiveness of teaching, and can also be used as a teaching tool, to give individuals or groups feedback designed to enable them to improve their performance in the future. (Bradney and Cownie 1999)

Institutional emphasis on feedback appears to concentrate on one of the most time-consuming methods, either handwritten or online comments on individual coursework. Although students may be more inclined to read online comments, there is copious anecdotal evidence showing that many students are concerned more or less exclusively with the grade they receive and do not even read, let alone consider, feedback comments. In many cases, where information about the mark obtained for an assessed piece of work is made available before the script is returned, students routinely fail to collect the marked script. Indeed, in a conference paper on combating plagiarism, one of the anxieties expressed by the speaker (Alison Bone speaking at the ALT Annual Conference in 2003) was the problem of uncollected student coursework remaining in Law School offices from one year to the next.

In balancing your academic workload it is worth bearing in mind that a better student experience of feedback may have to come from working smarter rather than working harder. As a starting point, it is helpful to ensure that students recognise all the opportunities for feedback with which they are provided beyond written comments on individual coursework, for example seminar and tutorial discussions. Face-to-face general feedback and examples of common errors in an exam or coursework can be provided promptly to all students in a cohort during a lecture or in a tutorial session. In the view of one expert in this area, there is no evidence that giving feedback to individuals is better than giving feedback to groups. General feedback posted on a VLE or feedback provided via email could be an effective means of providing initial feedback before assessed work is returned to students. Setting assessment tasks which require students to provide feedback on their own work can also be a very effective method of enabling students to develop skills of self-reflection and an efficient use of academic time.

The conclusion from the research indicates that if the quality and effectiveness of feedback on assessment is to be improved, you should encourage students to reconsider established assumptions about feedback and raise their awareness of the various sources, forms and functions of feedback.

The key messages for Anton and other academics considering 'assessment and feedback':

1. Although the need to demonstrate 'research output' is a key factor in career progression 'excellence' in teaching also needs to be achieved.
2. As a result of the National Student Survey (NSS) feedback on assessment has been identified as an area of priority in the learning and teaching strategies of many institutions.
3. In balancing your research and teaching, a better student experience of feedback will have to come from working smarter rather than working harder.

FURTHER READING

BOOKS

Bradney, A. and Cownie. F. (1999) *Teaching Legal System*, National Centre for Legal Education, Warwick: University of Warwick.

Research by Phil Race, quoted in Gibb G. (ed.) (1994) *Improving Student Learning, Theory and Practice*, Oxford: Oxford Centre for Staff Development.

JOURNAL

Bermingham, V. and Hodgson, J. (2006) Feedback on Assessment: Can We Provide a Better Student Experience by Working Smarter than by Working Harder?, *The Law Teacher, International Journal of Legal Education*, 40(2), 151–172.

WEBSITE

Dai Hounsell (2003) Professor of Higher Education at the University of Edinburgh and co-director of Enhancing Teaching-Learning Environments in Undergraduate Courses. http//www.ed.ac.uk/etl (delivering a paper on feedback at Kingston University Managing Change Conference, November 2003).

OTHER

Rust, C. (2001) Assessment Series, No.12, Learning and Teaching Support Network, (LTSN), York.

CHAPTER 30

Problem-Based Learning

BEN FITZPATRICK

> Anton would like to make use of problem-based learning as part of the law curriculum.

In a typical undergraduate law programme, the starting point of the learning cycle is the lecture. Students are presented with content – perhaps an outline of core principles, a work through of important cases, or a combination of both. They then follow up the lecture content through further research – perhaps a set of suggested readings including more statutes, cases, and secondary sources. The learning cycle usually culminates in some kind of smaller group activity – a tutorial or seminar – in which learners will *apply* what they have learned, typically to a range of problem scenarios, and/or to a set of more open-ended 'essay-type' questions. Ordinarily, there is a discrete learning cycle for each module – so, for example, lectures and seminars for tort are separate from lectures and seminars for contract or for public law.

There are a number of risks to this approach:

1. It proceeds from a *transmissive* basis, in which lecturers *give* content to students in lectures. It can be difficult for students to adjust to those aspects of the cycle which require them to act more independently, and for staff to adapt their practice in ways which allow that to happen.
2. The discrete learning cycles reinforce artificial distinctions between modules, and do not give learners a reasonable opportunity to see, explore and understand the links between them.
3. There is no inherent requirement for students to collaborate with each other. An individual student could, all things being equal, attend lectures and seminars without working constructively with another student.
4. Seminar problems involve low levels of authenticity, with scenarios being contrived to allow for exploration – at a level of some abstraction – of the legal issues under consideration. This stylised approach can be at the expense of more useful engagement with how the legal issues in question play out in the real world.

Problem-based learning (PBL) is an approach to learning and programme design which proceeds from a different basis. Rather than begin with the transmission of content by way of lectures, the PBL cycle begins with a group of students encountering a scenario of some description. It may be in the form of a set of facts, pieces of correspondence, a newspaper report, or an image: the key is that it acts as a trigger for students' interest. Students consider the trigger item in a discussion which is relatively open in terms of its content, but which has clearly defined steps (Moust, Bouhuijs and Schmidt 2007). The aim of the discussion is to arrive at a set of questions (sometimes referred to as learning outcomes) inspired by the scenario, which will form the agenda for that learning cycle. The discussion is facilitated by a tutor, whose role is not to tell students what the law is, or what the 'right' questions are, but to guide their discussion such that they reach suitable questions themselves.

Consider a scenario comprising a newspaper report about the passage through Parliament of a bill to regulate assisted dying. Let's say that the report highlights the critical scrutiny to which the bill is being subjected in the House of Lords, and that it incorporates the views of campaigners on different sides of the assisted-dying argument. This scenario might lead to a series of questions relating to (i) the current scope of the offence of assisting or encouraging suicide; (ii) prosecution policy and practice in cases of assisted suicide; (iii) policy arguments about the desirability of different modes of regulating assisted dying; (iv) the lawmaking process; (v) the roles of Parliament, and more particularly, the role of the House of Lords (and of second chambers in general), in lawmaking.

Once they have arrived at the questions, students spend the learning cycle engaging with whatever learning activities or resources are available to support their enquiries. They might be directed to certain readings, or they may be required to identify those readings themselves with support; they may attend lectures; and they may collaborate with their student colleagues in a variety of ways. The cycle concludes when the group reconvenes with the tutor and reports out on their findings in relation to the questions which they set at the initial meeting. And then the next cycle begins.

The PBL cycle might be represented as follows:

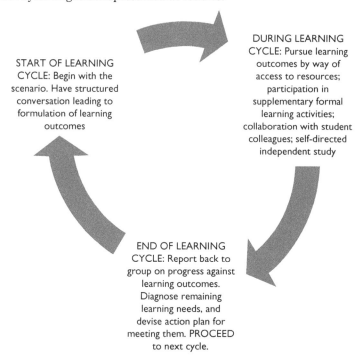

START OF LEARNING CYCLE: Begin with the scenario. Have structured conversation leading to formulation of learning outcomes

DURING LEARNING CYCLE: Pursue learning outcomes by way of access to resources; participation in supplementary formal learning activities; collaboration with student colleagues; self-directed independent study

END OF LEARNING CYCLE: Report back to group on progress against learning outcomes. Diagnose remaining learning needs, and devise action plan for meeting them. PROCEED to next cycle.

There is debate about the nature and potential benefits of PBL (Boud and Feletti 1997), but the following might be noted:

1. PBL can be genuinely student-centred (Barrows and Tamblyn 1980); students are responsible for managing their engagement with the scenario, with support and guidance, rather than direction, from the tutor. As a consequence, PBL can inculcate good habits in relation to independent study and contribute to a healthy attitude to self-directed lifelong learning.
2. Good PBL scenarios have high levels of authenticity, which can be motivating for students (Duch 2001). One aspect of authenticity is 'messiness'. Consider the 'assisted-dying' scenario referred to above, where students may construct an agenda for the learning cycle which spans issues of criminal law, public law, and legal systems. The habituation to and normalisation of messiness prepares students for how problems will present themselves in their future lives as professionals and as citizens.
3. Collaboration is intrinsic to PBL; the entire learning cycle is constructed around collaborative activities. Of course, collaboration is not unproblematic, but experiencing it can, at the very least, enhance students' employability.

Introducing PBL can also be challenging, for a variety of reasons:

1. It can be at odds with student and staff expectations of their respective roles in the learning process. Students may find it challenging to step up to the challenge of 'owning' their work in the way which PBL demands. Staff may find it difficult to adapt their role from content-transmitting subject-expert to *facilitator* of the learning of others (Savin-Baden 2003).
2. The 'messiness' to which PBL lends itself can challenge the orthodox boundaries between modules. While this can incentivise staff collaboration, modular structures themselves can contribute to an insular, territorial approach among colleagues, which militates against making that collaboration a reality.
3. The start-up costs for introducing PBL can be high. Materials and scenarios must be carefully designed to ensure their suitability for PBL; and it is desirable to provide development activities for staff and students to ensure a shared understanding of the aims of and processes associated with PBL (Schwartz, Mennin and Webb 2001).

PBL emerged from vocational disciplines such as medicine, so it is surprising that it continues to have a relatively low profile in law. Nonetheless, there is sufficient interest in PBL and in related forms of enquiry-based learning for there to be a range of experience in the legal education community on which would-be users of PBL can draw. Whether it is as a new way of supporting learning on a single module or, more radically, as a component of a new curricular philosophy, the judicious use of PBL has the potential to impact positively on student learning, and to have a transformative effect on how legal academics view their own roles.

FURTHER READING

BOOKS

Barrows, H. S. and Tamblyn, R. M. (1980) *Problem-Based Learning: An Approach to Medical Education*, Springer: New York.

Boud, D. and Feletti, G. I. (1997) *The Challenge of Problem-Based Learning*, 2nd edn, London: Kogan Page.

Duch, B. J. (2001) Writing Problems for Deeper Understanding, in B. J. Duch, S. E. Groh and D. E. Allen (eds) *The Power of Problem-Based Learning: A Practical 'How To' for Teaching Undergraduate Courses in Any Discipline*, Virginia: Stylus Publishing, 47–58.

Moust, J. H. C., Bouhuijs, P. A. J. and Schmidt, H. G. (2007) *Introduction to Problem-Based Learning: A Guide for Students*, Groningen: Wolters-Noordhoff.

Savin-Baden, M. (2003) *Facilitating Problem-Based Learning: Illuminating Perspectives*, Maidenhead: SRHE and Open University Press.

Schwartz, P., Mennin, S. and Webb, G. (2001) *Problem-Based Learning: Case Studies, Experience and Practice*, London: Kogan Page.

Reflection in Teaching, Learning and Practice

RICHARD GRIMES

> Anton has now made use of a range of approaches to his learning and teaching but remains eager to engage with reflective practice.

The word 'reflection', in its commonly understood sense, includes looking back at an image, an experience or an incident and thinking about what appears or what has happened.

The literature on pedagogy has increasingly, over the past 25 years or more, contained reference to the value of reflection as an integral part of the learning process (for example Boud et al. 1985). However this goes beyond the literal meaning ascribed to the words above and involves a deliberate strategy in which students (and for that matter teachers and, if applicable, practitioners) are expected to analyse their experiences and develop their understanding of relevant knowledge, skills and values in the light of that consideration.

A good illustration of how learning through reflection may work (albeit it in the context of working professionals rather than university or college students) can be found in the ideas of Donald Schön. His often cited concept of the high ground and the swamp shows how looking at the former provides the opportunity to look down and analyse whereas the latter sets out the reality which is often 'messy' and complex by comparison (Schön 1983). The experience of the swamp can be deconstructed and appraised from the relative luxury of the high ground. A cycle of learning where experience, reflection, further application and continuing post-experience evaluation is also used to describe the reflective learning process (for example Kolb 1984).

Were space to permit here we could have looked at these important ideas in greater detail and indeed at critiques of them. Suffice it to say however for present purposes that education theory broadly supports reflection as a key element and potentially effective component in the learning process.

Legal educators too have become interested in and appreciative of the value of reflection as a tool for self-development for students and teachers alike. The most recent review of legal education and training in the UK recognises the importance of experiential learning (LETR 2013). It is of course necessary to produce technically competent lawyers but society also needs those who are able to reflect critically on their work. This is central to the notion of continuing professional development. In one sense at least none of us ever stop being students!

There has been a rapid growth, particularly in the last ten years, of experiential and reflective learning methods in UK law schools (see LawWorks 2006, 2010, 2014). This has taken a multitude of forms from case-study-based simulation to live-client clinics. Learning 'clinically' is now a feature in over 70% of all UK law schools and has an increasing global presence too (Bloch 2010; LawWorks 2014). The word 'clinical' is used here drawing on the medical analogy – but with clients (real or simulated) rather than patients. But as will be seen below, reflection is not limited to a clinical approach (although it is very well illustrated by and central to the methodology) and can also be found in the more conventional setting of the lecture theatre or seminar room.

So what is reflection in this context? Simply put it is the process by which a person takes an experience (for example an exercise in legal research, a draft letter for a client or an essay submitted as part of a module assessment) and examines it critically with a view to understanding what went well and what might be done to improve comprehension and/or performance in the future.

The reality of working with academic colleagues and students suggests that reflection is neither intuitive nor straightforward. Asking or even requiring a student to reflect does not guarantee he or she will do so. Effective reflection appears to take place where it is incorporated as an integral part of a module or programme. This might be achieved through structured questioning – for example what would you do differently next time and why – and follow up monitoring to ensure the issues raised are addressed in future discussions or submissions.

For those looking for an overview of how to make reflection happen, Kerrigan and Murray (eds) have produced a very helpful guide to experiential learning (in the context of clinic) and address the reflective process in detail giving examples and suggestions as to how reflection can be facilitated. As suggested above it is as much to do with structure, study habits and learning group expectations as anything else. In the present context an experienced practitioner but fledgling academic would do well to read this book in its entirety as a starter in developing feel for effective learning and teaching before perhaps moving on to the more detailed theory on learning through reflection.

Perhaps the starting point to getting students to reflect is by linking this to specific learning outcomes and to the forms of assessment students are expected to undertake. The extent to which this is integrated across the curriculum will vary from one institution to another. Reflection might be a focus of isolated modules (for example a clinical option) or may appear as more central to a degree programme (for example the problem-based learning model used in all foundation and most optional subjects at York Law School).

What might a learning outcome requiring reflection look like? Take this hypothetical course entitled *the Law and dispute resolution*:

At the end of the module students should, using evidence from primary sources and academic publications, be able to identify the extent to which the law permits and promotes means of dispute resolution outside of formal litigation.

If assessing this (formatively and/or summatively) how can the students reflective capacity be captured? Following the above example the assessment might consist of two parts. The first, offered part-way through the module (to enable feedback to be given upon which the student can review what he or she needs to do to improve performance), is an oral presentation before peers and teaching staff when the means of dispute resolution are outlined with their respective benefits and challenges. Feedback would be given by the audience. The second, would be at the end of the module and take the form of a portfolio in which the student's claims as to what they have learnt are set out and the evidence for those claims appended – for example draft and annotated documents from case studies, a critical analysis of a parliamentary debate on the reform of civil justice and a description of what the student might do differently in revisiting the issues at stake in the future (particularly where tasks such as advising a case study 'client' are concerned).

The key messages for Anton and others when considering reflection as part of learning and teaching:

1. Like education more generally, reflection is part of a process and not a product or end in its own right.
2. The process is seldom intuitive but students (and others) can readily become accustomed to it.
3. To promote and support effective reflection there needs to be a structure through which reflective practice is both facilitated and measured.
4. The outcome referring to reflection (and generally) must, to be effective, be S.M.A.R.T. – specific, measurable, achievable, relevant and timely.

FURTHER READING

BOOKS

Bloch, F. (ed.) (2010) *The Global Clinical Movement: Educating Lawyers for Social Justice*, New York: OUP.

Boud, D., Keogh, R. and Walker, D. (1985) *Reflection: Turning Experience into Learning*, London: Kogan Page.

Kerrigan, K. and Murray, V. (2011) *A Student Guide to Clinical Legal Education and Pro Bono*, Basingstoke: Palgrave Macmillan.

Kolb, D. (1984) *Experiential Learning as the Science of Learning Development*, Engle-wood Cliffs, NJ: Prentice Hall.

LawWorks (2006, 2010, 2014) *The Law School Pro Bono Survey*, London: The Law Society.

Moon, Jennifer A. (2004) *A Handbook of Reflective and Experiential Learning: Theory and Practice*, London: RoutledgeFalmer.

Schön, D. (1983) *The Reflective Practitioner*, San Francisco: Jossey-Bass.

JOURNAL

Doran, G. T. (1981) There's a S.M.A.R.T. Way to Write Management's Goals and Objectives, *Management Review*, 70(11), 35.

WEBSITES

Legal Education Training Review (2013) *Setting Standards: The Future of Legal Services Education and Training Regulation in England and Wales*. http://www.letr.org.uk/wp-content/uploads/LETR-Report.pdf

CHAPTER 32

Organising a Specialist Conference

BEN LIVINGS

> Anton has been tasked with organising a conference.

Think carefully about what your proposed conference is trying to achieve. It may be that you have been doing some work in a particular area for a while, and want to bring together people with a variety of views from within the field, so as to build a research network in order to do more work, and in order to apply to funding bodies. The benefits of organising an academic conference are wide-ranging. Some of these benefits are to be expected, and flow naturally and directly from organising and then attending the event, others are unexpected. You may, for example, meet somebody who has a completely different take on the subject, which you want to pursue, or the contacts you make may lead to invitations to do collaborative work.

You may be able to find a colleague who wants to work with you on the organisation. If you are lucky, this will be somebody who shares your interest in the subject, and with whom you know you can work well. Of course, not everybody will be in this fortunate position. If there is nobody who is suitable or interested in helping to organise the conference, seek out advice from colleagues, particularly those with experience. There may be administrative support available, and you should take advantage of this assistance. However, the administrators may not be familiar with the particular type of event you are organising and you must communicate well and often, to ensure that everything is on track.

You need to decide on the format and duration of the conference. There are numerous types of academic conference, and a variety of roles that you might occupy in their organisation. Learned societies (such as the UK-based Society of Legal Scholars and the Socio-Legal Studies Association) organise large annual conferences, often nominally around a broad theme, but organised around distinct subject areas that are likely to remain relatively constant from year to year. These might correlate with subjects as they appear in modern, modularised law curricula, or they might be arranged around more theoretical approaches, such as feminist or critical legal studies. Each of these is likely to have an organiser, or convenor, either of a stream that runs throughout the duration of the conference, or of a single session, as well as an organising committee. Smaller conferences might be arranged around a session delivered by one speaker, or a panel, or it might be expanded to cover half a day, or even a whole day. It might therefore cover several sessions, either dedicated to one subject, or addressing a number of discrete themes that relate to the central theme. Holding it over one day is a good compromise, as this will allow for a good amount of time without the extra complications that holding it over multiple days will bring. One way to make the most of the limited timeframe is to have concurrent streams in some sessions, organised around several plenary speakers. The advantage of this is that more speakers can present, and delegates are more likely to find something of interest to them; the disadvantage is that the delegates cannot go to everything. However, it is better that people are forced to decide between sessions of interest than that they are given no choice, and have to go to a session in which they have no interest.

One of the factors that will influence the decision as to the format and duration of the conference is likely to be funding, which is an issue that needs to be considered from the start. The event could be expensive. If you are fortunate, your institution might be happy to fund the event, but you need to give them a reason to do so. When asking, emphasise the value of the conference to the institution, and to your work; try to be specific in detailing the sort of research outputs that you have in mind. Alternatively, you might be able to gain external funding for your event, and you should speak to the research administrators at your institution about organisations to contact, and avenues to explore. Even if you are unsuccessful in applying for external funding, going through the application process is good practice, and the success of the conference will stand you in good stead for future bids.

The funding available will be a significant factor in deciding upon venue and catering, but there are a number of other factors to be considered. Whilst local castles or other grand locations can make the event feel special, and appeal particularly to foreign participants, the venue should be easy to get to and there needs to be parking available (or other arrangements made). Think of the demands of the conference, both in terms of presentation spaces, and social spaces – people will want to have an opportunity to mix with other delegates. Where your event is organised at a dedicated conference space, say a local hotel or conference centre, it is likely that they will have packages that include catering. Wherever you are considering, visit and try to envisage every aspect of the conference as it will work there. Provided it is suitable, it may be a good idea to hold the conference at your own institution. You will have experience of how the different spaces work, and know how to use the equipment (and what to do if it goes wrong).

Don't skimp on catering. You don't need to wow, but you don't want to disappoint, or, worse still, precipitate a mass exodus from your carefully considered networking and social spaces as the delegates leave in search of food elsewhere. Catering can work out much more expensive than you might expect, even if all you want is a cup of coffee and a couple of biscuits. The corporatisation of universities means that they are frequently tied to particular contractors. As a junior academic, this aspect of university institutional organisation may amaze, frustrate and infuriate you in equal measure.

Pay some attention (and possibly cash) to publicising your event. Your institution, or whoever has funded this, wants it to be a success, and a conspicuous one, so make sure that it is. This is also good for your profile. You might want to design an e-flyer and use existing networks and mailing lists in order to contact people you think would be interested. Involve your institution's marketing department.

Contact potential presenters early (12 months before the proposed date is reasonable), especially if you want leading international names in the field to be involved in the conference. Whilst it is rare (depending on the person and subject area) to have to pay a presenter for their time, you may have to pay expenses. This can range from a taxi fare to international flights and hotel and related subsistence expenses. Here, you should budget for more than you expect to have to pay. Consider arranging travel and accommodation for the speakers. That way, you will avoid the cost of having to refund first-class return tickets from Australia and a week-long stay at the Ritz, or the embarrassment of having to point out that this is unreasonable, and refusing to pay it. You cannot, and should not want to, dictate precisely what your contributors are going to say. You have invited them for their expertise. That said, ask for abstracts so that you can arrange the sessions appropriately.

On the day, not everything will go exactly as you have planned (and this is inevitable). But often most, if not all, of those present will not notice, and some things will go far better than you had expected. Relax and enjoy the day. Talk to people during the conference, and be sure to communicate afterwards as well. The conference will raise your profile, you will get to meet interesting people and pursue avenues for further research activities.

The key messages for Anton and other academics considering organising a conference:

1. Consider the purpose of the conference: what you want to achieve.
2. Funding is crucial. Consider possible sources and stay within budget.
3. Look beyond the conference, at specific outcomes.

FURTHER READING

WEBSITES

The Glasgow 'How to ...' Guide for Researcher-Led Activity. www.gla.ac.uk/media/media_165114_en.pdf

International Association for Political Science Students, *How to Organize a Conference: Step by Step Manual.* www.iapss.org/downloads/publications/iapss_conference_manual.pdf

Lucey, Brian, *How to Organise an Academic Conference – 10 tips.* www.theguardian.com/higher-education-network/blog/2014/jan/17/how-to-organise-academic-conference?CMP=twt_gu

Muller, Nadine, *Organising Academic Conferences.* www.nadinemuller.org.uk/the-new-academic-guides/organising-conferences/

CHAPTER 33

Embedding Employability Skills (or Helping Graduates Get Jobs)

BEN MIDDLETON

> Anton's institution requires all programmes to embed employability skills.

At university open days, common questions asked by prospective students and their parents include 'how many of your graduates will get a job?' and 'how many of your graduates go on to become solicitors?' Each year the Destination of Leavers from Higher Education (DLHE) survey is issued and the results are incorporated into the Key Information Sets (KIS) that are published on every law school's web pages. This information also features heavily in league table calculations, particularly the Guardian League Table for Law and the Times University guide.

It is an often-quoted statistic that nationally, fewer than 50% of law graduates actually enter the legal profession. This is for a variety of reasons: many decide that a career practicing law is not for them and pursue alternative graduate-level employment. Some graduates do not become fully qualified due to the scarcity of training contracts. Increasingly, law firms are recruiting LLB and LPC graduates as paralegals and this can provide an alternative career route. But the law degree has always provided a liberal education that precedes the LPC and provides the wider skills required to enter graduate-level employment. The next genesis of legal education is on the horizon, with reforms currently being considered by the Solicitors Regulation Authority (SRA). Outside of the core requirements of the SRA and Bar Council's Joint Statement, which are to remain in force until at least 2017, different law schools are developing their law provision in a variety of ways.

It might be that your law school offers a traditional LLB, incorporating teaching of the foundation subjects but with little focus on some of the vocational skills that traditionally are the raison d'être of the LPC. At the other end of the spectrum, you might be at a law school that places substantial focus on vocational legal skills, perhaps where the LPC forms part of a student's degree programme. The reality is that this distinction is false: as Fitzpatrick (2014) states, academic and vocational skills are not distinct, but rather support one another. Whatever the direction of your institution, employability skills are likely to be embedded in several ways: (i) an integration of specific techniques in the teaching, learning and assessment strategies of the programme as a whole; (ii) the addition of discrete routes or modules focusing on a particular initiative, such as mooting, legal clinic, or work placement; (iii) an extra-curricular offer, including for example commercial awareness sessions, careers guidance, and guest speakers; and (iv) the provision of one-on-one advice and support to students in their quest for graduate employment.

In relation to the first point, there has been much written in relation to different approaches to teaching and learning in legal education. Generic skills, such as presenting to an audience, effective teamwork or independent problem solving, would be expected to feature on any law programme. For example, it is common for modules on the English legal system to incorporate legal research skills, and the majority of modules will teach and assess legal research and academic writing. Perhaps mooting forms part of the core curriculum; it might be possible to assess foundation subjects in this way. Perhaps your institution is deploying the use of problem-based learning to help engage students and discourage any tendency to 'compartmentalise' learning in discrete modules. There might be a focus on some of the vocational elements of the foundation subjects: rather than teaching contract law in abstract theory, it is arguably more useful to teach it in a practical way, with students working through real contracts and answering problems they are likely to encounter in the real world.

Secondly, there is also clearly a role for discrete modules that teach skills relevant to employment. Bespoke practical modules such as civil litigation or criminal litigation could be included. For many years, institutions have offered student-run law offices or clinics where students may work under the supervision of solicitors, providing legal information and advice to real clients. Client interviewing is a key skill that is increasingly being taught and assessed in this way. As an alternative to year-long placements, shorter placements could form the basis for the teaching, learning and assessment in a bespoke module.

While many of these laudable initiatives are invaluable to an undergraduate legal education and attractive to prospective students at the point of university selection, most are aimed at the 50% of students who eventually go into work in the legal sector. That is not to say that many of the acquired skills will not be transferable to general employment, but rather that there should also be specific recognition of alternative career options open to law graduates. For example, there is nothing to say that work placements must always take place in a law firm; casting the net more widely could benefit a larger group of students.

A third initiative is to encourage students to engage with extra-curricular activities which run alongside their law programme. Research has shown that unless students are aware of the benefit to them and/or are required to engage with an extra-curricular offer, the students who need it most might be the least likely to seek it out. If integration in the curriculum is possible, it will often be the most effective way forward. Many law firms are willing to run bespoke 'commercial awareness' sessions to help students with their application preparation. It might be possible to arrange mock interviews, inviting employers in to judge students' responses and provide feedback. Again, these need not be limited to law providers, although it might be useful to schedule early in a second year module to coincide with the point at which students are applying for training contracts.

Finally, a law programme must include a clear strategy for the development of generic skills such as CV preparation, application writing, interview coaching, career advice, guidance and mentoring. Usually this form of support is the preserve of a dedicated careers advisor, but there is much to be said for building this into the support mechanisms on a particular programme of study. When properly resourced, a dedicated academic tutor can provide invaluable mentoring to the would-be graduate employee. If any of these initiatives do not yet exist at your institution, the work put in to setting them up can yield rewards in terms of student engagement and employability. If they exist already, involvement in them can be incredibly rewarding and will provide a valuable addition to the CV of a newly appointed lecturer.

The key messages for Anton and other academics considering employability:

1. Try to devise strategies for incorporating employment skills into your teaching, learning and assessment.
2. Consider getting involved in mooting, client interviewing or law clinic, or develop work placements.
3. Be prepared to offer your individual support and guidance as a tutor.

FURTHER READING

JOURNAL

Guth, J. and Ashford, C. (2014) The Legal Education and Training Review: Regulating Socio-legal and Liberal Legal Education?, *The Law Teacher*, 48(1), 5–19.

Sylvester, C., Hall, J. and Hall, E. (2004) Problem-based Learning and Clinical Legal Education: What Can Clinical Educators Learn from PBL?, *IJCLE* (4) 39–63.

WEBSITES

Fitzpatrick, B. (2014) 'Legal Skills' in an Academic Context. http://benfitzpatrick1.wordpress.com/2014/03/23/legal-skills-in-an-academic-context-2/

SRA, Policy Statement: Training for Tomorrow (2013) http://www.sra.org.uk/sra/policy/training-for-tomorrow/resources/policy-statement.page

CHAPTER 34

Teaching Distance Learning Students

ROBERT HISCOCKS

> Anton has been asked to take responsibility over the next semester for delivering a criminal law module to a cohort of distance-learning students. He has taught the module to students attending the law school for their classes for two years but has never taught distance learning students before and is anxious to ensure that they get the best experience he can provide.

Not all tutors are comfortable in teaching distance-learning students. They are put off by the thought of having to master new technology and adapting their teaching style to what they feel will be the very different environment of online teaching. In fact, many of the techniques used in the physical classroom can be adapted easily for online teaching. The technology, once mastered, often turns out to be straightforward to use and there are many advantages to teaching online:

- With the growth of distance-learning studies, having experience in this field adds to a tutor's CV and can assist in promotions, job searches, and so on.
- It provides opportunities to interact with a wide variety of students from different backgrounds across the globe.
- It can enable a more flexible work environment: teaching can be done from anywhere with a broadband connection and some universities allow staff to work on their online teaching away from the university.

The starting point is to establish how classes are delivered. There are a number of delivery formats available: this will depend on the format(s) utilised by the university that are available to you and the degree of flexibility as to which formats you can use. Teaching distance-learning students can involve all or any of the following:

- Recorded sessions that students download and watch/listen to in their own time.
- Live online classes where students enter a virtual classroom on the VLE at a specified time and participate in a discussion with the tutor and fellow students.
- Discussion forums where students' queries are answered by tutors or by fellow students with the tutor taking a moderating role.
- Submission of practice assessments by students to be marked by tutors.
- Face-to-face classes that take place over one or more weekends or intensive blocks.

One of the main barriers to learning experienced by distance-learning students is the isolation they face in comparison to those students who attend classes regularly at the university. This can lead to problems with engagement on the part of distance-learning students and a higher dropout rate than with face to face classes. Additionally, where the course involves little regular structured teaching students can easily lose focus and fall behind in their studies. Two of your likely main challenges are to provide this structure and to engender a community feel within the cohort of students so that the isolation is diminished.

Where the teaching involves live classes in virtual classrooms via the VLE, this provides the closest equivalent to the structured regular classes that face to face students enjoy. Classes can be timetabled on a regular basis with a clear expectation created that students should attend. However, you need to be aware of some important differences between face-to-face and online teaching.

The precise format of the online classes will depend on the system used but typically the screen that students see when they enter the classroom will display some or all of the following:

- PowerPoint slides
- Chat boxes for students to write rather than speak their answers
- Facilities to link to webpages or other material
- A webcam picture of the tutor

In most instances, students will have a headset with microphone so they can talk to the tutor, although some students prefer to write questions or responses in the chat boxes.

Not all tutors use PowerPoint slides in face-to-face tutorial sessions as this can inhibit free contributions by students: they prefer to use whiteboards, or similar, to record such conclusions. In the virtual classroom, a pre-prepared presentation is useful to give structure to the class but you may want to include some blank slides to enable students' contributions to be recorded.

Chat boxes can be used to create virtual breakout rooms: You have the opportunity to split the group into smaller subgroups to discuss aspects of the topic under consideration and then report back to the main group in the same way as in a face-to-face class.

The problems that can be encountered in the course of teaching in the virtual classroom can be similar to those encountered in the face-to-face classroom, often somewhat amplified. For example, in any format of class, there is a danger of discussion being dominated by a few students who are keen to respond to all queries. In this situation, other students can shrink into the background and go unnoticed. You need to ensure that they are all brought into the discussion with the use of directed questions, and so on.

A virtual classroom can also be used for other forms of delivery outside of structured classes that can assist in encouraging student engagement both with the subject and with fellow students. These can include:

- Timetabled 'drop in' sessions where tutors makes themselves available at specified times to answer queries from students.
- Open sessions where the virtual classroom is made available to students to use as a virtual group study room to discuss topics amongst themselves without supervision by the tutor.

Turning to teaching via discussion forums can also can take a number of forms. Two principal ones are:

- Live chat forums, where a tutor will be available at a specified time to answer queries posed by students.
- Asynchronous forums where students can post queries at any time and the tutor will respond later.

However, discussion forums can be used in much the same way as the virtual classroom to encourage participation and engagement by students. Students can be provided with forums where they are able to discuss issues amongst themselves unsupervised by the tutor. Alternatively the tutor can monitor the discussion and intervene to refocus the students where they are going wrong.

One drawback that may deter students from using some of the facilities outlined above outside the formal classes is that they may feel inhibited from contributing freely where they feel that their discussions may be monitored by tutors (even if the tutors make clear that they do not intend to do so). A solution here would be for the tutor to encourage students to set up their own groups on social media (WhatsApp/Facebook or whatever media they prefer) that they know they can control. This will of course depend on the students (or at least one or two of them in the first instance) to be proactive about creating this group. A starting point is to encourage one or more of the students to be responsible for collecting contact details for all the class and to facilitate this by circulating to the students that person's contact details.

The key messages for Anton and other academics considering teaching distance learning students:

1. Take the opportunities available to increase your skill set and widen your experience.
2. Remember that distance-learning students often face problems with engagement, driven partly by a sense of isolation from their fellow students.
3. Make use of the technology available through the university VLE and also generally available to students to encourage them to collaborate inside and outside of class.

FURTHER READING

BOOK

Carroll, J. (9 July 2014) *Tools for Teaching in an Educationally Mobile World*, Abingdon: Routledge.

Lehman, R.M. and Conciecao, S.C.O. (29 November 2013) *Retaining and Motivating Online Students: Research-Based Strategies and Interventions that Work*, San Francisco: John Wiley & Sons.

JOURNAL

Simpson, Ormond (2013) Student Retention in Distance Education: Are We Failing Our Students?, *Open Learning: The Journal of Open, Distance and e-Learning*, 28(2), 105–119.

CHAPTER 35

Supporting Student Law Societies and Extracurricular Activities and Students

EDWARD MOWLAM

> Anton is keen to learn more about the student law society and how he can support extracurricular activities.

Student law societies often play a fundamental role in law-school life. The best student law societies provide experience in a range of worthwhile activities, developing vital skills and fostering engagement and a sense of collegiate harmony amongst all of the school's stakeholders – in my view they are indispensable. Other groups, formal or informal, which encourage extracurricular activities and bring students together fulfil much of the same role and much of what is said in this chapter applies to the full range of groups, clubs, societies and student activities.

Assistance from academics and school support staff can be critical to a society's success. The question is how much academics and other support staff should involve themselves in the extracurricular activities of students. Too much can be an unwelcome imposition upon students. Too little, and many of the initiatives which a law society can provide may never materialise.

This chapter aims to cast light on these issues and offer guidance as to best practice when dealing with student societies and related activities.

At a time of increased 'customer' focus in higher education, and repositioning students as 'consumers', extracurricular activity is an important way of law schools providing extra value to the student experience.

Advising and assisting students with their extracurricular can also enable academics to establish themselves in a law school and to raise their profile. Sam Butterworth, Sports and Societies Officer at Bradford University Student Union, writes on student societies, 'I support and represent both Clubs and Societies to the University to ensure their initiatives ... are championed and *remain student led*' (my emphasis, quoted on ubuonline.co.uk). Clearly it is important to let the students do their thing, but they can be 'nudged' or encouraged to act upon tactfully presented suggestions.

Many schools appoint an academic as lead liaison between staff and student societies. This role requires a light touch providing a welcoming environment in which students will stick around long enough to benefit from the attention; keep them intellectually nourished, try to prevent 'mishaps' but be prepared to clean up the mess that may be left afterwards. This, for the supportive academic, usually requires leg-work, at least in the infancy of an executive committee involving some, or all, of the following:

- Promote advantages to executives of inaugurating or maintaining a law society, and promote advantages to potential members of engaging with a law society.
- Act as returning officer for elections to the executive committees.
- Guide registration(s) of newly formed society/executive committee.
- Help draft pro forma letters and documents for a range of purposes, such as securing external sponsorship, arranging events or inviting guest speakers.
- Facilitate initial introductions to people and places.
- Sign up to and help secure the finances to enter and facilitate moots, client interviews and arbitration competitions. Connections to legal professionals are also invaluable should a judge be required for such competitions, and academics can provide invaluable assistance as a mentor to hopeful competitors.
- Book suitable rooms and venues.
- Support the establishment online and/or social media presence.

Secure in the knowledge that students can rely on such support the executive members should feel encouraged to become more engaged, more adventurous and more integrated into the everyday workings of the school. The more appropriate the support, the more society members may do for the law school. They are more likely to get involved in open-days, careers fairs and to promote talks and events organised with their patronage. I have been informed that the activities of law societies have made their way in to National Student Survey responses, which implies that the more extra-curricular activities of worth on offer the greater the potential for favourable view of the institution at large.

Who is right for the student law society liaison role? The individual must be personable, an efficient administrator, with a working knowledge of social media. An academic with authority and student esteem, unflappable and possessing an unwaveringly sunny disposition. Dr Hercules, as Ron Dworkin might imagine. But failing that, if you're inclined to get involved, to assist and advise, to suggest and help plan, to hone your administrative or organisational skills, then do it. Even if it's voluntary work in lieu of contribution to the university's alumni fund.

A law society can take many forms, there is no perfect template. The most auspicious foundation emanates from student need and demand with, sometimes, a little 'nudging' from staff, to fuel the groundswell. To this end good PR cannot be overstated. Well-aimed promotion of a law society's aspirational activities and first-hand accounts of empowerment, success and fun that may be had, all conveyed with a sense of humour and a light touch, worked in Bradford. As the society grows ensure that those who have contributed are recognised. Be it on websites, or a group photo on a prominent noticeboard. Most student unions have an awards ceremony to recognise commitment and success so help draft nominations and co-opt a student union member to file it.

One effective method of endearing yourself to executives and other enthusiastic society members is to involve them in your institution's open-days, or other such marketing events. If remuneration, preferably in the form of cash and a free dinner, is not provided for their involvement, then argue for it with the powers-that-be. Let the students know that they are valued within your institution. This will also help to ensure the society's longevity, as other students will see a potential reward for their involvement, and future students will be made aware at an early stage of the society's existence.

Extracurricular activities add immensely to the university experience. Student societies may seem like hard work, peripheral to the core function of a law school and even a little passé. But underestimate their importance at your peril. In a field as competitive as law, the individual graduate must stand out. The experiences provided by the sort of activities mentioned above can be instrumental in this regard, with obvious resultant benefits to both student and school.

Other activities to support are things like mooting and other types of competitions, debating, film clubs or indeed anything else that students might suggest (within reason). These activities might fall within the student law society's remit or they may be separate but they will be of benefit and should be supported where possible.

The key messages for Anton and other academics considering supporting student activities:

1. Get involved!
2. Societies must be student-led and student-orientated.
3. By bringing together enthusiastic individuals through extracurricular activities, many of the students' aims and ambitions may well be achieved with relatively little effort.

FURTHER READING

WEBSITE

National Student Law Society. http://www.nsls.co.uk/

CHAPTER 36

External Engagement – Enterprise

CHRISTOPHER J. NEWMAN

> Anton, drawing on his practice experience, is keen to develop the external engagement portfolio of the law school.

It is axiomatic to state that graduates of all disciplines need to possess an awareness of commercial skills and enterprise. Given the recent contraction of the public sector within the UK and the emphasis of economic regeneration of the private sector, such skills are going to become ever more vital (Rae et al. 2012). Given the intense competition for training contracts and pupillages, where demand significantly exceeds supply, students are increasingly looking to legal academics to provide guidance on ways in which they can gain any advantage in a progressively more difficult employment market. It is suggested that a key approach to be adopted is that of engaging with stakeholders outside of academia.

This discussion will examine the ways in which external engagement can lead to significant opportunities, both for enhancing the experience of students within the law curriculum and also for promoting collaboration outside of the traditional environs of academia. Such collaboration has usually operated within the traditional confines of the legal profession for example a placement within a law firm, but this piece will argue that collaboration with a broader range of stakeholders will enrich the law curriculum and provide students with much needed enterprise awareness, a commodity which is highly prized by graduate employers. The discussion will conclude with suggestions for embedding this external facing approach to enterprise within the curriculum.

External engagement is a phrase that has slipped into the academic idiom over recent years and, broadly speaking, defines any relationship either on an institutional or individual level, between a university and an organisation not connected with academia. Initially this might have been perceived as solely involving a private-sector company. Rather than being a two-way process, the collaborative endeavour was usually commercial in nature and seen as a direct transfer of knowledge from academia to business (Harloe and Perry 2005). External engagement, however, has come to mean something broader, with a wide variety of potential partners interacting with universities for a wide variety of different reasons. The National Co-ordinating Centre for Public Engagement states that engagement is, by definition a two-way process, involving interaction and listening, with the goal of generating mutual benefit (www. publicengagement.ac.uk). This notion of mutual benefit is a key element in collaborative ventures.

The somewhat cynical view traditionally taken in respect of enterprise, as a purely commercial imperative, masks the genuine purpose and context of external engagement. It is argued that enterprise is itself a much broader construct than simply the generation of income. Undoubtedly it can be a manifestation of commercial activity, but it can also be social entrepreneurship, whereby a social problem is identified and entrepreneurial principles are employed to provide a solution for the local community. This type of external engagement leads to the creation of a cohort of students who have learned the skills knowledge and personal attributes that are necessary when trying to apply creative ideas and innovations to practical solutions. Rae et al. (2012) identifies these generic skills as initiative, independence, creativity, problem solving, leadership and being able to act resourcefully to effect change. It is suggested that these skills are precisely the ones that are craved by legal employers. Using external engagement to embed enterprise skills, it is argued, is a crucial part of the employability matrix.

As stated earlier, the paradox inherent within this discussion is that legal education has a rich history of engagement with law firms, and there is a huge body of literature championing the advantages of clinical legal education. The notion of enterprise within the context of legal education may seem counterintuitive; however, it is hoped that the above definition illustrates how such a notion is crucial to the 21st-century law graduate. Given the changes that the employment market has undergone and that the law curriculum is set to undergo (for full details see Guth and Ashford 2014), it is argued that legal academics need look beyond the traditional forms of engagement usually undertaken by law schools.

When addressing the ways in which such engagement can be undertaken, this discussion will not seek to offer insights and solutions that are revelatory or revolutionary. The main point to consider is that external engagement activity is likely to be underway within the institution. This approach is not without its difficulties but once explored may yield positive results. Utilising the existing networks and processes within the institution for external engagement is an obvious first stage. It is, however, not the only method by which external engagement can be achieved and there are a number of pro-active ways in which law schools can reach out to a whole range of organisations in order to develop the enterprise culture within the student body. Academics should be prepared to explore (and indeed exploit) every opportunity to create and develop external networks.

Having identified these networks, the next challenge is to construct an effective strategy for managing and utilising the networks. It may be that the students are able to access external organisations within a dedicated option module, enhancing the prestige and importance of engagement activities whilst also embedding them within mainstream legal education. There are, however, numerous ways in which engagement and collaborative ventures can be cascaded out to students. One approach might be to have academics and students working as co-collaborators on externally facing projects, taking the students through the whole process of network building and relationship management. It may be that the students themselves initiate the contact and are encouraged to incorporate academic input only so far as it is necessary.

Whether the external relationships are fostered by mechanisms that are already in place within the institution or as a result of independent, ad-hoc activity from individual members of staff, the advantages of broadening out the scope of external facing activity are manifold. Developing strategies for capturing and managing these external engagement activities will provide law schools with a crucial resource to enable students to truly compete in the current employment market. The real benefit to law schools could be a long term one. The students themselves, once successfully employed and if convinced of the value of the experience, could become a new generation of collaborators. By broadening the scope of collaboration, previous students working in a whole range of organisations could help in the creation of a truly self-sustaining approach to external engagement.

The key messages for Anton and other academics considering issues around external engagement:

1. External engagement is a crucial way in which students can be exposed to key the enterprise skills valued by graduate employers.
2. Whilst the majority of law schools will have experience of exploring external collaborations within the legal environment, there are advantages to looking beyond the legal sector for more diverse networks.
3. There are numerous ways in which students can be exposed to the benefits of external engagement activities. The scope for innovation offered by diverse engagement with an external organisation is attractive to students, academics and employers alike.

FURTHER READING

BOOK

Gibson, David A. (2009) *The Streetwise Guide to Being Enterprising*, Cork: Oak Tree Press.

JOURNALS

Guth, J. and Ashford, C. (2014). The Legal Education and Training Review: Regulating Socio-legal and Liberal Legal Education?, *The Law Teacher*, 48(1), 5–19.

Harloe, M. and Perry, B. (2005). Rethinking or Hollowing Out the University? External Engagement and Internal Transformation in the Knowledge Economy, *Higher Education Management and Policy*, 17(2), 29.

Rae, D., Martin, L., Antcliff, V. and Hannon, P. (2012). Enterprise and Entrepreneurship in English Higher Education: 2010 and Beyond, *Journal of Small Business and Enterprise Development*, 19(3), 380–401.

CHAPTER 37

External Examiners

CHRIS GALE

> Anton has been told that he should consider becoming an external examiner.

Most universities say that the external examiner system is a vital part of the quality assurance of their programmes. The external examiner system originated in 1832 with the establishment of the University of Durham, the first in England since Cambridge was founded 600 years earlier. Durham used Oxford examiners to assure the public that its degrees were a similar standard to Oxford's. (Cuthbert, Mike (2003) '*The External Examiner: How Did We Get Here?*' Presentation to the UKCLE/ALT workshop on external examiners, 6 June 2003).

As more universities were founded in the United Kingdom from the 1880s to the present day, there was a requirement that examinations be conducted by internal and external examiners. They are usually appointed to courses/modules roughly aligning with their areas of expertise. The system is also found in countries whose higher education systems were developed from United Kingdom practice, or strongly influenced by it, including New Zealand and India.

QAA's Quality Code (UK Quality Code for Higher Education) – Chapter B7: External examining (October 2011) sets out the expectations regarding the appointment, training, work and reporting rights of external examiners. As these include the possibility of flagging serious issues direct to the vice chancellor, the external examiner is ignored by a university department or faculty at its peril. The codification of work under the Quality Code replaces the previous system where each university had a slightly different version of the external examiner theme. Attention is specifically directed to process, systems and standards.

Although it can be seen that an external examiner is of considerable importance, there remain anomalies. Very occasionally, advertisements are made to attract candidates to the role. More usually, appointment comes through being known personally to members of a subject area in the appointing university, or to having a national profile which has brought the appointee to the attention of the appointing university.

Individuals can register with the CHULS (Committee of Heads of University Law Schools) website (www.chuls.ac.uk) setting out their areas of expertise but this system is rather old and clunky. Subject associations or 'learned societies' in each discipline area may form an *ad hoc* point of reference, but there seems no certain way of getting the aspiring candidate in touch with a university looking for an external examiner with his/her speciality. Happenchance is the order of the day. There is a law section in the Jiscmail list (www.jiscmail.ac.uk).

Another anomaly is that this supposedly important role is very poorly paid at most universities. Pay is often based on the number of modules overseen and can be as little as £150 per year in a (usual) four-year appointment. More can be and is paid in some places, but around £500 a year should be regarded as reasonable. Additional perks are, of course, seeing how other places operate, networking, a day or two in a different location, overnight accommodation and hospitality. It is unlikely that the pay works out to be more than £20 to £25 per hour at best and sometimes less as the work involves approving instruments of assessment, examining piles of marked scripts, attending examination boards and often having a say in minor changes to modules and programmes. There is, however, the dubious satisfaction of being recognised in the appointment and of 'doing your bit' for the higher education community. It is traditional that institutions allow employees to take a reasonable amount of time away to fulfil their external examiner duties at two institutions at least, without having to dip into their holiday allowance – they need people from other institutions to undertake external examining work at their own, so self-interest rather than generosity is the likely driver!

For junior staff such as research assistants, the harsh but simple truth is that as the appointment of an external examiner, despite the dreadful rate of pay, is seen as a 'senior appointment', no university is likely to be interested in someone at the outset of their career as its external. They can position themselves by developing networks, and so on, but it is work for tomorrow rather than today. In a first external appointment, it is likely that someone would be mentored by another external examiner on the programme so, given the capacity and current subject knowledge of junior practitioners, there is no real reason why they should not be appointed, but they are probably going to have to accept that it is not going to happen. It is ironic as, at that point of their career, a person is usually very much up to date with subject matter with its pedagogical underpinning, is keen and eager, may be a new Fellow of the Higher Education Academy or about to become one and maybe also has the time to devote to the post a more senior academic does not.

Someone who has been in legal practice before coming into higher education, is at least 'at the races'. They may well have colleagues who would be prepared to recommend them, junior as they may be in HE terms. Workload and other responsibilities may well preclude becoming an external examiner from being a priority on people's lists, but they should make sure it is somewhere on that list. Exposure to other institutions can sometimes help make sense of one's own. Street Law and other practical legal experience will certainly give someone access to new contacts in other universities and although external examining is not likely to be the focus of their first conversations with them, they should make sure it gets in somewhere.

Very senior academics may think external examining to be beneath them, but those who do get involved often can have their choice of appointments and are still in need of networking opportunities!

External-examiner duties can be time consuming. Usually you will be required to approve assessment questions and make comment on their suitability in the context of the institutions requirements and regulations, the level of the module and the module and programme learning outcomes. You will then need to consider a sample of work from the institution and will be asked to comment on the level of work as compared to the sector as well as the university's own standards and national standards such as FHEQ levels and the QAA Benchmark Statement. While you will not have to attend all examination boards or assessment committees you will usually be expected to attend at least one and to submit a report – usually in a standard format. Do not be afraid to share both positive and negative feedback and think about what sort of constructive comments you would like to receive on your assessment questions and marking. Comments in relation to which action can easily be demonstrated are usually the most helpful.

The key messages for Anton and other academics considering becoming an external examiner:

1. Join any networks you can.
2. Tell colleagues and friends in the HE community you would like an external examinership – there is a cap on numbers each individual can take and they may be prepared to recommend a colleague.
3. Spread the word at conferences or any other gatherings you attend.
4. Being an external examiner carries significant responsibility so make sure you have the time to carry out all your duties properly.
5. Do not be afraid to feedback your thoughts, both positive and negative.

FURTHER READING

WEBSITES

UK Quality Code for Higher Education – Chapter B7: External Examining (October 2011)

www.chuls.ac.uk

www.jiscmail.ac.uk

PART III

Jack

Jack is 25 when we first meet him. He works in an institution that regards itself as 'teaching focused' with an emphasis on widening participation; providing opportunities for students who might not otherwise have experienced higher education. Jack has spent three years teaching courses part time at similar institutions in the region, and also taught on the CILEX programme at a nearby college of further education. Jack is keen to develop his teaching profile and is considering doing a PGC offered by his institution. He is also keen to try out different teaching techniques and on using technology in his teaching but is fairly clueless when it comes to what is available. Jack spends a lot of time with students, giving feedback and acting as personal tutor. He sees pastoral care as really important and a key motivator for his career in education.

Jack was drawn to the role for the extra freedom he anticipated compared to his previous employers – particularly compared to his time at the local college. Jack is motivated by a sense of social justice and enabling people from whatever background to become economically and socially mobile through education. He would also like to seek recognition for his teaching and is considering writing a textbook.

Jack is seeing the number of students at his institution fall, and increased pressure to respond to the National Student Survey – which his institution scores well in. Jack's institution is also keen to distinguish itself from private providers and Jack's former employer, the nearby college, which is growing their HE provision. To do this, the institution is increasingly asking Jack to develop his – by now – impressive record of teaching innovation into a research agenda. Jack is developing legal education research but feels he is too often under-resourced with funds to attend conferences and lacks sufficient time to do his research. He is also struggling to balance this demand with his continued desire to develop high-quality teaching materials, and to support his students. He's increasingly frustrated and unhappy.

CHAPTER 38

Facilitating Small Group Discussions

FRANCIS KING

Jack has recently taken up his first HE appointment and is teaching mainly small groups of students.

This chapter seeks to provide an overview of some of the positive, as well as the more challenging, aspects of working with small groups in legal education, and aims to provide some strategies and advice for facilitating or leading small group discussions.

The traditional format for small-group work in law, whether referred to as a tutorial or a seminar, tends to be that of a seminar-style: Brown (1996) identifies these as sessions which allow for the discussion of material that is relational to, or associated with, the module lecture programme and is conducted between a tutor and a group of students. These small-group sessions are consonant with the Socratic method of teaching, which sought to develop students' self-awareness and attitudes to thought, as well as enhancing their intellectual and oral skills.

Brown and Atkins (1988) recognise that there are many positives for both student and tutor in these sessions, where the ultimate aim is 'to get students to talk and to think': Students are able to develop communication skills, demonstrate problem-solving in more creative and original ways, build on previous learning experiences in a more relaxed and supportive environment, and engage in deeper level discussions with a subject-specialist.

However, this exemplar of small-group pedagogy can often seem infeasible in practice, with many sessions falling flat due to a number of common issues: time constraints often mean that quite complex problems are being worked through relatively quickly, with little opportunity for 'deep' discussion; the 'over-prepared student' can discourage involvement from the rest of the group and monopolise tutor time; conversely, insufficient student preparation constrains the ability to conduct more collaborative discussions; and similarly, poor student attendance and/or participation can defeat even the most enthusiastic academics among us. As Guth (2009) acknowledges, it can be difficult, as the tutor in the room tasked with 'teaching' a module, to avoid filling the silence and talking too much in small-group sessions.

In considering strategies for dealing with these difficulties, the starting point should be with the module design. The learning outcomes for the module will define the module and its content: The teaching team then consider a strategy that will ensure that the teaching methods align with the learning outcomes for the module, but this discussion can also include practical considerations such as time and task. This means that the team consider the development of material that can be worked through within the given time period, in groups of that size, and that aligns with both the relational large-group teaching content, and the assessment strategy for the module. These should be matters for the module leader, and their team, to consider when designing the small-group materials.

The module leader could also co-ordinate the team in a way that would enable students to have a more consistent learning experience across all of the small groups for the module. This could be achieved through regular team briefings relating to the teaching materials and activities, as well as consistency in the team's approach to issues such as time-keeping and class preparation. The module leader therefore would weigh the balance between academic integrity and equivalence of experience by ensuring that the material meets the module objectives and learning outcomes, while considering consistencies in the delivery.

It is also important to develop personal strategies in order to ensure that there is an ideal learning environment which will allow for the 'deeper' discussions that the Socratic method seeks to achieve. Brown and Atkins (1988) recognise the importance of student-centred approaches or strategies, which would avoid repetition or re-delivery of module materials but provide opportunities for students to become more active participants during the session. Race (2001) also identifies with this form of 'facilitation' of the group, rather than 'instruction', and considers techniques or strategies to be employed by the facilitator of small group discussions which would encourage a more dynamic and collaborative approach to learning. These strategies are varied and include: partner dialogue, where students work in pairs to discuss the problem and its possible resolutions; role play in class, where students would act through the scenarios in character; and self-directed approaches, where students would suggest potential problems themselves and work through solutions together, or conduct forms of peer-assessment in pairs or groups in order to discern the assessment criteria for the module.

These models rely on the ability of a good facilitator, rather than a teacher, to allow students the freedom and autonomy to develop their own communication and problem-solving skills in an environment where the facilitator, as subject-specialist, can provide interaction and guidance where appropriate. Achieving this balance can be difficult, however, as such dynamic approaches may result in an imbalance in student experience across groups, where some groups engage more actively than others. These strategies also rely heavily on student attendance, participation and preparation which, as acknowledged above, can prove to be problematic. Other simple strategies which can increase interaction and energy in class include the use of writing materials and visual aids, such as whiteboards, flip-charts and post-it notes. These strategies allow for the generation of ideas and solutions to problems, while providing an element of anonymity or group interaction.

Brown and Atkins (1988) also confirm the importance of engaging with discipline-specific strategies, as these have been developed to complement the requisite behavioural and intellectual characteristics for each discipline. For problem-solving in law, this can be recognised most often as the IRAC method: recognising the relevant legal **I**ssue, identifying the **R**ule or rules of law that relate to that issue, **A**pplication of the rule to the given problem scenario, and **C**oncluding with some advice for the parties concerned. This can prove to be an ideal structure or framework for the group facilitator to use in generating suggestions and discussions within the group. It provides an opportunity for the group to work through set problem questions, which tend to be fairly typical in legal education, and the visual prompts previously mentioned could complement this further, bringing more energy and collaboration into the session.

The move away from identifying with ourselves as 'teachers' may seem unsettling but the role of facilitator is far more nuanced and will rely on expertise of more than the subject matter. In empirical research conducted on seminar students, Rudduck (1978) observed that student productivity reduced where the 'teacher' talked too much, was too knowledgeable and discouraged students from making mistakes. Conversely, student productivity rose where the 'teacher' defined problems, rather than solutions, showed that they were not infallible, and encouraged student creativity and originality. Rudduck identifies that this role as 'teacher' delineates a relationship of authority between student and staff member, with the teacher being 'an authority', that is, a subject expert, and 'in authority', as a representative of the institution.

Race (2001), in identifying with the phraseology of 'facilitation' and 'leadership' recognises the inescapable nature of a leadership position in such situations, but proffers strategies which allow for a symbiotic relationship between subject expertise and group leadership, as appropriate. In identifying with good leadership behaviours for small-group work, he encourages a form of leadership which guides discussions with an awareness of the group dynamics, making space for creative thought, and inviting student participation in order to consider the appropriate responses to hypothetical or real-life problems. This form of leadership, in combination with some of the strategies outlined above, and well-designed module material, should prove fruitful in facilitating collaborative and interactive small-group discussions for law.

The key messages for Jack and other academics considering how to make their small group teaching as effective as possible:

1. Small-group sessions present excellent opportunities for engaging students in deeper learning activities but are also beset by a number of common pitfalls.
2. Work with your module leader to ensure academic integrity is balanced with equivalence of experience for your students, and develop your own strategies to facilitate group discussions.
3. While facilitating the group you will be seen as 'an authority', as well as being 'in authority' – this will require you to draw on your strengths as a subject-specialist, and as a group leader.

FURTHER READING

BOOKS

Brown, G. and Atkins, M. (1988) *Effective Teaching in Higher Education*, London: Routledge.

Race, P. (2001) *The Lecturer's Toolkit*, 2nd edn, London: Routledge Falmer.

Rudduck, J. (1978) *Learning Through Small Group Discussion*, Guildford: Society for Research into Higher Education.

JOURNALS

Brown, S. (1996) The Art of Teaching Small Groups, *New Academic*, Autumn 5(3), 3–5.

Guth, J. (2009) The Case for Time Turners – the Practicalities of Being a New Law Lecturer, *The Law Teacher*, 43(2), 185–199.

CHAPTER 39

Innovation and the Use of Film in Legal Education

HUGO DE RIJKE

> Jack is eager to explore innovative teaching methods, in order to engage his students more and produce better results. He is considering using film in order to engage students in legal learning.

What do we mean by innovation in legal education? In general, innovation can be viewed as the application of better solutions to meet new requirements or existing needs. In this respect innovation differs from invention (the creation of products or processes) and also from improvement, since innovation refers to doing something different, rather than doing something better. There are many definitions of innovation, which largely depend on context. In legal education, innovation usually refers to the use of more effective ideas, methodologies and technologies in the teaching, learning and assessment process. Examples include student-centred learning, experiential learning (e.g. work-based learning, dispute-resolution skills and law clinics), online distance learning, blended learning (blending internet technology with face-to-face learning), blogs, social media, television, films, animations, videos, online games, mobile applications and numerous forms of assessment.

Innovative pedagogies are generally regarded as a positive means of increasing student access to courses and materials and also for increasing student engagement, thus achieving greater student satisfaction and achievement. For example, The Higher Education Academy's work in this area focuses on 'creative pedagogical use of digital technologies in strategic practitioner development for engaged student learning'. The rate of change and innovation continues to accelerate, led mostly by technology. This process is self-reinforcing, as it increases the capacity for technological innovation, which raises the expectations of students as consumers for more innovation.

Consequently there is some pressure upon legal academics to recognise such opportunities and take advantage of them, so that their students remain engaged, satisfied and achieve their potential. In a perfect world, this reflects well upon everyone concerned. Nevertheless, change for change's sake is not always desirable. It is important for the academic to try out different innovations, whilst balancing their skills and attributes with the interests and expectations of the students. What works for one law teacher will not always work for another.

This chapter deals with the use of film as an innovation in legal education. Film is one of the most ubiquitous cultural products of society today. In particular, the film industry has long been preoccupied with legal culture and has drawn heavily from the human drama, emotion, showmanship and suspense presented by legal narratives. Countless law films have been produced around the world for the past 75 years, offering a wealth of teaching and research material for academics and students. For much of this period, the use of popular culture to teach law has been regarded by the legal academy as 'low-brow' and lacking in serious content. More recently, however, it has been recognised that film can be used effectively as an engaging tool to teach legal concepts and skills, increase student interaction and enhance performance.

It should not be forgotten that society derives virtually all its knowledge of law from popular culture. This includes students who are inspired by law films to embark on a law course and who subsequently enjoy watching such films as part of their studies. In addition, it must be acknowledged that students now expect to be both educated *and* entertained. Surveys reveal that the millennial generation who grew up with the internet are resistant to lengthy textual reading and cite watching films amongst their highest priorities. Showing extracts from films is therefore an excellent way to engage the interest of large or small groups and to encourage discussion of the legal aspects of those films.

Many legal themes and issues arise from the interconnections between law and film. A large number of these relate to law as portrayed in film, such as representations of truth, justice, advocacy, lawyers, jurors, judges, witnesses, sentencing and the death penalty. At a practical level, extracts from film can be used as pedagogical aids to illustrate legal concepts and skills, such as *Philadelphia* for examples of courtroom techniques when teaching advocacy. Another interesting approach is the analysis of transcripts of notorious trials as examples of legal storytelling, adapted into films such as *Let Him Have It* and *Wilde*. A further significant interconnection is the censorship and classification of film through obscenity and other laws, including the remit of the British Board of Film Classification and the powers of the Motion Picture Association of America, revealed in *This Film Is Not Yet Rated*.

For teachers and students of film and the law, there is excellent scope for in-depth research, analysis and critical evaluation. For instance, students may explore society's cultural fascination with lawyers and the law, examine how films question the ideals and values associated with the law, identify the impact of law upon film or assess the impact of film upon law. Students are frequently surprised to discover that films dealing with injustice can lead to important changes in the law, such as the impact of *Rosetta* on employment law for teenagers in Belgium and *FGM* on female genital mutilation in Kurdistan; or even lead to a successful appeal against conviction for murder, as in *The Thin Blue Line*.

Legal themes in films often raise contentious issues, which facilitates enthusiastic debate among students in lectures and seminars. For example, the notion of justice includes vigilantism, which leads to ethical dilemmas, as illustrated in *A Time to Kill*. Representations of lawyers and judges reinforce (with some exceptions) common stereotypes of the 'good' or 'bad' lawyer, and representations of jurors reveal the scope for prejudice, as in *12 Angry Men*. Representations of capital punishment in films such as *A Short Film About Killing* and *Dead Man Walking* invoke arguments for and against the death penalty, including its repeal in some countries and the significance of the European Convention on Human Rights.

Films also present excellent opportunities for innovation in learning methods, including the use of role-play to gain an understanding of legal performance, witnessing and storytelling. For example, law films highlight professional behaviour and conduct, which is useful for advocacy and mooting. Legal performance is also apparent in films when lawyers are displaying showmanship or grandstanding, and when witnesses are 'playing to the gallery'. Furthermore, films highlight the importance of witnesses and their crucial evidential role in providing narrative dialogue for the 'plot' of a legal story and in influencing the outcome of a trial. Showing students a film extract of an event such as a crime being committed allows them to consider the reliability of witnesses, through a simple task where they answer detailed questions about what they saw in the film. Consequently students are able to reflect upon the accuracy of their recollection if called as a witness in court. Likewise, students can test the findings from psychology that a true story is as likely to receive a 'false' verdict as a 'true' verdict, and vice versa. In groups of three, one student tells a true story about herself, another tells a false story about herself, and the third student 'judges' which story is true and which is false. Students engage enthusiastically in such exercises and gain a great deal of practical knowledge and understanding in the process.

In conclusion, using film in legal education provides important links with the past, emotional depth and human engagement, which are not always prioritised in other technologies.

The key messages for Jack and other academics considering innovation and the use of film in legal education:

1. Innovation in legal education refers to the use of more effective ideas, methodologies and technologies in the teaching, learning and assessment process.
2. Try out different innovations – what works for one law teacher will not always work for another.
3. Using film in legal education provides excellent opportunities for innovation.

FURTHER READING

BOOKS

Greenfield, S. and Osborn, G. and Robson, P. (2010) *Film and the Law*, 2nd edn, Oxford: Hart Publishing.

Freeman, M. (ed.) (2005) *Law and Popular Culture*, Oxford: OUP.

JOURNAL

Pawlowski, M. and Greer, S. (2009) Film and Literature in the Legal Classroom, *The Law Teacher*, 43, 49–61.

WEBSITE

www.heacademy.ac.uk/workstreams-research/workstreams/innovative-pedagogies

CHAPTER 40

Approaches to Law

KEVIN J. BROWN

> Jack is considering different approaches to law, and the approach that is right for him.

One might assume that the most important decision for an academic at the beginning of their career is deciding in what area of law to specialise, but a fundamentally more important decision is what approach to the law to adopt. The choice will be shaped by the individual's experiences, education and worldview. The decision need not be final and many academics' approaches develop over time, although for the most part not dramatically. Academics like others are creatures of habit. A particular approach becomes second nature; it is how we see the law. It is therefore worth reminding ourselves on occasion that our particular perspective is one of many and that there is much to be gained from having an appreciation of the alternative approaches to legal research and teaching to be found in academia.

One of the traditional approaches to legal scholarship is black-letter analysis. Here the law is interpreted through positivist principles and doctrines, which seek to identify, organise, and synthesise the law from its various sources including common law, statute and treaty. Critique of the law is primarily focused on the goal of achieving a more coherent and rational set of rules. Critics of the black-letter approach accuse adherents of operating in a disciplinary vacuum ignoring the political and social influences on the law and presenting to students 'a particular and partial view of the world as neutral and natural' (Hutchinson 1999, 308). Whilst a black-letter approach holds less sway over legal research in the United Kingdom than it once did, it remains pervasive in legal education. Evidence for this is found in the many popular undergraduate textbooks adopting the approach.

Analytical jurisprudential approaches have long accompanied black-letter scholarship as staples of legal education and research in the United Kingdom. This involves a philosophical exploration of the law and its institutions. Scholars in this field address fundamental questions of what law is and what the purpose of law should be. Debates on particular points can span generations of scholars with approaches encompassing the abstract, the conceptual and the practical (Veitch et al. 2012). There has been a tendency in legal education in the United Kingdom to corner off jurisprudence to a specific module often taken later in the degree programme. This has the effect of discouraging students from applying tools of jurisprudential analysis throughout their studies. Some law schools now seek to counter this by introducing students to jurisprudence from the outset. Partly as a result of how jurisprudence has traditionally been taught in many British universities, when it comes to research, legal academics in the United Kingdom are prone to shy away from in-depth engagement unless it is their chosen specialism. This causes them to potentially miss out on useful insights into their topics of research.

In the 20th century, scholars unhappy with a perceived inherent conservatism within the black-letter and analytical jurisprudential approaches to the law established the legal realist and subsequently the critical legal scholarship movements in the USA and latterly the United Kingdom. Early proponents of these approaches sought to demystify the law and its institutions. In a challenge to previous methods of analysis, the study of the law is placed within its historical, political and social contexts. The tendency of the law and its institutions to perpetuate wealth and power and marginalise those requiring social justice has been and remains a strong focus of such scholarship (Stone et al. 2012). This includes approaches to the law that are grounded in feminist, gendered and queer perspectives and those which seek to examine the relationship between law, race and ethnicity. Whilst explicitly Marxist perspectives on the law are not as common as they once were, the study of the relationship between law, poverty and deprivation remains strong and arguably in an age of austerity is more important than ever. A good source of support for academics venturing into this field in the United Kingdom is the Critical Legal Conference that is held annually attracting around 200 delegates.

A significant proportion of legal academics would today label themselves as adopting a socio-legal approach to education and research (Collier 2004). The Socio-Legal Studies Association founded in 1990 in the United Kingdom has over 1,200 members with its annual conference attracting around 350 delegates. Socio-legal shares commonalities with critical legal scholarship, placing research and teaching of the law in the context of broader social and political theories. A distinctive feature of the socio-legal approach is the use of social scientific research methods to analyse the operation of the law including the use of qualitative and quantitative techniques. Adopting such an approach requires additional skills particularly if the academic is to engage in empirical work. Training is available within some universities, whilst there is a range of texts available for those venturing into the field for the first time (see for example Banakar and Travers 2005). The empirical socio-legal researcher may find there are greater opportunities to access funding from organisations that value research supported by data. This includes research studies commissioned by non-governmental organisations, national and international governmental bodies.

In large part thanks to the work of the critical legal and socio-legal movements, legal academia in the United Kingdom has shown an increasing willingness to cross disciplinary boundaries in its exploration of the law. Interdisciplinary approaches seek to provide better answers to research questions than single disciplines can provide. Recent influential developments with strong interdisciplinary foundations include the law and literature (Ward 2008) and the law and economics (Posner 2014) movements. Institutional support for such endeavours can be found in interdisciplinary research and teaching centres which are currently popular within the university sector. Access to financial support for collaborative projects may be available from research councils and other bodies, which in recent years have sought to promote interdisciplinary research.

It is fair to say that legal education in the United Kingdom, particularly at the undergraduate level, lags behind research in the extent to which alternatives approaches to law are explored. Some law schools (e.g. Kent) explicitly incorporate critical approaches into their degree programmes, whilst in many law schools one can find modules that seek to provide alternative perspectives on the law. However, the tradition of black-letter legal pedagogy remains strong. There are a number of factors behind this including resistance from some academics to change, the lack of undergraduate textbooks adopting alternative approaches in some subjects areas and the restrictive teaching and assessment formats favoured by many law schools. With many universities encouraging research-led teaching it is worth academics asking themselves whether there is more they can do to promote their approach to law in their teaching.

To conclude, in most law schools today one will find a kaleidoscope of approaches to law among the faculty. The black-letter lawyer, the jurisdprude, the 'crit' and the socio-legal scholar all bring their own perspectives to a particular legal issue. Keeping an open mind and taking time out of our busy schedules to attend seminars, read papers by colleagues and even chatting over the watercooler can pay dividends by broadening our horizons and enriching our approaches to education and research.

The key messages for Jack and other academics considering their approach to the law:

1. Do not just focus on what subject area to specialise in, but what approach to legal scholarship to adopt.
2. Reflect on whether you can better incorporate your approach to research into your teaching.
3. Engage with colleagues who adopt other approaches to law or colleagues from other disciplines with shared interests.

FURTHER READING

BOOKS

Banakar, R. and Travers, M. (eds) (2005) *Theory and Method in Socio-Legal Research*, Oxford: Hart Publishing.

Posner, R. (2014) *Economic Analysis of Law*, New York: Wolters Kluwer Law and Business.

Stone, M., Wall, I. R. and Douzinas, C. (eds) (2012) *New Critical Legal Thinking: Law and the Political*, Abingdon: Routledge.

Veitch, S., Christodoulidis. E. and Farmer, L. (2012) *Jurisprudence: Themes and Concepts*, Abingdon: Routledge.

Ward, I. (2008) *Law and Literature: Possibilities and Perspectives*, Cambridge: Cambridge University Press.

JOURNALS

Collier, R. (2004) We're All Socio-Legal Now – Legal Education, Scholarship and the Global Knowledge Economy – Reflections on the UK Experience, *Sydney Law Review*, 26, 503–536.

Hutchinson, A. C. (1999) Beyond Black-letterism: Ethics in Law and Legal Education, *The Law Teacher*, 33(3), 301–309.

CHAPTER 41

Teaching and Assessment Can be Inclusive Too

JACKIE LANE

> Jack is reflecting upon how to ensure that his teaching and assessment is as inclusive as possible.

Teachers are certain to encounter students who have a learning disability in the course of their career, but they should not be concerned that this will take up an inordinate amount of their time and resources since there are simple ways of supporting such students, partly through the use of modern technology, but also through simple adaptations to teaching and assessment methods which address the needs of those with disabilities. All students should be treated as individuals who deserve equality in the classroom. Those learners may be dyslexic, or may have any of a range of learning difficulties or disabilities. Students with autism or Asperger syndrome are increasingly likely to find their way on to higher education courses, and tutors should be prepared and informed, ready to adapt to the challenges of ensuring inclusivity.

As a first step, disabled students should be referred to the disability office in the university or college for an initial assessment, and recommendations will be made for extra time in exams, permission to record lectures, access to lecture notes prior to the lecture, a dedicated note-taker or whatever else is considered desirable for that student to gain equality with their peers. However, these standard recommendations cannot be a panacea for overcoming their learning difficulties, so you as the tutor will need to reassess your teaching and assessment methods to ensure greater equality among your students.

The theory of universal design for learning (UDL) has three central tenets which are, roughly, that there should be multiple means of representing course content, that students should be assessed in a variety of ways and that there should be a variety of teaching strategies and means of interaction with the course material. This model creates a more inclusive paradigm, seeing learners as on a continuum rather than as disabled and non-disabled.

The first of these could be achieved through using PowerPoint presentations to accompany verbal lectures, or utilizing the VLE to provide information in a range of formats such as text, video or audio which the student can access at a time and pace to suit them. The provision of e-books allows the student to manipulate information and to access assistive technology supports such as text-to-speech programmes. The provision of multiple formats allows the student to select the one that best suits their learning styles and needs, whether they have a learning disability or not.

The second tenet of UDL refers to assessment and you can make simple adjustments to ensure that assessments are as fair to the disabled student as to the non-disabled. Flexibility is essential and this may even mean that exams are discarded in favour of other types of assessment. The disability office's recommended adjustment of 25% extra time, or provision of an amanuensis, cannot possibly provide equality of opportunity for the seriously dyslexic student in an exam, so it is down to the assessor to design such equality into their assessment methods. Adjustments such as providing exam papers in a larger font or on a particular coloured paper are only part of the solution and the tutor should consider different types of assessment. The good news is that, whether you have disabled students or not, a flexible and inclusive approach to teaching and assessment will benefit *all* students, so you do not have to worry about lack of time to deal with individual issues since you will be acting for the collective good of your whole student cohort.

Verbal presentations (individual or group), poster presentations or a viva are all ways of getting away from the traditional written assessment and help to create a more level playing field for the dyslexic student who will usually find the written word something of a challenge. Students with autism or Asperger Syndrome, however, will often struggle with social interaction and may therefore perform badly in assessments involving team work, social interaction or verbal skills, but may also find exams hard to cope with. Exam questions, when used, should ideally be clear, specific and preferably objective – multiple choice questions or those requiring short answers are ideal. Vague essay questions, typically beginning with a quotation and asking the student to 'discuss' are not. These could be the topic of a formative assignment, however, subject to the provision of a clear structure that the student can work around. Remember that you are testing knowledge in an exam so devise ways of enabling the student to demonstrate that knowledge. Flexible assessment methods can address some of the barriers to the expression of knowledge.

Moreover, autistic students will often suffer excessive anxiety in a large exam room so consider whether they could be tested through other means if at all possible. The suggested reading will give you some useful ideas, but you could consider assessing wikis or blogs, journals, verbal and/or poster presentations or take-home projects. You could also consider providing speech recognition facilities for students when there is no alternative to an exam, but where an amanuensis is not appropriate.

The third tenet of UDL involves inclusive teaching strategies. Lectures present a variety of accessibility barriers to students with learning difficulties and they may value the provision of lecture notes or the opportunity to record a lecture to revisit later. Lecture outlines on which the students fill in details have also been found to be beneficial. The university may be fortunate enough to have assistive technology labs where tools such as voice recognition software are available and this possibility could be usefully explored.

Finally, providing multiple, flexible options for engagement is fundamental to stimulating learning and that will involve getting to know your students well and being able to understand their learning styles and areas of confusion, allowing you to tailor your support more appropriately. This will take time and effort but the rewards will be great. Learn to value difference and really care about enabling students to do the best they possibly can. Forget conformity, embrace flexibility and work towards equality so that all students can achieve their goals with your help.

The key messages for Jack and other academics considering furthering inclusivity for students with learning disabilities:

1. Be prepared to be flexible in your assessment and teaching methods.
2. Arm yourself with information on disabilities so that you can act accordingly and be empathic.
3. Value differences.

FURTHER READING

BOOKS

Betts, S., Betts, D. and Gerber-Eckard, L. (2007) *Asperger Syndrome in the Inclusive Classroom: Advice and Strategies for Teachers*, London: Jessica Kingsley Publishers.

Birnbaum, B. (2005) *Using Assistive Technology for Instructing Students with Disabilities: A Survey of New Resources*, Lampeter: E. Mellen Press.

Hodge, B. and Preston-Sabin, J. (1997) *Accommodations or Just Good Teaching? Strategies for Teaching College Students with Disabilities*, Westport, CT: Praeger.

Seale, J. (2006) *E-learning and Disability in Higher Education: Accessibility Research and Practice*, Oxon: Routledge.

JOURNAL

Orr, A. and Bachman Hammig, S. (2009) Inclusive Postsecondary Strategies for Teaching Students with Learning Disabilities: A Review of the Literature, *Learning Disability Quarterly*, 32(3), 181–196.

WEBSITE

The National Autistic Society. www.nas.org.uk

CHAPTER 42

Using Animations with Students

CAROL WITHEY

> Jack is seeking to further develop his innovative approach to teaching with the use of animation.

Law lecturers often worry about how to maintain student attention in lectures. There are various strategies for engaging students through the use of animation. PowerPoint presentations are one of the most relied upon lecture tools and the visual appeal of slides can be enhanced in several ways. An obvious enhancement is to link to external websites. This is simple to do and just requires pasting the URL link into the relevant slide. In this way students can view news items, statistical sites, YouTube videos, animations and other relevant material.

The visual appeal of a PowerPoint presentation can also be enhanced with animated images. There are several sites that permit downloading of free royalty free images, such as Animation Library: www.animationlibrary.com/ and Amazing Animations :http://www.amazing-animations.com/. These sites organise the animations into categories, including occupations, people, props and buildings, and there is bound to be an image or cartoon character that relates to the PowerPoint text. Some websites also include royalty free sounds.

A specific form of animation is the 'smiley'. Smileys are available with almost every conceivable emotion, and come in a vast range of poses and actions. Many websites allow free download of smiley and animated emoticons. These websites were primarily developed to enable users of mobile phones to add smileys to text messages, but the animations are also ideal for PowerPoint presentations. Websites with a huge range include www.freesmileys.org and www.mysmiley.net

Downloading instructions are always provided, but it is usually quicker to hover over the image, right click and save the image to desktop. The smiley can then be inserted to the relevant slide. The animation will appear static but will 'come alive' when the presentation is viewed.

For very creative lecturers and tutors, a time consuming but satisfying project is to create videos, cartoon strips or animations that depict aspects of a course, including visual representations of legal cases. Apple users should try iMovie and the applicable software for Windows is Movie Maker: www. windows.microsoft.com/en-gb/windows-live/movie-maker. These programmes allow the user to create videos from uploaded images. I have used iMovie to create revision films for Criminal Law using LEGO® characters to depict defendants and victims. https://www.youtube.com/user/carolwithey/videos

Cartoon websites include Powtoon: www.powtoon.com and *BitStrips*: www.bitstrips.com. *These are fun to use and come with standard characters and scenes, or characters and scenes can be created to reflect real people and situations. Most cartoon websites only permit non-animated strips.*

The real enthusiast might want to create animated cartoons. A popular Apple programme is iStopMotion; www.boinx.com/istopmotion/mac. There are many websites to choose from and most have free packages for both creating and sharing content. Popular sites include www.toondoo.com; www.powtoon.com; www.dvolver.com; www.wideo.com and www.goanimate.com. There are clear instructions regarding how to create animations, and users can usually select from standard backgrounds, characters, props and sounds. Voiceovers can sometimes be added to characters.

The above visual enhancements can be used in conjunction with PowerPoint or can be uploaded or linked to external websites, or to the virtual learning environment of your institution. According to Bahrani and Soltani (2011) cartoons are an effective way to maintain student engagement during lectures and seminars and they help to enhance learning because the modified language in a cartoon is accessible to all students. However, they also comment that cartoons should not become distracting and should be used sparingly; otherwise their effect will be lost.

Lectures and seminars can also be made more interesting by the introduction of interactive poll voting. This is a good way to introduce some variety into a teaching session and research has shown that it helps to maintain student engagement and assists learning; Draper et al. (2002); Boyle and Nicol (2003); Withey (2011).

There are several companies that use the 'clicker' system. This electronic voting system (EVS) or personal response system (PRS) requires purchase of the hardware clicker devices. The disadvantage of this system is that unless students are given the devices to take home, they have to be handed out each session and collected at the end. One of the most popular devices is the Response Card clicker from Turning Technologies: www.turningtechnologies.co.uk.

The accompanying TurningPoint software allows the tutor to devise polls, and these can be embedded into PowerPoint slides. In recent years the technology has progressed so that students are now able to poll vote by texting their selection from a mobile phone, tablet or laptop. The advantage of this system is that it is less disruptive to the class given that students are already in possession of their voting device. One of the most popular companies is Poll Everywhere: www.polleverywhere.com. The site is user friendly and there are instructions for creating polls and for embedding them into lecture and seminar materials. Multiple choice questions can be set, as can free questions that allow students to text short answers. The results of a multiple choice poll can be displayed in a graph in real time, as individual students vote, or the results can be shown after all the votes have been registered. Most companies have a range of subscriptions to choose from. Poll Everywhere is free to use for classes of 40 student responses. There are also Higher Education plans that allow the institution to purchase a subscription on a wider campus basis. Turning Technologies have now introduced ResponseWare, which allows their voting software to be used in conjunction with phones, laptops and tablets, thereby cutting out the need to purchase clickers. I have used the clicker system and the phone system with my Criminal Law students and have compared student perceptions of both systems; Withey (2011). Out of the 79 students that responded to a survey, 94% preferred the clicker system and 6% the phone system. The main objections to the phone system came from students who sent their votes via text, because they had to pay for the text and there was also some resentment regarding the use of a student's own device in lectures. With the increased use of laptops, smart phones and tablets over the last few years, this may not now be such an objection. I prefer to use the phone system as it is more convenient and less disruptive to lectures, given that students are already in possession of their voting device. My research also required students to state whether there were any benefits from poll voting in lectures. There were 93 comments in total and 23 of these were to the effect that it tested or clarified their understanding of the lecture material. There were 18 comments that poll voting introduced variety and helped to focus attention, and 16 students said that it made the lecture interesting. Students were asked whether lectures should continue to have a 15-minute poll voting session and 97% answered that they should.

I have used all of the above animation resources. All of these tools have helped to engage students and they are also a good revision aid, especially when animations depict legal cases. This helps students to memorise both case names and their facts. However, devising polls and developing cartoons is a time-consuming process, so be prepared for some hard work!

The key messages for Jack and other academics considering using animations with students:

1. Animations are a great way to engage students and maintain their attention.
2. Animations can help enhance learning and are a good resource during the revision period.
3. There are many websites for developing cartoon strips and animation videos.

FURTHER READING

JOURNALS

Bahrani, T. and Soltani, R. (2011) The Pedagogical Values of Cartoons, *Research on Humanities and Social Sciences*, 1(4), 19–22.

Boyle, J. T. and Nicol, D. J. (2003) Using Classroom Communication Systems to Support Interaction and Discussion in Large Class Settings, *Association for Learning Technology Journal*, 11(3), 43–57.

Draper, S.W., Cargill, J. and Cutts, Q. (2002) Electronically Enhanced Classroom Interaction, *Australian Journal of Educational Technology*, 18(1), 13–23.

WEBSITES

Withey, C. (2011) Engaging Students Through Electronic Voting Systems – Clickers and Mobile Phone Systems. www.slideshare.net/ukcleslidespace/engaging-students-through-electronic-voting-clickers-and-mobile-phone-systems

www.youtube.com/user/carolwithey/videos

CHAPTER 43

Developing Students' Legal Writing Skills

Lisa Webley

> Jack is keen to develop his students' writing skills.

Many law students find it hard to express themselves in writing, so do many academic staff too. Yet writing an essay, problem question answer, counsel's opinion or dissertation, far from being the task of getting information on to a page, is a process so fundamental to thinking, reasoning, analysing and refining arguments that it is surprising that we do not spend more time helping students to develop their (legal) writing. How we write is not simply, if simply is the right word, an expression of our linguistic dexterity. The writing process goes to the heart of students' abilities to develop their thoughts, marshal their evidence and present their arguments so that the substance is of a quality we rate.

Many of us worry about how to engage students with the writing process. Some students could do with help with English grammar and may need to be referred to the academic support unit. Most find writing less than enjoyable and struggle to translate their feedback into practical steps for improvement. Academics sometimes feel nervous about their ability to help students given that they too may find it hard to get beyond writer's block. Where should we start?

Firstly it is important to acknowledge that many people find writing difficult in new contexts. Legal writing is not that different from many others forms of technical writing but many law students will not have had much experience of it prior to coming to university. Many will have the impression that good legal writing involves long sentences using flowery and arcane language. Some may even be disappointed when they learn that it is preferable to use plain English and not Latin gadgets! It may be useful to dispel some of these myths, to acknowledge student anxiety, share some of our own experiences as a writer, and to underline that clarity, strong arguments and authoritative evidence are important features in written work, just as they are in oral presentations and advocacy.

Secondly, the writing process involves a number of important phases. Good writing is easier when the writer is clear on the task to be performed. So, dissecting the question (essay); setting an outline research question (dissertation); and working through the fact pattern to determine agreed and contested facts and an absence of important information (problem question) are good skills to help students to develop. Students can be focused on this phase via an interim assessment, providing an opportunity to discuss the meaning of the task on an online discussion board, or through a seminar or poster-style presentation. Some may find it helps to start a document, place the title at the top and then in a couple of sentences (essay, problem question, counsel's opinion) or a paragraph (dissertation, extended essay) set out their understanding of the task. This could become the starting point for their introduction at a later date.

The next phase is for students to establish what they already know. This step is often passed over rather too quickly, but they will often have lecture notes, text-book notes or other sources that they can review straight away and paraphrase within the document that they have begun above. To add value, they may wish to explain not just what they know but how their knowledge helps them to answer the question to assist with application. This could be repeated once further text-book reading has been completed. They could be tasked with writing down things they think they need to find out, to develop key words for their research phase below, plus set out a brief plan of how they will undertake their research at the next stage.

Often the main research phase of the task will come next. This can be the prompt for students immediately to head for Google. This can be harnessed to good effect by ensuring that they are all *au fait* with Google Scholar and make use of that before branching out from Google Scholar to Lexis/Westlaw and other relevant databases. We may need to flag the importance of keeping full and accurate citations including page references and to be clear on when they are quoting or paraphrasing. Effective reading and note-taking is part of the thinking process and it may be helpful to set a task to help with this too, asking students to read the introduction, the methods section (where relevant) and the conclusion of an academic source, and to write brief notes on: who wrote the article; what was the article about; how did they conduct their research (where relevant); what were the author's main conclusions that are relevant to the essay/problem question; and then, very importantly, how do the author's conclusions help to answer the question that they have been set? Then, if the article is directly relevant to the question, students could be asked to read the whole article, but only to note down additional material that is absolutely on point and then only if they can explain how it helps them to answer the question. A similar task can be set for a piece of legislation or for a case. These notes could all be made into the document above.

Our students will already have written quite a lot by now and all of this material forms the foundation of their final answer. It may be worthwhile to encourage a brief halt to the note-taking phase, to allow time for students to read through their document and reflect on its contents. Many students find it helpful to annotate their document with details of reoccurring themes or points of law and then convert these into sub-headings (they can be temporary) and rearrange their notes so that they are thematic rather than ordered by source. We are now entering what many consider to be the writing phase proper: the paragraph development phase in which they develop a paragraph or so for each of the themes or points of law. A simple paragraph structure may help them if blocked: a sentence that sets out the point they wish to make (their conclusion on the issue); a few sentences that explain that point with reference to the evidence (all the material that they have read is now their evidence base); a sentence in which they say what is their conclusion as regards the question given the preceding discussion. Select paragraphs could be swapped with a peer for feedback with reflection on: the clarity of the point; how convincing are the argument and the evidence; and how strong is the concluding sentence in explaining relevance of the point to the question. For those with a more advanced level of writing, analysis can be developed further with the simple trick of taking the concluding sentence to the top of the paragraph, redrafting the middle section of the paragraph as an evidenced justification for how the conclusion was reached and then adding a new higher-level conclusion to round off the paragraph. This stage can be repeated again and again to ramp up the critical analysis.

Some writers struggle with the introduction and the conclusion to their work, and it may help to explain the introduction as the signpost (to the task and the themes or points that will be made in what follows) and the conclusion as the section in which all of the concluding sentences from previous paragraphs are drawn together into one final answer to the question. There is usually a need to stress to students that a first draft is a stage on the way to a finished document, but is not the end of the writing journey, the importance of finishing and polishing, checking quotations and citations, checking the task requirements and also deadlines and submission procedures. By dividing legal writing into a set of processes students may see that writing is integral to every stage, and in turn they may have developed their diagnosis, research, argumentation and critical analysis skills too along the way.

> The key messages for Jack and other academics considering how to develop their students' legal writing skills:
>
> 1. Writing is rather than In a process that is fundamental to developing arguments and analysis.
> 2. The writing process can be split into a set of stages. These include determining the nature of the task; establishing what the writer already knows; research; reading and note-taking; theme development leading to argument development; redrafting to develop analysis; finishing and polishing.
> 3. Students can be set tasks to help them with any of these stages and allow them to develop skills allied to legal writing.

FURTHER READING

BOOKS

Haigh, R. (2012) *Legal English*, 3rd edn, Abingdon and New York: Routledge.

Higgins, E. and Tatham, L. (2010) *Successful Legal Writing*, 2nd edn, London: Sweet and Maxwell.

Salter, M. and Mason. J. (2007) *Writing Law Dissertations: An Introduction and Guide to the Conduct of Legal Research*, Harlow: Longman.

Strong, S. (2014) *How to Write Law Essays and Exams*, 4th edn, Oxford: OUP.

Webley, L. (2013) *Legal Writing*, 3rd edn, Abingdon and New York: Routledge.

CHAPTER 44

Working with the Library

EMILY ALLBON

Jack is exploring opportunities to work with the library.

Unlike the majority of subject librarians (also called liaison librarians etc.) in higher education, librarians supporting law have traditionally been offered a certain 'protected' status. This is largely on the basis that the standards written by the Society of Legal Scholars on what is expected of a university law library (*A library for the modern law school: a statement of standards for university law library provision in the UK*) require a law librarian to be in place in order to determine law library policy and manage the law library. These standards cover the library collections, space and levels of support, and inform course validations. Law libraries have often been termed as the law students 'laboratory' – essential in terms of the space itself but also the wide variety of materials within.

Recent years however, have seen universities making huge efficiency cuts, with libraries often first in the firing line for restructures. Subject specialism is seen as less important in this new HE sphere – pure law librarians are becoming rarer, with many seeing their role diluted as they struggle to deal with responsibility for many completely unrelated subjects in addition to law. Some universities have abandoned subject librarians altogether, creating crack teams of 'teaching librarians' who can be rolled out to adapt generic training across the whole university. For law, this is a concern; having that extra line of support to help students struggling to navigate their way through the maze of obscure abbreviations, law reports and legal databases is essential.

If you are a relatively new academic you might be a little unsure how to get the most out of your relationship with the library, and perhaps even hazy about what librarians do outside of the 'buying books' capacity. Librarians are all about information: seeking, organising and managing, thriving on procuring the right snippet at the time it's needed.

If you are module leader and would like to beef up the research element, or simply prepare your students better in key skills areas then consider embedding some sessions from your librarian into the course. You might even think about a co-teaching arrangement. Librarians will work with you to tie in content which will be helpful for assessments.

The HEA ran several workshops in 2014 highlighting case studies where librarians and academic staff collaborate for teaching legal research skills. We heard about how such skills are interwoven into substantive subjects thanks to such a partnership (Yeatman 2014), and a variety of approaches were evident in an earlier workshop (Auchmuty 2014) from total integration, to a law school where the law librarian felt largely invisible.

Librarians have a great enthusiasm for the teaching part of their role, often developing classes using less traditional methods, for example flipping the classroom and incorporating technology. Remember – making legal research skills teaching interesting is quite a challenge and law librarians need to pay close attention to the pedagogy in order to engage young lawyers in the principles required. Librarians are adept at teaching general information literacy skills also – ensuring students know how to evaluate and use the information they find – especially important for law.

Don't be overwhelmed and feel a complete curriculum re-design will be required – sometimes a quick half-hour appearance by the librarian in a lecture will just be enough to remind students of the key resources. Beginning a subject like EU law, where all the sources can seem alien at first, is an ideal opportunity to ask for library assistance – they can take the students through the key databases to find different examples of cases, treaties, directives and regulations as well as help them see how to find things like national implementation measures. This should give the students greater confidence in tracking down the authorities you have referred them to.

Law librarians are very committed to professional development; with a strong network in the UK called the British and Irish Association of Law Librarians (BIALL), which means they know what is going on at other libraries in the UK and internationally. The network includes librarians from law firms, barrister's chambers, the Inns of Court and the government, as well as libraries like the Law Society and Advocates Library in Scotland. Crucially this means that they are very aware of the skills required of our students in their future careers, and the issues concerning how they acquire these. BIALL directly addressed the decline in legal research competency skills amongst trainees at law firms by writing the BIALL Legal Information Literacy Statement, which was noted within the Legal Education and Training Review (LETR).

They make ideal allies for academic staff – not only can they assist with teaching of legal research skills, plagiarism, referencing and citation and critical thinking, they are generally pretty switched on in relation to technology and social media tools. Remember librarians are on the front line and will often have an insight into the problems students are facing early on; students will often see them as a brain to pick without exposing their perceived ignorance to their lecturers.

Geekiness and librarianship goes hand-in-hand; librarians generally love new technologies and many librarians have carved out specific expertise around their teaching practice and technology, including social media tools. In my earlier role as Law Librarian at City I created the Lawbore resource, which exploits various technologies to offer students a space to find out what's going on, learn about opportunities and gain support during their law studies via videos, talking slideshows and articles. This started out as a 'library thing' but was embraced by the law school as a whole so was able to blossom into a resource with much wider application. I have worked with various academics to 'bring content to life' with different tools.

For your own research, you may feel confident you know all the best places to look for related literature, but it's always worth having a word with the librarian too.

Content in legal databases changes all the time – your librarian will have an ear to the ground for any new services that may be useful to the law school's academic staff and students. If you haven't used a particular service before, or your skills have got a little rusty, don't be shy in coming forward to ask for some tips – getting help might save you hours of frustration as you grapple with the advanced searching techniques required. Don't think this is just limited to paid-for resources either; librarians are usually very familiar with any free tools that make organising and managing your research more efficient.

The key messages for Jack and other academics considering working with the library:

1. Go and speak to your law librarian early on – tell them about yourself (what you teach, areas of research, things you're interested in).
2. Think about the viability of incorporating some research skills practice within the modules you teach.
3. Don't underestimate! Librarians have diverse skills, which they are happy to put to use for the benefit of their academic staff and students.

FURTHER READING

WEBSITES

Auchmuty, R. (2014) Teaching Research Skills to Law Students: A Workshop of Best Practice, *HEA Social Sciences Blog*. http://blogs.heacademy.ac.uk/social-sciences/2014/02/25/teaching-research-skills-to-law-students-a-workshop-on-best-practice/

BIALL (2013) BIALL Legal Information Literacy Statement. http://www.biall.org.uk/pages/biall-legal-information-literacy-statement.html

Lawbore. lawbore.net

Society of Legal Scholars (2009) A Library for the Modern Law School: A Statement of Standards for University Law Library Provision in the United Kingdom – 2009 Revision Prepared by the Libraries Sub-Committee of the Society of Legal Scholars. http://www.legalscholars.ac.uk/documents/SLS-Library-for-a-Modern-Law-School-Statement-2009.pdf

Yeatman, L. (2014) Embedding Legal Research Skills into the LLB Curriculum, *HEA Social Sciences Blog*. http://blogs.heacademy.ac.uk/social-sciences/2014/06/03/embedding-legal-research-skills-into-the-llb-curriculum/

CHAPTER 45

Engaging with Schools and Prospective Students

JESSICA GUTH

> Jack has been asked to get involved with Open Day activities and school visits. This is not something he has done before and he is unsure of the expectations.

Universities are competing for students. Whether we like it or not, that is the reality. Institutions are therefore seeking to engage with potential students at an early stage and build up relationships with those students in the hope that they will choose to apply and then select that institution. One key driver for any sort of outreach activities with schools and colleges is therefore to secure future students. In order to do so, we need to sell them the institution, the location, the programmes, the teaching, the accommodation, the support networks and everything else that goes with coming to university. Often we have to do this in schools which do not traditionally send most or even many of their pupils to university and where many of the pupils have little understanding of what going to university might mean. This highlights a further dimension of schools outreach work and one that I personally value and enjoy far more than getting students to commit to applying to my institution – that of raising aspirations. The work we do with schools can have a profound impact on the young people we meet and we should never underestimate that power.

At a very basic level all institutions engage with potential students through open days. Some institutions have open days which are structured and designed specifically for school groups to come and visit as well as days for individuals (and their parents). If asked to participate in an open day, find out what is expected of you. Are you to be a point of contact and information at a subject specific stand for example or are you expected to give a presentation on the courses or particular aspects of courses your institution offers? Find out who else will be there and what their roles are so that you can refer any questions if you need to. If possible have a look at any brochures or material which is to be given to prospective applicants so that you have the information easily to hand and can easily direct people to it. Also make sure you know where on campus things are happening and when and familiarise yourself with a campus map!

If you have student helpers, say hello to them and ask them how they see their role. Often they do a far better job than we can to convince applicants that your institution is the right one so if they are engaging their audience leave them to it but stand by for questions which require academic input.

Many institutions offer their applicants another opportunity to visit the institution and gain more information about their chosen programme or programmes. These usually include the opportunity to have a tour of the campus and the faculty in which the student would study as well as to meet the staff. Remember that applicants are often shy and unsure of what is expected. We do this several times a year; they might only do it once or twice in their life. Do not expect them to come up to you and ask lots of questions (although some will!) but approach them, ask them about their ambitions and plans, explain how we can help get them there and try and engage them as much as possible (without scaring them, you also need to know when to leave them alone!).

Both open days and applicant visit days are a great way to engage with prospective students and to explore with them whether your institution is the right one for them and whether they are likely to make the grades and thrive. However, at these events you will only see people who have already decided they want to go to university and are already considering the possibility of applying to yours. At some open days the sales pitch nature of the day is therefore rather obvious but that should not stop you from engaging with applicants about what they want.

Other activities are more geared towards getting students interested in university study either generally or for specific courses. The might include school visits to deliver specific subject content or taster sessions or to lead skills sessions or simply to provide information about studying at university or your specific institution. They might also include running taster days or information sessions on campus or inviting schools to other on-campus activities. Whatever form they take remember that you are talking to an audience of young people who may not have seriously thought about going to university or, even if they have, what exactly that might mean. Things we take for granted will be completely alien to many of them. Make sure you avoid using jargon and explain how things work clearly. Students are often concerned about entry requirements, subject choice, finance and what sort of support networks are available. Once they have got their head around those issues they also often want to know about course details.

Any presentation you deliver to prospective applicants must be pitched at the right level and you might want to make sure that you have different presentations with different levels of detail so that people whose school you have visited, who have come to an open day and then attend an applicant visit day, do not get the same presentation three times! Think about the purpose of the presentation and then add appropriate levels of detail. Leaving your own or generic contact details so that questions can be asked later is also a good idea. It allows the shy student to come forward in their own time and ask their questions privately.

Going into schools is also a good opportunity to chat to teachers to make them aware of programmes and particular features. The more they know about you and your institution, the more likely they are to mention those things to their pupils.

The key messages for Jack and other academics considering engagement with schools and prospective students:

1. Get involved – it can be lots of fun and hugely rewarding.
2. You are there to sell the institution but be honest. Explain why you think your institution is right for the people you are talking to and why you like working there.
3. Make sure you have information on all the programmes you are representing and ideally take something along that you can give them – a brochure, a summary sheet or a copy of the presentation.

FURTHER READING

JOURNALS

Fleming, M. J. and Grace, D. M. (April 2015) Eyes on the Future: The Impact of a University Campus Experience Day on Students from Financially Disadvantaged Backgrounds, *Australian Journal of Education*, 59(1), 82–96.

Rowland, J. (2015) Library Outreach to Schools and Colleges at the University of Bradford. Teaching Students, Networking with Librarians, *SCONUL Focus*, 62, 28–30.

Your own institutions' marketing material whether in print or online.

CHAPTER 46

Building a Research Profile

ROSEMARY HUNTER

> Jack's institution is increasingly asking him to develop his impressive record of teaching innovation into a research agenda.

Before directly addressing the issue of building a research profile, it is important to understand the broader context for the institutional pressures to develop a research agenda to which you find yourself subject. At university level and upwards, there is a 'dual economy' of separate policies and funding sources for research and teaching, yet academics are expected to integrate the two areas in their own practice and unsurprisingly often experience tension between the demands of each (Tennant et al. 2010, 169–170), but there is evidence that the level of these demands is increasing. A number of writers have analysed recent changes in higher education associated with the 'neoliberal turn', which have resulted in intensification of academic workloads, new requirements for academic performativity and the creation of new academic subjectivities (see e.g. Collier 2005; Fanghanel 2012, Chapter 1; Thornton 2011). HEIs have a material as well as reputational interest in their staff producing high-quality research: it brings in income from externally-funded grants and from HEFCE through the periodic REF exercise. Individual academics also have a material incentive to undertake research as in most universities publications are the surest route to promotion.

It tends to be assumed that academics actively want to do research, which may explain why there is relatively little literature on how to become a researcher, compared to masses of literature on how to become a university teacher. For the more hesitant researcher, the key is to focus on an area about which one is enthusiastic, and ideally passionate. Several authors have noted the advantages of pursuing scholarship in learning and teaching as a way to reduce the tension between teaching and research, as well as to contribute more widely to good teaching practices (e.g. Fanghanel 2012, Chapter 5; Nagy 2011; Tennant et al. 2010). Legal education research is a well-established area of study for REF purposes, and also has considerable potential for another commodity valued in research assessment – impact.

Åkerlind (2008) identifies three steps in building a research profile: becoming confident as a researcher (developing one's internal sense of confidence and competence), becoming recognised as a researcher (gaining external recognition of one's competence and success and becoming an acknowledged part of a research community) and ultimately becoming known and respected in one's field. For law academics, the first step is increasingly accomplished by undertaking a PhD. But attempting to complete a part-time PhD alongside your day job may prove to be a lengthy and potentially demotivating process with few rewards along the way. You would certainly be advised, however, to undertake a PGC course, which will introduce you to some of the scholarship on learning and teaching and also provide you with a community of peers and more senior contacts in the higher education field. In the absence of a PhD supervisor, you would also be advised to find a research mentor or mentors (who may but need not be in the same department or even institution) who can provide advice, read draft articles and so forth.

Cownie (2004, 85) refers to necessary qualities of persistence or perseverance in relation to research. One must develop one's own research agenda; manage one's time to undertake research and writing in the absence of external structures and in the face of other – often more immediate – demands on one's time; have the patience to keep chipping away; be disciplined and self-motivated; and have the determination and drive to complete projects and see the results in print. All of this is very much assisted by the existence of a supportive institutional research culture, including the regular availability of study leave. But in the absence of such formal supports at departmental level, self-generated, informal 'communities of practice' can be very useful in overcoming intellectual isolation, enabling engagement in productive conversations and helping to drive research (see e.g. Nagy 2011; Ng and Pemberton 2013). These can be set up within a department or can be cross-disciplinary or cross-institutional, and take the form of reading groups, work-in-progress seminars, or even social gatherings among researchers working in a particular area.

'Communities of practice' also recognise the fact that all research involves participation in conversations – face-to-face or at a distance, actual or virtual, immediate or over time – with other academic researchers. One aspect of those conversations involves reading what others have published on one's topic, and responding to that work through one's own publications. This helps to answer the questions of what and where to publish. Research in law is generally published in the form of refereed journal articles, chapters in edited books and monographs. Textbooks are not generally part of an academic conversation but have a different purpose, and thus do not generally count as research. In building your research profile, you would be best advised to put your plans for a textbook on hold for the time being in favour of journal articles. The textbook can come later (you may certainly factor it into your longer-term plans). What will also come later, as your work starts to become known, will be invitations to contribute to edited collections or special issues of journals. Such invitations should always be considered in light of one's research plans: does it fit with my plans and my intellectual interests, or will it take me off on a tangent or prevent me doing something I wanted to do? On the other hand, might the proposed tangent be a potentially fruitful one? A new and interesting direction I hadn't previously considered? Is it worth the risk? But before any invitations arrive, and for future unsolicited work, you will want to place your articles in journals where they will be read by the audience you want to reach. This may be a specialist journal, for example *The Law Teacher* in the case of legal education research. Research mentors can be asked for advice about which journal(s) to target for a particular piece of work. They can also be useful, initially, in helping to interpret and respond to referees' reports.

The other essential aspect of engaging in academic conversations is attending and presenting at conferences. Åkerlind (2008) notes that conference attendance may have different goals at different times: initially to develop confidence in giving a paper, then to develop a network and to become known and recognised. Many departments offer only limited conference funding, but you should try to attend at least one key conference each year. Again, a research mentor can be helpful in identifying which conference would be most useful to you. You should also join all relevant learned societies/ associations, which will give access to information about forthcoming conferences and workshops, discounted conference fees, and a variety of other membership benefits and resources, often including small grant opportunities. If grant-getting is or becomes part of the institutional pressures placed on you, such small grants are a very good way of gaining experience in applying for competitive funding and getting started on the track to more substantial grant applications.

The key messages for Jack and other academics considering building a research profile:

1. Turn your passion about teaching and student support into a research agenda.
2. Establish a support structure for your research in the form of mentor(s) and an intellectual community.
3. Engage in conversations with other researchers through publications and conferences.

FURTHER READING

BOOKS

Cownie, F. (2004) *Legal Academics: Culture and Identities*, Oxford: Hart Publishing.

Fanghanel, J. (2012) *Being an Academic*, London: Routledge.

Tennant, M., McMullen, C. and Kaczynski, D. (2010) *Teaching, Learning and Research in Higher Education: A Critical Approach*, London: Routledge.

Thornton, M. (2011) *Privatising the Public University: The Case of Law*, London: Routledge.

JOURNALS

Åkerlind, G. S. (2008) Growing and Developing as a University Researcher, *Higher Education*, 55, 241–254.

Collier, R. (2005) 'We're All Socio-Legal Now?' Legal Education, Scholarship and the 'Global Knowledge Economy' – Reflections on the UK Experience, *Sydney Law Review*, 26(4), 503–536.

Nagy, J. (2011) Scholarship in Higher Education: Building Research Capabilities Through Core Business, *British Journal of Educational Studies*, 59(3), 303–321.

Ng, L. L. and Pemberton, J. (2013) Research-Based Communities of Practice in UK Higher Education, *Studies in Higher Education*, 38(10), 1522–1539.

CHAPTER 47

Postgraduate Certificates in Higher Education

JESSICA GUTH

> Jack is enthusiastic to develop his teaching profile and skills.

'Teaching matters in higher education institutions. Although quality teaching encompasses definitions and conceptions that are highly varied and in constant flux, the initiatives aimed at improving the quality of teaching are spreading within institutions' (OECD 2010). There seems to be increasing pressure on institutions to demonstrate that their academics can teach. One way to do that is to require all teaching staff to hold a teaching qualification or be a Fellow of the Higher Education Academy. Michael Bromby in this volume has written about the HEA so this chapter focuses on teaching qualifications. Many institutions offer their own version of a Postgraduate Certificate in Higher Education Practice (or something similarly titled) and many of these certificates are aligned with and accredited by the HEA so successful completion will lead to Associate Fellow or Fellow Status.

Many new academics do not have much choice in terms of where they complete the certificate as they will simply go through the process at their own institution. If you do however have some choice, consider carefully the mode of delivery, the focus of the programme (so is there really any point in learning lots about distance learning if your institution does not offer distance learning programmes and you have no intention of teaching on such programmes) and speak to the people running the course to find out whether it is the right one for you.

Most PGCs will be made up of some face-to-face class time as well as significant directed learning which is usually based around your own teaching practice. Modules usually include courses around the design of modules, teaching techniques, assessment and also elements focused on higher-education policy and other related issues. To find information about the kind of things you might study, just look at several course outlines online.

New academics often struggle with the demands of a new role and are not therefore likely to be keen to take on extra study duties and some PGC programmes receive better feedback than others. For those without any teaching experience they can be helpful in explaining the sort of activities which are possible and in encouraging teachers to try new things. However, they can also have the opposite effect. As a new teacher, if spending the first few weeks in a classroom, studying 'best practice' at the same time can undermine confidence and result in a sense of 'I'm doing it all wrong'. It is therefore worth remembering that 'teaching excellence is a highly contested concept' (Skelton 2009) and that just because you are doing something which is different that does not mean it is wrong!

Other concerns about PGC programmes is that they are not discipline specific enough and gloss over or ignore disciplinary differences. This may be true but I do not see this as all that problematic. Considering what happens in other disciplines can enhance our own teaching and I would therefore suggest that you highlight disciplinary differences by raising questions about how the issues under discussions might play out in different contexts. Like most things, these courses are what you make them and the more you engage the more you will get out of your studies. At the very least you will get a rich bank of ideas for what to do in the classroom but you are also likely to gain an understanding of some of the theoretical frameworks which underpin our teaching. That enhanced understanding will help you make decisions about your teaching, from designing modules or even programmes to the delivery of individual sessions.

Given that there are already likely to be varied and constant demands on your time, you will need to find a way to make the most of the programme without overloading yourself with work. The more closely you can therefore link your studies and assignments to your teaching practice the better. Writing about whatever issue you are asked to address in the context of your own teaching will make it more meaningful and more useful. Use the space you are given to really think about your teaching and who you are as a teacher, get into the habit of reflecting on your teaching (and work generally) and you are likely to benefit from participating long after having received your certificate.

My own PGC experience was mixed. I found some of it very useful and some of it not but after a few weeks of whinging about the waste of time that it was I decided to use the questions being asked to structure my own thoughts about my work and to take the initiative and reflect. Once I did that the experience was positive even though I did not think that much of what I was being taught was that relevant to what I was doing. My own thinking and reading made it relevant. The other aspect that was useful for me was that I got an insight into policies and processes relating to teaching at my institution. The advantage of doing a PGC at your own institution rather than elsewhere therefore might be that as well as learning about, for example the theoretical aspects of module design, you are also likely to gain an understanding of the administrative and timing requirements to design new modules at your institution. This can save you a great deal of time and confusion later down the line!

It is also worth remembering though that just because someone has a teaching qualification they are not necessarily a good teacher. Assessments can be passed even without much belief in what is written for assessment so PGCs can be and sometimes are seen as just a hoop to jump through. Taking that approach is possible but in my view, is an opportunity missed. Most of us want to do a good job and having conversations with people who are in a similar position to you as well as with people with extensive experience in higher education teaching and learning can only help you be better at your job.

The key messages for Jack and other academics considering undertaking a PGC:

1. Many universities now require all their teaching staff to have a teaching qualification.
2. Doing a PGC can help you reflect on your own practice and improve it.
3. It can feel like a waste of time, particularly if you have been teaching a while, but it does provide insights into different types of practice and might give you ideas to try out.

FURTHER READING

BOOK

OECD (2010) *Learning Our Lesson: Review of Quality Teaching in Higher Education*, Paris: OECD.

JOURNALS

Åkerlind, G. S. (2008) A Phenomenographic Approach to Developing Academics' Understanding of the Nature of Teaching and Learning, *Teaching in Higher Education*, 13(6), 633.

Knight, P. (2006) Quality Enhancement and Educational Professional Development, *Quality in Higher Education*, 12(1), 29–40.

Ramsden, P. (2003) *Learning to Teach in Higher Education*, London: Routledge.

Skelton, A. M. (2009) A 'Teaching Excellence' For The Times We Live In?, *Teaching in Higher Education*, 14(1), 107–112.

CHAPTER 48

The EdD Experience

ELIZABETH MYTTON

> Jack is considering how best to progress his career and one of the issues that has come up is whether he should do a doctorate. He is not that interested in doing a substantive piece of legal research as he is not sure how this will further his career in the sector he wishes to work in. A colleague has suggested a Doctor of Education as a possible alternative.

The purpose of this commentary is to provide some insight into the experience of a Doctor of Education (EdD) qualification (in the case of the author awarded by the University of Southampton) and how it works within a range of university career paths. Career paths in the academy are complex entities where many opportunities for professional development exist and changes of direction and emphasis are common. Barnett (2000) refers to 'supercomplexity' in explaining the structures of higher education. Insights into current changes in university law schools are provided by Mytton and Gale (2012) who highlight that legal academics' career paths are also changing and becoming more varied.

The career benefits of a professional doctorate such as the EdD are many. In terms of university careers, there are blurred lines regarding career paths which are not mutually exclusive and often intersect. The seminal article by Birks in 1998 provides an insightful starting point from which to proceed in understanding the academic and the practitioner. Yet, the academy has changed exponentially since that publication. Building on her own EdD research, Mytton (2003) explores the lived experience of the law teacher and how different career paths shape the academy and law schools in particular. Having been head of a law department and chair of the committee of heads of university law schools, as well as holding senior positions in the academy such as deputy dean of a business school, and now as a professor of legal education, her career development demonstrates a strong case for the EdD.

Higher-education structures, including law schools, form an intricate web in which administrative, research, leadership, academic practice, legal practice and management roles all contribute to dynamic career paths. The administrative career route through the academy is gaining momentum with increasing parity between academics and administrators. It is clear that in higher-education institutions, it is not unusual for administrative staff to contribute to teaching in areas such as human resources and marketing, and undertake what hitherto may have been academic areas of responsibility and for academics to have a portfolio of administrative and academic responsibilities. Often there is little training or personal development for academics to move between and fully engage with all aspects of HE. An EdD provides insights into all of them.

Institutional dynamics and spheres of influence which impact on the legal academic provide the framework for a flexible career structure. In terms of building an academic career, the initial decision to undertake an EdD is a little tricky. Perceptions need to be taken into account. When considering a doctoral path it is realistic, at the outset, to acknowledge that a key feature of the academic research world is the PhD. The EdD can be seen, unjustly, as a soft option without the academic rigour of a PhD notwithstanding the doctoral level criteria set by the National Qualifications Framework for England and Wales. There are also jurisdictional differences regarding the level of academic awards which confounds the perception. That said, the EdD has relevance and application across different areas of responsibility. Whilst the PhD goes to the essence of academic research, the EdD is at the cornerstone of academic theory and practice and as such valuable for those seeking careers which draw on those elements of HE.

The educational doctorate has strengths. For example, the law academic with an LLB and an LLM will have developed a subject specialism and academic engagement in that discipline. To then engage in a different subject area at doctoral level such as with an EdD requires an immediate and effective leap from one discipline to another necessitating many intellectual adjustments in terms of academic training, academic practice, vocabulary, research methods, methodologies, and research techniques. This necessarily requires a highly developed interdisciplinary approach which is also useful when moving from a teaching/research environment to a management role because it facilitates a broader and more flexible understanding of what HE is about and how it can and should be managed.

The benefit of the EdD course emanates from its structure and flexibility. It enables the doctoral researcher to maintain social equanimity as compared with the PhD experience which can be a more solitary endeavour. The EdD is designed to combine taught subjects and individual research. A typical model enables EdD students to undertake joint sessions especially research methods with other doctoral students, thus integrating them into a research community. The course seems easier to manage in terms of managing diaries, combining work and home-life balance, applying theory to practice and every day professional development. The EdD seems to have a sharp focus and a practical alignment with one's everyday tasks in higher education – the day job. It seems to be a course which also has particular relevance to and empathy with one's teaching colleagues. The interface between the EdD and academic management is clear. As such the EdD is a logical choice for people already working in the HE sector, particularly if they see their career path as one which has a strong HE administration and management focus alongside teaching and research.

A doctorate has benefits in terms of enabling the researcher to engage with a specialist area and the academic research community in that field of study. Publications, research status, reputation, papers, academic standing, can all emanate from a PhD. The EdD also imports these attributes yet somehow it works slightly differently. It enforces the ability to understand good teaching, learning and professional practice. Whilst the academic researcher explores the possibilities of new knowledge throughout the PhD and beyond, the EdD achieves this whilst its additional strengths lie in the acquisition of enhanced professional practice. In a teaching community, the inter-disciplinary nature of the EdD provides the vocabulary, skills and attributes to engage with academic professionals at all levels of the organisation from a range of disciplines. It also improves the ability to understand different learning styles and how to enable students to learn effectively from an effective communicator who can respond to different learners.

In conclusion, the EdD provides a valuable toolkit with which to build a career. It enables the holder to be pragmatic and to lead change. It helps make sense of complex higher education structures and a range of ways to manage and lead projects at different levels throughout the organisation. It provides flexible opportunities for career development and most importantly it creates a substantial network based upon collegiality.

The key messages for Jack and other academics considering a professional doctorate:

1. If you are interested in education, an EdD is a viable alternative to a PhD.
2. An EdD might provide a specific career track into university management.
3. An EdD provides a valuable toolkit to build a career in HE.

FURTHER READING

BOOK

Barnett, R. (2000) *Realizing the University in an Age of Supercomplexity*, Buckingham: OUP.

JOURNALS

Birks, P. (1998) The Academic and the Practitioner, *Legal Studies*, 18(4), 397–414.

Mytton, E. (2003) Lived Experiences of Law Teachers, *The Law Teacher: International Journal of Legal Education*, 37(1), 36–54.

Mytton, E. (2005) Legal Education: The Integrated Law School, 4 Web JCLI, http://www.bailii.org/uk/other/journals/WebJCLI/2005/issue4/mytton4.html

Mytton, E. and Gale, C. (2012) Prevailing Issues in Legal Education within Management and Business Environments, *International Journal of Law and Management*, 54(4), 311–321.

CHAPTER 49

Social Media, Blogging and Tweeting

PAUL BERNAL

> Jack is interested in blogging and using social media in his professional academic life.

Social media – in particular blogging and Tweeting – offers unprecedented opportunities for legal academics. At the same time it can be a distraction from 'normal' academic work and has potential pitfalls that must be avoided. The rewards, however, outweigh the risks, and most legal academics should consider embracing the use of social media. It can help with the development of ideas, with career progression, with becoming part of a wider academic community, with the dissemination of research – and, as well as all that, can be highly enjoyable.

There are many different kinds of social media: new ones are being developed all the time. Though blogging and Tweeting are the most important for legal academics at the moment, there are others that might be of interest. LinkedIn has interesting discussion groups and is good in terms of professional contacts. Facebook is by far the largest and most familiar social network – with well over a billion users worldwide – and so has the greatest reach, but it is generally less professional and focused than is useful for most academic purposes. Moreover, there is less of a developed legal and academic community than on Twitter. This, however, may well change – with social media, things are potentially subject to rapid and unpredictable change.

The word 'blog' is a shortening of 'web-log'. The original idea of a 'blog' was a record, kept on the web – a journal, a diary or a set of public notes. That idea has broadened into something much bigger but the essence remains the same: pieces of writing put onto the internet for people to see. Blogs are short, fast, and generally made available to the public – and they are very easy to create and use. There are free blogging 'platforms' such as WordPress and Blogger that allow you to create your own blog in minutes, and then posting something to that blog is as easy as creating a word-processing document. You can add links, pictures, videos and other media; there is a huge amount of flexibility.

The key to good legal academic blogging is to take advantage of the features of the system: its speed, ease of use and 'publicness'. All these things contrast blogging from 'proper' academic writing, which is by nature slow and painstaking, has long and often convoluted processes from thought to print, and is often read by very few people, and none outside academia. Blogging can help an academic to sort out ideas – and to test them on other people, some expert, some not so expert. It can be a great way to learn to express yourself in clear, accessible and concise language, and to be able to summarise your ideas in a coherent way – a blog post might be 600 to 1,200 words, rather than the 7,000+ for an academic article.

The speed of blogs makes them ideal for dealing quickly with topics as they come up – responding to the news, dealing with political or legal crises, commenting on cases in their immediate aftermath rather than many months later when there is far less interest. Blogs can publicise and summarise more 'serious' academic publications. If you have an article published, writing a blog post about it can help you find more readers – and potentially more citations. With open access, online journals, you can include a link to the publication within the blog post.

There are many different kinds of blogs other than the personal blog: university-run blogs, professional blogs run by people in practice, blogs for specific fields of law such as the UK Constitutional Law Group Blog and so forth. Each kind of blog has particular features and a particular style – and unlike personal blogs, they often involve some kind of an editorial process. You may be invited to write for one – or the person running one may ask to 'repost' your blog post on their blog. At its best, blogging is very cooperative and interlinked. One key to this is the use of Twitter.

Twitter is a 'micro-blogging platform': each 'tweet', a bit of text up to 140 characters long, is a tiny blog post. Tweets are immediate and public – though the first people to see any tweet are those who 'follow' the tweeter. After that, a tweet can spread, either by being 'retweeted' by someone, or found through a search. The point of Twitter, though, is the 'community'. When you follow someone, you see their tweets, and vice versa – and there is a significant legal academic community on Twitter, people who keep in touch with each others' tweets. 'Live tweeting' from conferences, for example, lets people learn when they can't attend – and builds up the feeling of community.

Tweets can include links – to blogs, to news stories, to anything on the internet. It has become a source of information, a builder of community, a way to make links and a way to disseminate information – and to publicise your blog. Write a new blog post, then tweet about it to get people to read it – and encourage comments. This all combines to give you a 'digital presence' that can help you to be found and your work to be read. This can help increase your impact and engagement – something that every university likes to see. Blogging and tweeting can also help with media work: media people read blogs and follow twitter, and if they think what you write is interesting, they can contact you. A good blog post may even make its way into a newspaper or magazine.

Engaging with social media is not without downsides. It can waste time – successful blogging requires persistence and regularity. If you run a personal blog, posting at least couple of times a month really helps; this needs to be understood from the outset. Some people won't understand your use of social media – and that can lead to unsupportive colleagues, who think that you're not really doing your job. It can be possible to prejudice future publications if you blog about research before you submit a piece to a journal. Journals may not view the research as original if you have blogged about it before: check the rules of the journals you are targeting. You need to be careful with the law – defamation, public order, and communications laws all apply online, as well as the perennial issues of copyright and plagiarism. One thing particularly relevant may be contempt of court – when you're tweeting or blogging contemporaneously from court, for example. The advantages of blogging – its immediacy, the lack of a need for an editor, the premium on brevity and making it accessible – can, on the flipside, make mistakes more possible.

There are other risks – everyone has heard of internet trolls, for example. Depending on the subject you write about, you may come across sexism, racism and homophobia, or be contacted by cranks and conspiracy theorists. These need careful navigation.

Even so, it is worth it – and there are other advantages. You can say things that you can't really say in an academic form. You can use humour, satire and parody. You can be speculative, daring, and even political – but you need to be careful how you do this. There is a delicate balance to be found – but when done well, blogging can show that you are more than just a dry academic. Social media is a way to escape the ivory tower, something that is likely to be good for academics both professionally and personally. It can also be a lot of fun.

The key messages for Jack and other academics considering social media, blogging and tweeting:

1. Blogging can disseminate ideas and bring more readers and citations of academic work.
2. Combined with tweeting, it can help you to become part of a wider academic community, making contacts and creating an online presence.
3. It can help work with the media and the public and improve impact and engagement.

FURTHER READING

JOURNALS

Bernal, P. (2014) A Defence of Responsible Tweeting, *Communications Law*, 19(1), 12–19.

Rowbottom, J. (2012) To Rant, Vent and Converse: Protecting Low Level Digital Speech, *Cambridge Law Journal*, 71(2), 355–383.

WEBSITES

CPS Guidelines on Prosecuting Cases Involving Communications Sent Via Social Media. http://www.cps.gov.uk/legal/a_to_c/communications_sent_via_social_media/index.html

Fullick, M. (2011) *Should You Enter the Academic Blogosphere? A Discussion on Whether Scholars Should Take the Time to Write a Blog About Their Work.* http://blogs.lse.ac.uk/impactofsocialsciences/2011/11/30/should-you-enter-the-academic-blogosphere/

Selwyn, N. (2011) *Social Media in Higher Education.* http://www.educationarena.com/pdf/sample/sample-essay-selwyn.pdf

CHAPTER 50

Gaining Recognition for Teaching

Michael Bromby

> Jack would like recognition for his growing teaching expertise.

Academics, by and large, are seen to be 'qualified to teach' their subject based upon the completion of higher degrees, research in a particular field and general academic experience. These skills, whilst necessary to understand and develop further the academic field, do not necessarily equate to an ability to teach the subject per se. Higher education is an atypical form of education where those who deliver the teaching and learning experience are not required to possess a teaching qualification. Indeed, primary and secondary education teachers are required to undertake initial teacher training to demonstrate the required attributes of Qualified Teacher Status.

Significant changes to university recruitment, particularly to junior lecturers who have only recently completed a PhD or other higher degree, have resulted in an increase in Postgraduate Certificate in Learning and Teaching in Higher Education (or similar) being either offered or made a requirement when hiring new staff who will deliver teaching. Such courses, upon completion, offer the evidence that academics are 'qualified' to teach and are becoming prevalent across all types of higher education institutions.

Recognition, however, differs from qualification. A qualification may be seen as the base standard which should be attained by all within the sector, whereas recognition is a level above that suggests some higher ability to deliver a better, more improved, efficient, or even enjoyable experience. Recognising staff is one way of being able to measure quality in learning and teaching.

Gibbs lists 'quality of teaching staff' as one of the 'presage dimensions of quality', which are the variables which exist in a university context before a student enters higher education to learn, and lists 'quality of teaching' as a 'process dimension of quality' which are the variables that characterise what is going on within the learning and teaching environment. Quality enhancement, therefore, is a driver for recognising staff which can then be quantified or used as an indicator.

Recognition can take a variety of forms. Within a university, recognition may take place in the form of awards or promotions. Awards from departments, schools, colleges or the university may or may not exist, depending on the budget, focus or initiative of management. Likewise, promotion based upon excellent in learning and teaching may or may not be a recognised pathway or route to promotion in every institution. For law teachers, a small number of awards exist nationally such as the Law Teacher of the Year run by Oxford University Press, the Attorney General's Pro Bono Awards which recognises the work of law clinics, and subject associations such as the Association of Law Teachers, the Society of Legal Scholars and the Social Legal Studies Association. Whether national or internal, these forms of recognition are inherently unattainable to all. Even if the competition is open to all, there can only be one winner for each year or cycle and therefore there are only a small percentage of winners and runners-up who are recognised through these awards and promotion routes in comparison to the total numbers of staff who may wish to be recognised for being of demonstrably good quality.

The Higher Education Academy (HEA) is a national body which aims to enhance learning and teaching in higher education by supporting to improve the student experience. It has a number of functions, including staff recognition which is offered by this body in a number of different ways, including fellowship, awards and professional development.

The UK Professional Standards Framework (UKPSF) is managed by the HEA as a nationally-recognised framework for benchmarking success within HE teaching and learning support. This framework is used to recognise quality by awarding one of four categories of fellowship to those who demonstrate capabilities in a number of core areas: Areas of Activity, Core Knowledge and Professional Values, which are detailed in the 'descriptor' for each category of fellowship. In an impact study, several respondents to a large survey stated that the framework was seen as providing leverage for staff tasked with leading learning and teaching work in an institution. They also mentioned its value as a means of asserting one's identity as a teaching-focused academic, as well as a means for recognising teaching, particularly in an institution with a strong research focus. They mentioned too that the UKPSF helps to 'get people talking about education', providing a common language and a focus within a discipline and across disciplines.

Associate Fellow is aimed at new academics, early career researchers with some teaching responsibilities, support staff such as librarians or learning technologists or part-time tutors who may largely be employed in practice or elsewhere outside the higher education environment. This descriptor is particularly suited to law librarians or practitioner-tutors and regular guest lecturers who are not necessarily engaged in design of planning of learning activities or involved in assessment and feedback.

Although not hierarchical, the next descriptor of Fellow particularly suits academics with a few years' experience in learning and teaching who are using appropriate methods for evaluating the effectiveness of their teaching and are engaging with quality assurance and quality enhancement processes.

Senior Fellowship requires a sustained record of organisational leadership to be demonstrated and is aimed at staff who have a departmental or wider teaching and learning responsibility. Heads of law schools, pro bono or clinic directors, programme leaders and key influencers or subject leaders who lead or manage specific aspects of learning and teaching provision are likely to gain this level of recognition.

The final descriptor for Principal Fellow requires effective record of impact at a strategic level in relation to teaching and learning which may be institutional, national or international. This is the highest level of recognition available within the framework for highly experienced and/or senior staff with wide-ranging academic or academic-related strategic leadership responsibilities in connection with key aspects of teaching and supporting learning.

The Higher Education Academy accepts applications directly, or, alternatively, many institutions now have an internal accredited pathway for fellowship, either linked to a PGCertLTHE or stand-alone for more experienced or senior staff. Recognition by an external body offers a mechanism by which staff engaged across a wide spectrum of learning and teaching can demonstrate that their activities stand up to scrutiny, and the very process of obtaining recognition itself leads to self-reflection on academic practice, in turn leading to quality enhancement.

The key messages for Jack and other academics considering applying for recognition in learning and teaching:

1. Recognition is available at a number of different levels.
2. HEA fellowship may be used as evidence for promotion.
3. Recognition leads to quality enhancement.

FURTHER READING

WEBSITES

Gibbs, G. (2010) Dimensions of Quality *The Higher Education Academy*. https://www.heacademy.ac.uk/sites/default/files/Dimensions_of_Quality.pdf

Oxford University Press. Law Teacher of the Year. http://global.oup.com/uk/academic/highereducation/law/goodwill/lawteacher/

The Higher Education Academy (2011) UK Professional Standards Framework. https://www.heacademy.ac.uk/professional-recognition/uk-professional-standards-framework-ukpsf

The Higher Education Academy (2013) Measuring the Impact of the UK Professional Standards Framework for Teaching and Supporting Learning (UKPSF). https://www.heacademy.ac.uk/sites/default/files/resources/UKPSF_Impact_Study_Report.pdf

The National Union of Students, National Student Awards. http://www.nusawards.org.uk/

CHAPTER 51

Legal Education Research

FIONA COWNIE

> Jack would like to develop a research agenda based on his teaching expertise.

Reading legal education research should be something that all law teachers do, whether or not they are interested in actually carrying out this type of research themselves. Legal education research talks about issues that are relevant to all law teachers. How should we teach our subjects? What should law schools be trying to do for their students? How do law schools fit into the academy and at the same time produce graduates who are attractive for the legal and other professions they may wish to enter after leaving university? All of us who are involved in law teaching should be reflecting on these questions and working out what we think about them. Nowadays, if you become a lecturer, universities require you to go on a training course which is likely to look at these issues as they affect all disciplines, but it's unlikely that training courses will have sufficient time to cover much discipline-specific content, so we need to do that for ourselves. And we need to keep on reading legal education research, long after we have completed the training course. Otherwise, we'll get out of date, just as we would if we stopped reading the literature in torts or contract or whatever other area of law we specialise in. The Bradney book recommended below aims to explore just the sort of questions that we as law teachers ought to be thinking about.

For some people, an interest in legal education research goes beyond reflecting on the literature. They want to carry out some research themselves. Researching legal education offers opportunities to think about a huge variety of different things. You can analyse the best way to teach or assess a subject, or explore the attitudes of students to learning law. Or you might want to think about higher education policy as it affects law schools and law teachers; does the government's emphasis on employability skills enhance or detract from the law degree? But whatever you decide to think about, there are some common issues you need to be aware of.

In the eyes of some academic lawyers, researching legal education is only a hobby. It doesn't involve a substantive legal subject, so in their view, it isn't really what academic lawyers should be doing. You may come across people espousing these views, and it can be intimidating, especially if you are hoping to use your published research as part of your application for promotion! However, the truth is that researching legal education is as intellectually demanding as researching any other academic subject, and the outputs of that research can make as valuable a contribution to the development of law as a discipline as researching contract or torts. Legal education research outputs are also eligible for submission to research assessment exercises, so they can contribute to your promotion possibilities, just like other research outputs. Just as there are professors whose reputations rests on their research in restitution, there are professors whose reputations rest on their research into legal education. But they do not treat legal education research as a hobby! (The Cownie pieces in the 'Further reading' below explores these issues further.)

And that is the second fundamental issue about legal education research. You need to approach it as professionally as you would any other kind of legal research. That means being intellectually rigorous in exploring your subject, doing thorough literature searches, just as you would with a conventional legal topic. But in this case, much of the literature with which you need to be familiar is outside the discipline of law. Higher education studies is a whole sub-discipline itself, and you need to become knowledgeable about that literature, know the work of the leading scholars, read the leading journals, such as *Studies in Higher Education* and use the academic literature to justify your arguments in just the same way as you would if you were writing any other legal article. To get an idea of the possibilities of legal education research, you might like to read the Twining article contained in the 'Further reading' below, which is a classic piece of legal education research, and then look at some of the literature referred to in the Bradney book.

The main reason that you should never treat legal education research as a hobby is obvious. All academic research should be intellectually rigorous. But in the case of legal education research, there is another reason. In the past, some people *have* treated it as a hobby. They have basically described what they do, or think should be done, in a law lecture or tutorial, and have published articles (or sometimes even whole books) about legal education which are purely descriptive, with no (or few) references to the relevant literature, and without including any critique. Because of this, legal education research has had a reputation for being poor quality, and if you are serious about it today, you need to show very clearly that your research is just as serious as any other research produced in the legal academy.

Once you have decided that you're going to do some research into legal education, you have to decide what aspect of legal education you're going to look at, and what approach you're going to take, in terms of method. As far as topics go, as we noted at the start of this section, the choice is very wide. If you want to see the kinds of research that has already been published on legal education, you might like to look at a specialist journal, such as *The Law Teacher* but you might also like to look at *Legal Studies*, which also publishes a significant amount of legal education research. If you are looking for inspiration, reading the higher education journals can give you lots of ideas about what researchers in other disciplines are currently discussing, which you might then think about applying to legal education. Or you might want to look at the *Journal of Legal Education*, which is an American journal, and can also provide inspiration from a different perspective. In terms of method, some legal education research, such as the Twining and Bradney pieces referred to below, are based on library research and reflection by the author. But much legal education research involves gathering empirical data and analysing it. If you do that kind of research, you need to consider method just in the same way as any other social scientist would do. The Watkins and Burton book referred to in the 'Further reading' is a good place to start thinking about the methodological issues facing anyone who wants to carry out empirical research in the context of the discipline of law.

Whatever you decide to do, whether you decide that your research interest lies elsewhere, but you want to read and reflect on legal education research, or you want to contribute to the debate by carrying out research yourself, legal education research is full of possibilities.

The key messages for Jack and other academics considering legal education research:

1. All law teachers should be reading and reflecting on legal education research.
2. Approach researching legal education in the same rigorous way as researching law itself.
3. Only if you do that will your research be valuable (and respected by others).

FURTHER READING

BOOKS

Bradney, A. (2003) *Conversations, Choices and Chances: The Liberal Law School in the Twenty First Century*, Oxford and Portland, OR: Hart Publishing.

Burton, A. and Watkins, D. (eds) (2013) *Methodologies in Legal Research*, London: Routledge.

Cownie, F. (2010) The Legal Academy and Legal Academics, in P. Cane and H. Kritzer (eds) *Oxford Handbook of Empirical Legal Studies*, Oxford and New York: Oxford University Press, chapter 39.

Cownie, F. (1999) Searching for Theory in Teaching Law, in F. Cownie (ed.) *The Law School – Global Issues, Local Questions*, Aldershot: Dartmouth, chapter 3.

JOURNAL

Twining, W. L. (1967) Pericles and the Plumber, *Law Quarterly Review*, 83, 396–426.

CHAPTER 52

Despite My Job or Because of My Job: Impact and Research

Jane Ching

> The institution is increasingly asking Jack to develop his impressive record of teaching innovation into a research agenda. Jack is developing Legal Education research but feels he is too often under-resourced with funds to attend conferences and lacks sufficient time to do his research. He is also struggling to balance this demand with his continued desire to develop high quality teaching materials, and to support his students.

There is a tension for many academics, particularly perhaps in teaching focused institutions and even more so for those whose teaching is in the vocational sector, between teaching and research. Those who succeed frequently do so despite their jobs, rather than because of them. There may be two career paths: principal lecturer for course leaders, leading into management; and readership for researchers, leading into professorship. Some institutions have both teaching and research-focused routes into readership and professorship. Both are likely to evaluate 'esteem' or 'impact'.

'Impact' is often in the context of the Research Excellence Framework 2014 (REF) for the UK which allocated 20% of its evaluation to 'reach and significance'. This was assessed by case studies demonstrating 'social, economic or cultural impact or benefit beyond academia that … was underpinned by excellent research produced by the submitting institution within a given timeframe'. First, it is up to your institution to decide which case studies they submit for the REF exercise. Secondly, the impact has to be 'beyond academia'. Thirdly, there is a sequence: research first, impact as a result. In education, the sequence is often the reverse: an innovation takes place, and is evaluated as research after the event. Finally, the impact has to be susceptible of being demonstrated and has to have occurred within the relevant timescale. All of which, if we assume a similar approach will be taken in the future, involves forward planning and finding ways to track and evaluate impact. Research evaluation is a complete sub-discipline with its own methodologies and *Research Evaluation* journal.

Of course, the impact you want your research to make may be entirely different. Educational innovation, research and scholarship have an impact on students, on colleagues and on the institution. Published research has an impact on your career and public profile. It provides an outlet that can have impacts (positive or negative) on your wellbeing and family life. And so on.

But, given the competing pressures on you and on your time, the challenge will be to find space for you to do research that can have impact of any kind. Harness your strengths as well as your anger. You will need stamina to keep up the impetus of your research, and you will need an emotional involvement in or commitment to it.

Also harness anything that you can demonstrate to have a positive benefit for your institution. It will be difficult to argue that you should not have time and space to do something that will, for example, improve recruitment or retention. Target what you can by way of external activity. Go to a conference for a day, rather than the whole thing. Look for workshops that may be free or less expensive. These might be run at other institutions in your region or by organisations such as the HEA or LERN. If your teaching is applied in any way, try events for legal practitioners, where you meet potential collaborators, or gatekeepers for empirical research projects. Research which benefits the legal practising community clearly has the potential for impact in the REF sense. Although many of the professional organisations have their own in-house researchers, they also put projects out to tender, and research funding of any kind can be used to buy out your teaching time. It can also have REF impact.

Activities that you might think of as being profile raising can be useful in the long haul towards doing research that has impact in the REF sense. Write for the student or practitioner press and websites. Try your local paper or radio station. Sign up with your press office to be an 'expert'. Write letters to the press. Offer to review books or peer review articles. Start a blog. Tweet. Some of these activities, which can be fitted around your other commitments can have impact in themselves (see some of the blogs, for example) or can be used to recruit collaborators for projects. Read other people's blogs and tweets to allow them to recruit you into their multi-institutional projects. You might think of this as involving a pyramid, with reading, networking and talking to people on the widest layer; short articles and presentations in the middle, and the top being one substantial project a year.

Develop a research agenda around the things that matter to you (student support, teaching materials). You may be able to balance your desire to research with your desire to create high-quality teaching materials and to support your students, if you use action research methods which can be absorbed into your teaching/pastoral work (see McNiff 2013). It turns the 'despite' into a 'because'.

However, if you are working towards REF impact, then you will need a very specific plan, over a five-year period. I suggest that you think about this, from the outset, in terms of topping and tailing.

The 'top' involves some preliminary investigation on your part. Find out, first of all, who has responsibility for research in your school and go and talk to them. Many academics are delighted to mentor others, but they can only do so if the mentees make themselves known. Find out who else in your school is interested in educational research. If no one, go and find out who is interested in educational research in other schools in your institution. Once there are two or three or four of you, you create a momentum and can support each other as well as work together on research projects.

Find out how the institutional infrastructure works. The last thing you need is for hard work to be excluded from the REF count because it was approved as a 'teaching' project rather than a 'research' project.

The tail is my suggestion that you also think, before you start, about the kinds of impact you want to aim for. This will shape your project. For example, a project that looks at improving student participation in outreach and clinic work has more obvious REF impact than a project that seeks to improve student participation in sport. Look at examples in the literature (see Nutley et al. 2003) to see what has been treated as 'impact'. Think about how you will track impact. This may be by keeping up with citations of your own work by others, or by looking at comment in the press, or by keeping up with others who have adopted your recommendations or your evidence-informed teaching model.

All research has impact – including impact on ourselves as researchers – or it would not be worth doing. The more difficult question is the right kind of impact, at the right time, demonstrated in the right way.

The key messages for Jack and other academics considering making an impact with their research:

1. Harness your emotions. Research requires stamina and if you aren't interested or even angry in your research, you won't finish it.
2. Make yourself difficult to ignore. It opens doors.
3. Decide what kind of impact is important to you and shape your research projects with that impact in mind. Make plans, before you start, to track the impact of your work.

FURTHER READING

BOOK

McNiff, J. (2013) *Action Research: Principles and Practice*, London: Taylor & Francis.

Nutley, S., Percy-Smith, J. and Solesbury, W. (2003) *Models of Research Impact: A Cross-sector Review of Literature and Practice*, London: Learning and Skills Research Centre. www.tlrp.org/rcbn/capacity/Activities/Themes/Impact/LSDA_models_of_research_impact.pdf

WEBSITE

Research Excellence Framework (2011) *Decisions on Assessing Research Impact*. www.ref.ac.uk/pubs/2011-01/

CHAPTER 53

Looking for an Academic Job? Wanting to Develop Your Academic Career?

Jon Reast

> Jack is seeking to move from his 'teaching-focused' institution to a research-intensive university and is looking for advice on job hunting.

The context of this chapter is as a recruiting manager, seeking a relatively new academic colleague or one seeking to develop their career.

In any UK university or HE College, there are four broad streams of activity in which academics engage: teaching and learning (the obvious one); research and knowledge transfer (academic publications, as well as activities which translate research or academic knowledge into something of value for external organisations); external paid consultancy and/or training work; and academic administration. One of the other chapters in this book specifically looks at the role of course leader, for example.

From the perspective of a recruiting manager in academia, the emphasis on each of the streams of activity outlined above will depend upon the type of academic institution being recruited to. The UK, with over 150 universities has a rich range of higher education provision. A broad simplification follows! Some universities typically those in the top 50 (Times Ranking) tend to be much more research focused, the very top end described as research intensive. Those in the 50–75 perhaps focusing on a contribution of research and teaching and learning, and those in the 75–100 probably less research focused but providing good-quality teaching and learning, and probably more focused on providing practical consultancy and training provision to local organisations. The recruitment criteria being applied and described in job descriptions and recruitment advertising will therefore reflect the type of institution and the focus of its activities. Advertising for academic posts in the majority of universities takes place within jobs.ac.uk and within the Times Higher Education Supplement (either physical copy of online version).

In entering or developing your career in a research intensive or research-focused university, the expectation is typically that you would have a PhD or are on-route to completion of a PhD. This qualification is still seen somewhat as a 'research apprenticeship' providing a sound understanding of literature reviewing research philosophy, but also project definition and research methodology. It would very much be hoped or expected that candidates would have published to a national or international level with outputs from their PhD studies. Initial publications tend to be gained with the supervisory team. The recruiting manager, if recruiting such an 'early-career' researcher has the expectation that the holder of a PhD together with some initial publications will have the potential to continue publishing at an improving quality and rate throughout the coming years. The applicant will almost certainly be quizzed strongly about the nature of their 'academic contribution' delivered via the PhD and subsequent publications. The recruiting panel will want to ensure themselves that the candidate has a strong grasp of their research and its importance. Additionally, the panel (typically comprising of three to five academic staff) would like to see some evidence of teaching and learning experience having been gained whilst completing a PhD. Whether entering the research intensive/focused sector or any other sector, academic staff will typically be expected to undertake a programme or qualification (perhaps a postgraduate certificate) in order to ensure that they have a good professional approach and capability around teaching and learning.

As early-career staff look to be promoted or apply for more senior roles, they will need to show progression in terms of the quality and quantity of their research publications, provide evidence of being able to teach to a good quality across a reasonable number of subject areas (or modules), and ideally evidence an ability to provide some form of 'academic management' – perhaps module leader on a few modules, possibly programme or course leader (largely the same thing, different terms in different institutions) and ideally showing some capability to innovate in module or programme design and delivery.

From the outline provided above, it should be clear that making a switch from industry or the professions into a research-intensive university is very difficult/impossible without also showing research capability via PhD and publications. There is more potential in a 'hybrid' university, where research as well as teaching and learning are more equally valued. If an applicant has been working as a legal professional, but has alongside this undertaken some lecturing responsibilities, then they are well placed to gain a post in a 'hybrid' organisation. Clearly then, if you are working in the professions and would like to switch into academia, try to build a portfolio of experience (lectures, guest presentations) in order to develop your CV and facilitate the move. Enhancing your CV along the way minimises the risk to the recruiting manager, ensuring that you can teach. It is likely that in a hybrid type of university you will be encouraged or required to undertake a PhD and therefore you might consider preparing a proposal and/or enrolling as a part-time PhD student prior to making a job application. This will not only show intent but also evidence some capability in this direction. Dependant on which specific organisation you are applying for and their aspirations it might be that many would still be looking to recruit the type of 'researcher' candidate outlined in the first section but there is undoubtedly more opportunity to switch from the professions into a hybrid than into a research-focused university. In terms of developing your career in a hybrid university, seeking promotion, there is more likelihood of valuing a variety of contributions across the four activity areas of teaching and learning, research, consultancy and academic administration.

Teaching and learning-based universities and higher-education colleges, offer the easiest opportunity for those coming from industry or the professions to enter. The recruiting manager will be looking for professional qualifications, an ability to teach and inspire students, and an ability to provide a considerable amount of real world experience. Building up a portfolio of teaching experience whilst still in the professions is always advisable. Since this gives a taster of a future career and whether it will suit the candidate and evidences capability to the recruiting manager. Candidates are still likely to be expected to undertake a teaching qualification.

One of the differences about working in a teaching and learning-focused institution is that teaching 'contract hours' (or time with students) tends to be higher. In the same way that working in a research-focused institution, or a hybrid institution can be very fulfilling, this is also true of the teaching-focused institution, candidates need to be motivated by working with and developing the knowledge, understanding and capability of students, since this is what they will be doing/or a good proportion of their time. Academic management is also likely to be a significant part of responsibilities, so being efficient and organised is a real bonus. Teaching-focused institutions, whilst not doing so much research, may have a desire to make some movements in this direction but time availability for staff to do research alongside teaching commitments can be limited.

Whichever career route is being sought, being organised, efficient and a ruthless time manager always helps!

The key messages for Jack and other academics looking for academic jobs:

1. Make sure you are clear about what the expectations of any institution you are thinking of applying to are.
2. Be organised.
3. Make sure that you clearly highlight all the skills and experience you have.

FURTHER READING

WEBSITE

jobs.ac.uk

CHAPTER 54

Applying for a Move to a Research-Intensive HEI

JONATHAN DOAK

> Jack is seeking to move from his 'teaching-focused' institution to a research-intensive university.

The question as to what precisely constitutes a 'research-intensive' university is necessarily ambiguous. For the sake of simplicity, the term is used within this chapter to describe the general characteristics of a Russell-Group type of university: one that produces high quality REF-style research activity across a range of disciplines, and places considerable institutional emphasis on maintaining and enhancing its international reputation for research.

There are two important myths that ought to be dispelled at the outset. First, a research-intensive university will not necessarily mean a light teaching or admin load. Despite the label, research-intensive universities are also competitors in the student market, and – like all universities – seek to deliver a model of education that is student-centred and which will yield the institution positive results in the National Student Survey and newspaper rankings. It is widely understood that a focus on research must not sacrifice the quality of the student experience; innovation in pedagogy and the delivery of high-quality teaching are now very much expected across all universities. The emphasis placed on research may mean that individuals have more opportunity to engage in 'research-led teaching', by designing courses and modules around salient themes in their research, but this does not equate to less onerous expectations in terms of either the quality of teaching or the contact hours. The second myth that ought to be dispelled is that research-intensive universities are the exclusive preserve of great research; outstanding researchers can be readily found within new universities, many of which also attach an important strategic priority to research excellence. Likewise, not all research-intensive universities offer the same experience; some will offer better opportunities than others, and even within the Russell Group there are areas of strength and weakness across the different law schools.

In very broad terms, however, research-intensive universities tend to allocate more resources towards supporting the production of high-quality research. This may include, for example, the provision of more extensive libraries, an enhanced range of electronic resources and databases, and the use of non-academic support staff to assist with activities such as grant applications, research design, dissemination and the generation of impact. Some universities also offer staff personal 'research accounts' which they may choose to spend on attending conferences, purchasing books or journals, or to offer casual employment to students as research assistants. Workload models are often used to ensure that each academic has a specified number of hours set aside for research, and most universities operate a research leave scheme that allows a staff member to take a semester or year out to develop their research every three to four years. Early-career researchers may also be offered reduced teaching or admin loads to develop their research profiles. Incentives (e.g. reduced teaching/admin loads; extended research leave) may be used strategically to encourage researchers to complete a major publication on time or to facilitate a large, collaborative funding application.

The drive to obtain favourable REF outcomes leads to three significant pressures that are often associated with working in a research-intensive university. These are (1) ensuring the quality of research; (2) income generation; and (3) impact.

The first of these, research quality, relates to the benchmarks of quality laid down in the current REF, namely originality, significance and rigour. As part of their recruitment processes, it is not uncommon for research-intensive HEIs to scrutinise publications in some detail; some will ask their existing staff to rate applicants' outputs on the basis of the REF criteria. Interviewees can be expected to be questioned about the quality of publications, and should adopt REF-style terminology to make a case as to their quality. Questions relating to substance/argument or methodology are also commonplace, particularly if someone in the same field is sitting on the panel. Those who aspire to work within the setting should generally prioritise lengthy, in-depth, analytical publications that are likely to feature in a well-renowned journal over and above book reviews and case-notes, or shorter pieces in publications aimed primarily at legal professionals. Quality invariably usurps quantity as a measure of excellence.

The second challenge relates to the generation of research income. The funding pot has undoubtedly become depleted in recent years, and with the climate of austerity set to continue for some time, the competition for grants is greater than ever. Whilst most research-intensive universities have a network of support staff who will assist in navigating the array of calls and the often cumbersome process in applying for them, success rates remain low – particularly for sole applicants or those at an early point in their career. On joining a research-intensive institution, it is undoubtedly beneficial for new colleagues to make themselves known not only to other staff within their own department, but also to colleagues in other departments with similar interests. The best opportunities for securing grants often arise through being invited to participate in a large project as a co-investigator by an experienced colleague who may be based in another department or faculty.

The final challenge relates to research impact, which counted for 20% of the departmental scores of REF 2014. This figure is likely to increase in the future. Research impact is essentially the production of evidence to show that research actually counts for something in the 'real world': academic activities are not confined to analysing the intricacies of the theories of Rawls or Dworkin, but that their research carries a clear and demonstrable impact beyond the academy. This might, for example, include influencing the reform of law or public policy. Ironically, some of the newer universities outdo their elder counterparts on this front, since they may have a long history in areas such as professional training and engaging in knowledge transfer activities. A track record in generating impact is not expected for young scholars, though it is important to demonstrate a willingness to engage with the impact agenda. Indeed, the increasing emphasis placed upon it may be good news for those applying from new universities or the legal profession who may have pre-existing networks in place and previous experience of translating theory into practice.

In summary then, the decision to seek a position in a research-intensive university is a personal one. As noted above, it is by no means the only path to building a reputation as an expert in a field, but the process of actually 'doing' research may become easier if that research activity is well supported through resource allocation as well as by other colleagues – most of whom are facing the same challenges. Early-career researchers, in particular, may have a little more space to develop their ideas compared with those in a less research-intensive environment in that workloads may be reduced to help them to achieve research-related probation targets. The downside is that there is no escape from the 'research'; academics at all levels will typically have annual targets in terms of producing outputs and submitting grant applications. Scholars who only wish to dip into research on an occasional basis, or aren't sure if they want to spend the remainder of their careers immersed in it, are unlikely to be rewarded by a move into such an environment. On the other hand, those who genuinely enjoy research and wish to make it the primary focus of their careers, may find that a move to the right research-intensive university to be extremely rewarding and to offer enhanced opportunities to develop their profiles as researchers.

The key messages for Jack and other academics considering applying for a move to a research intensive HEI:

1. Do not assume that teaching or admin responsibilities are always lighter in research-intensive universities.
2. Some research-intensive universities can offer a higher level of support for individuals, particularly those in the early stages of their careers.
3. The expectations of research-intensive universities are that staff will publish high-quality work, generate income, and develop research impact alongside their teaching and admin roles.

FURTHER READING

BOOK

Barnett, R. (ed.) (2005) *Reshaping the University: New Relationships Between Research, Scholarship and Teaching*, Maidenhead: McGraw-Hill International.

JOURNALS

Broecke, S. (2012) University Rankings: Do They Matter in the UK?, *Education Economics*, 23(2), 1–25.

Elen, J., Lindblom-Ylänne, S. and Clement, M. (2007) Faculty Development in Research-intensive Universities: The Role of Academics' Conceptions on the Relationship Between Research and Teaching, *International Journal for Academic Development*, 12(2), 123–139.

Siems, M. and Mac Sithigh, D. (2012) Mapping Legal Research, *Cambridge Law Journal*, 71, 651–676.

WEBSITE

Russell Group. http://www.russellgroup.ac.uk/

PART IV

Nadia

Nadia is 27 when we first meet her. She finished her PhD a year ago and is now working as a research assistant. She has now applied (and will get) a lectureship at an institution that describes itself as 'research focused'. Nadia teaches undergraduate students who have a strong academic record, and is also teaching an increasing number of postgraduate students, particularly from Asia. Nadia mostly teaches tutorials on courses which already exist and are led by others but is asked to develop her own PG course. She is keen to explore socio-legal and contextual approaches to law and legal study and incorporate those into her teaching.

She has research targets both in terms of income generation and in terms of outputs and is trying to develop a book proposal based on her PhD work. Nadia is a focused researcher and wants to apply for a substantial research grant and gain experience in managing research teams including international collaborations. She will in due course join an editorial board of a leading journal, edit special issues of top journals and take on editorship as overall editor. She is excited about the possibility of supervising her own PhD students.

She will need to demonstrate some administrative roles and external activities in order to progress to SL at her institution and eventually to reader/professor. She has made enquiries about how to get onto the executive of various professional associations.

Nadia's strengths are her research skills and academic/intellectual ability and her enthusiasm for her work. She tends to work long hours and her main priority is her research. She has confidence in her abilities as a researcher but is far less sure about her abilities as a teacher. She is a competent administrator but sometimes struggles with university processes. She is not particularly interested in a management career in HE; she wants to be a research professor although she accepts that some management responsibilities are inevitable – she wants them to be research focused though.

CHAPTER 55

Applying for Lectureship with PhD/Research Experience

LIZ OLIVER

> Nadia is currently working as a research assistant, having completed her PhD one year ago. She is now applying for her first lectureship.

There is a tendency to assume that once a person has completed a doctorate and taken up a research-assistant position within an academic institution; the 'natural' next step in their career is a university lectureship. There is, however, nothing 'natural' about this transition at all; on the contrary, it is very much the outcome of human endeavour. This is the case even for those who appear to slide seamlessly into a first lecturing job (which is perhaps more common in the discipline of law than in some other academic disciplines). Here too, a concerted behind-the-scenes, often team, effort will likely have been expended to prepare and position a successful applicant. The first step towards applying for a lectureship, therefore, has to be a decision; sometimes by the applicant alone, more often by the applicant and those around them, to exert some concerted effort to this end.

Whilst an obvious career path for a doctoral graduate is an academic one, this is of course not the only one. A candidate who has experience of working as a research assistant and of conducting her or his own doctoral research might consider carrying out research for other types of organisation, or moving into a different occupation altogether (Vitae, no date a). Such steps would require efforts of a different sort to articulate and position the abilities and skills that flow from doctoral study and working as a university research assistant. The focus of this chapter is on achieving a lectureship but it is worth noting though that this is a choice between options.

The decision to become a lecturer therefore should be consciously taken and preferably well in advance of 'needing a job'. 'Portfolio-building' in preparation for lectureship applications begins throughout the early career, during which shrewd decision making can benefit the wise apportionment of valuable time between competing priorities. Guidance from a PhD supervisor or academic mentor may assist with prioritising (the pitfalls of exploitation presented as 'opportunity' notwithstanding). Many of the activities and experiences that demonstrate suitability for the role of lecturer (completed PhD, publications, participation in academic networks through conferences and seminars, small and large-group teaching experience) will be gained through doctoral and early-career appointments. The advice of an established academic who has sight of the field within which an early-career researcher seeks to develop her or his career will be particularly helpful when developing a publication strategy; in considering, for example, whether to prioritise publishing a thesis as a book or to work up some of the chapters for publication in a peer reviewed journal. Academics with editorial roles can provide insight into which journals to target and how to approach them.

Sources of generic advice about how to identify academic jobs, to present CVs, complete application forms and perform at interviews and presentations are accessible online (Vitae, no date b) and sometimes through university training and development departments. Rather than rehearse these, the focus of the following discussion is on intellectual ambitions and 'fit'. At an interview I was once asked 'what do you want to be famous for?' A lectureship position sets the incumbent on a track of academic leadership, be it in the design of curricula, the supervision of doctoral researchers or in the future vitality of academic disciplines or fields. Even within an increasingly managerialist environment, the role of a lecturer is to be autonomous, to have a plan and to make their mark. This involves becoming aware of who one is as an academic, what one wants to achieve with their research and their teaching. This positioning within academic debates and disciplines will of course continue to shift and change over time (as indeed will the debate itself and the expectations of appointing institutions) but it should be borne in mind that the ethos of academic law schools differs between institutions. The most dynamic research environments will have critical mass in a particular area, or a distinct research culture. Applicants will be challenged to consider how their aspirations for research and teaching would sit with those of their potential colleagues. For example, if a researcher seeks to further develop socio-legal and contextual approaches to law and legal study and to incorporate those into her or his teaching, they should identify the locations where their expertise and enthusiasm will be fruitful.

Resilience is essential to continue with the journey towards appointment. The process of 'thinking oneself into a job' demands intellectual and emotional energy. Establishing and articulating an academic agenda can feel exposing, whist contemplating employment in another location might involve planning, budgeting and negotiation with other members of a family or household. Against the backdrop of such investment, unsuccessful applications are all the more disappointing. Feedback on application forms and interviews, where sought and constructively given, can help applicants to assess whether their energies are being targeted realistically. Such feedback can be source of confidence to continue applying or guidance to change approach or direction.

Maintaining employment in the university sector between graduating with a doctorate and beginning work as a lecturer is very likely to entail contractual insecurity. Much has been written about this uncertain and fast-changing career stage (for example McAlpine 2012; Oliver 2012). Universities offer a mass of temporary forms of employment often on a 'teaching only' or 'research only' basis. The effort involved in navigating a path through a succession of intense appointments, whilst keeping a personal research portfolio on track and applying for further short and long-term jobs should not be underestimated. Moving between early-career research positions is characterised by frequent re-locations encompassing shifts in geographical, intellectual and networking positions (McAlpine 2012). This is particularly challenging at a point in the life course where financial and familial decisions around cohabiting, civil partnership, marriage and children might be taken.

As we have seen lectureship positions are a route to research and teaching leadership; this career transition is however demanding and requires both individual resilience and wider professional and personal support.

The key messages for Nadia and other academics considering applying for lectureship with PhD/research experience:

1. Applying for a lectureship requires a conscious and concerted effort with support drawn from academic mentors and personal relationships.
2. Portfolio-building occurs throughout doctoral research and early career appointments.
3. Achieving a lectureship entails having a research and teaching agenda and demonstrating fit with the recruiting department.

FURTHER READING

JOURNALS

Elmes, J. (2014) How to Get Your First Research Paper Published, *The Times Higher Education Supplement*, 4 September 2014. www.timeshighereducation.co.uk/news/how-to-get-your-first-research-paper-published/2015485.article

McAlpine, L. (2012) Academic Work and Careers: Re-location, Re-location, Re-location, *Higher Education Quarterly*, 66(2), 174–188.

Oliver, E. A. (2012) Living Flexibly? How Europe's Science Researchers Manage Mobility, Fixed-Term Employment and Life Outside of Work, *International Journal of Human Resource Management*, 23(18), 3856–3871.

WEBSITES

Vitae [no date a] Researcher Career Stories. www.vitae.ac.uk/researcher-careers/researcher-career-stories

Vitae [no date b] Applying for Academic Jobs. www.vitae.ac.uk/researcher-careers/pursuing-an-academic-career/applying-for-academic-jobs

CHAPTER 56

Teaching from Other People's Materials

MICHAEL JEFFERSON

> Nadia has got her first job as a lecturer and is being asked to contribute to teaching by taking tutorials and some lectures on a module run by a colleague.

Only one immediate thought – it's absolutely necessary for novice PGR students who are thrown in at the deep end of teaching with little or no training! A few times through with someone else's material absolutely gives the confidence back that we actually do know what we're talking about ....

The above is a quote in 2013 from a postgraduate research (PGR) student who taught a small number of seminar groups, each of around 14 undergraduate students, to the author's seminar sheets, lectures and virtual learning environment (VLE) and more than possibly his student textbook. She is now a fully-fledged lecturer elsewhere.

At some time in your career, almost certainly at the start and maybe later too, you will face the challenge of teaching classes using material prepared by others. Perhaps this is standard practice at your institution for all staff in the first few years from appointment; or it could be that someone is ill or on leave of some kind, for example a sabbatical, maternity, and you are instructed to read out someone else's lecture notes to a large class which cannot be rescheduled. The below assumes that you are being asked to teach small groups and not give lectures.

Just as there is no one way into a career in teaching law, so there is no one route into using material provided by others. Things have changed over the years and it will now be rare, very rare, for a new member of staff to be told, as I was in my first job, to prepare 48 lectures and 16 seminars on criminal law and not be afforded any assistance (including the syllabus)! Law schools are much more professional than they were; yet they do offer a degree of freedom, that degree being perhaps influenced by the type of institution at which one is teaching, the 'team mentality' of the people teaching the same subject (or lack of it) and the energy of colleagues. The nature of the institution (e.g. Oxbridge, redbrick, 'new', Birkbeck, BPP, University of Law, Kaplan...) will also influence the nature of the experience. This chapter is divided into some general points followed by a problematisation of whether there is one and only one right way.

Nowadays new teachers of law including Graduate Teaching Assistants (GTAs) however named (i.e. PhD students who for money teach and perhaps mark law subjects especially one or more of the seven undergraduate foundations of legal knowledge, 'FOLK', subjects such as contract and tort law) can expect some kind of induction into the school and a meeting with colleagues before the start of teaching about the organisation of the course and one at the end to review the course. There may well be weekly or fortnightly meetings with the leader of the module (often named a convenor or a coordinator) to go through the suggested answers, if there are ones, to seminar or tutorial classes. A contact person within the law school often called a 'mentor' may be nominated as the 'go to' person in the event of queries of an academic nature. If you are not provided with such assistance, complain! Most teams will also be open to proposals from the most junior members of staff for new questions, whether for the seminar/small group programme or for the various assessments; indeed, they may well be highly grateful for such suggestions.

You may think that with suggested ('model') answers and the like that there is little room to manoeuvre but depending on the law school, the course (there may be very little freedom when teaching on the Bar Professional Training Course or Legal Practice Course) and the teaching team there may be a more or less complete freedom as to *how* the material is taught. Let's assume that you are given seminars to teach in a FOLK subject. Unless you are directed as to the manner in which you must get through the material, you have a free hand over delivery. For instance, you may wish to do something which you have come across while you were a student; this may be quite innovative at the institution at which you are. By way of example, you may wish to divide the students into two teams which argue one way or the other as an answer to a question, whether of the essay or problem variety. Another method not often used in older establishments is to ask students or a selection of them to write the main points to an answer on flipcharts, post-it notes or a whiteboard. At some time you may well (and again institutions differ) be the subject of peer observation by a member of that teaching team or by someone else, perhaps as part of your induction or training. You can demonstrate your teaching methods to good effect to both colleagues and students in these ways, and this may lead to a permanent contract if you are not already on one. University departments used to be subject to the government-run Teaching Quality Assessment (TQA) regime, which ranked teaching as 'excellent', 'satisfactory' or 'unsatisfactory' in each university school. That has died away but each university will run similar internally-led exercises; your law school may be subject to review under the auspices of the Quality Assurance Agency and will normally be subject to a periodic (often quinquennial) review including one or more external panel members. In all cases, whether external or internal review, some attention will be devoted to what happens on paper and at times what happens in practice.

The tutor/seminar leader new to the subject is unlikely to be handed the whole undergraduate subject to teach (lectures, seminars, assessments, VLE, liaison with the external examiner) but will start with a handful of seminars. The tutor may be an old hand at teaching or new to such tasks. It is to be hoped that the head of department has gone through the timetable with the tutor so that the latter is not teaching a subject they do not want to teach (which is not unusual) and a module which will shortly expire (again, not unusual). Some heads seem to assume that a new tutor can take on a subject without help and the convenor may not be particularly helpful or perhaps not even often available. In my view, not just is each institution different but so is each module coordinator despite efforts at standardisation. Moreover, one's other commitments in the law school may be just as vital, for example is one writing a PhD, a REFable article? One's commitments outside school such as children are of course highly important and at times may be more so than answering the same email from students. Work–life balance is of course wonderful in theory but practice may bedevil the best promises, especially when teaching looms or marking must be undertaken within a severely impracticable deadline. The tutor may also in the first year of teaching be expected to undergo a university-wide training course. Again, the work–life balance point is important. It should be remembered that while matters are changing, few experienced law lecturers certainly in the 'old' universities have any recognised teaching qualifications at all. If control is lax, then there is the Scylla of not knowing what to do and the Charybdis of what might be called over-preparation (e.g. in one of my subjects one publisher now (2015) publishes 11 large and medium student textbooks, the lengthiest being 1,316 pages), and it is not unknown for new members of staff instructed to teach that module to read as many books on the topic as there are. However, even if the module leader is uncooperative, there should be at least one other member of staff which one can latch onto and learn from. Indeed, the freedom given by a 'hands off' coordinator may be conductive to the development of teaching ideas new to the school, if not to the academic community. The author believes that confidence comes through doing and that if one does not try something new and do it to the best of one's ability, one does not build up resilience to, for example, student evaluation questionnaires, which can undermine confidence gained at a cost.

The advice therefore is: get stuck in, don't be afraid (even to fail) and try to enjoy what you are doing. You'll probably recall when you are older that the first couple of years of your teaching life were the best, and you'll remember those students better than ones you taught last year.

> The key messages for Nadia and other academics considering teaching from other people's materials:
> Early in your career as a law teacher, whether on an academic or practitioner course, you will almost certainly have to teach using other materials, often in the form of written seminar sheets and material on the Virtual Learning Environment. (You may also be asked to mark students' work, whether formative, summative, or both.) This can be a learning process and you become a reflective practitioner of the art of teaching.

FURTHER READING

JOURNALS

Cobley, C. and White, S. (1994) Specimen and Model Answers in Law Teaching, *The Law Teacher: The International Journal of Legal Education*, 28(1), 36–55.

Game, A. and Metcalfe, A. (2009) Dialogue and Team Teaching, *Higher Education Research & Development*, 28(1), 45–57.

Howarth, D. A. (1969) An Experiment in Team Teaching, *The Law Teacher: The International Journal of Legal Education*, 3(2), 63–67.

CHAPTER 57

Devising New Modules

David McArdle

> Nadia is asked to devise and deliver a new undergraduate module, available to students in the final year of studying either an LLB or a BA law degree. Nadia would like some advice on what sort of course she should design.

Given the drive for research-led teaching, those involved in the delivery of law degrees can properly expect to have the opportunity to teach a module which dovetails with their research specialisms. The day-to-day demands of legal education delivery mean that, outwith the most rarefied of atmospheres, they can also be reasonably expected to teach on one or more of the 'Foundations of Legal Knowledge' which professional bodies such as the Law Society or the Bar Council require students to have passed before they can be considered for entry to the legal profession. However, the need to ensure that an appropriate level of module choice is available to students means staff members can also be expected to develop and deliver modules that do not particularly reflect their own research areas and which build upon the comparatively straightforward material that the foundation modules offer. This is particularly the case in law schools with relatively few academic staff members: the demands on one's time may be limitless and the student cohort may be small, but the need to offer an appropriate range of subjects for them to choose from remains.

Whichever category a new module falls into, devising them is inevitably time-consuming and (for early-career academics especially) a daunting prospect. But it also provides a unique opportunity to reflect on what academics do and how and why we do it. It is often stated, not unproblematically, that the undergraduate study of law is an academic pursuit rather than a vocational one and that the aim of a law degree is not to instil students with the discrete skills they will need in the 'real world' of work but to help those individuals become original, critical thinkers with the skills to make sense of the world around them. The reality is that these dichotomies do not exist, and that drawing such distinctions is a fanciful and irrelevant exercise. There is little point in teaching a law module that encourages higher-level thinking skills if, at the end of it, there is no evidence that students know 'what the law says' about the issues covered, and while it is not the task of legal educators to avowedly inculcate values demanded by the legal or any other profession, there are in existence certain transferable skills that all graduates are expected to have, and law schools can be expected to help law students develop them no less than their colleagues in other modules. Creating new modules involves taking all these demands into consideration.

That said, the very concept of the 'transferable skill' is a problematic one. The English/Welsh professional bodies say law students are expected to complete their studies with an ability to (inter alia) apply knowledge to complex situations; recognise that alternative but equally valid solutions to problems can exist; select key relevant issues to research using standard online and library-based resources; use the English language effectively and to be proficient in word processing and other IT skills. Such overtures can be expected from equivalent authorities the world over, but 'whilst all of this is admirable and deliverable, nothing is said (by the legal professions) about how students acquire this knowledge' (Virgo 2011, 222). While this gives academic staff members a great deal of flexibility in how to impart said skills, there is no evidence that the legal profession wants universities to teach those skills at the expense of imparting legal knowledge (the ability to deliver an assessed PowerPoint presentation being of decidedly limited preparation for tendering a plea in mitigation before Keighley Magistrates), and generic skill delivery should not be privileged over the learning of legal knowledge or the development of legal research abilities. Most of what are called 'transferable skills' are just as effectively learned through the simple expedient of being alive, having a job, playing a sport and so forth. So pervasive are they that creating and delivering new modules will involve covering those 'transferable skills' by default, and in the course of module design there is little need to spend much time ensuring that is the case. If university administrators demand that it is spelled out, so be it; for the most part it will be enough simply to make a mental note of where the transferable skills are covered, in case anyone should ever ask. But designing new modules should not involve investing too much time on the 'transferable skills' agenda.

Of far greater import for the new module leader is to think about what legal researchers 'do' and what is expected of the students in this regard. Thinking about what is required of a 'legal researcher' allows tutors to remove the distinction between LLB and joint honours students (which is decidedly artificial by the time they reach their final years of study), between those wishing to enter the legal profession and those who interests lie elsewhere, and between undergraduate and postgraduate students – in those final years colleagues can expect to have undergraduate and taught postgraduate students on the same module, with little practical distinction except in the difficulty of the exam and coursework questions and with the two cohorts having separate tutorial/ seminar groups. Regardless of which category one's students fall into, there is much merit in explicitly considering what skills are required by competent legal researchers and how you are going to help those students achieve them within your particular module. Ultimately, the role of the lecturer is to inspire students to think critically and in depth, to understand what the law 'says' and what the alternatives are, and to question everything but accept nothing until the evidence is overwhelming. But those lofty ideals also have to be reconciled with the far more prosaic need to strike a balance between learning the law and thinking critically 'about' the law. These should be central to module development too. Additionally, law schools need to ensure that, across the duration of their studies, students are exposed to a variety of legal research methodologies. Staff members should be collectively encouraged to ensure that particular modules are taught from historical, feminist and comparative as well as doctrinal perspectives; the leadership role expected of professorial staff should carry with it a willingness to explore different philosophies of law and different strategies for teaching it, and to develop the expertise necessary for delivering those modules successfully.

But whichever approach is taken to teaching and assessment and regardless of the substantive content of the module, the need to get law students to 'think like lawyers' must be a lecturer's focus. Seminars or tutorials are the most effective way of helping students develop these thinking skills, and particular care must be given to their planning and delivery. Virgo (2011) outlines six 'modes of thinking' that can assist in this regard: helping students' ability to describe, apply and interpret the law is central to what law lecturers do; but description, application and interpretation require an ability to think imaginatively (perhaps by encouraging them to approach problems from different and unexpected legal perspectives). The ability to identify the policy decisions which underpin those rules is also important, for it is a truism that law does not exist in a vacuum and knowing why 'the law' says what it does, how those policy decisions were reached and what are the alternatives are fundamental to a legal education. Students 'need to develop the skills and techniques to be able to criticise the law' (Virgo, 224), and when considering seminar strategies and thinking how to deliver lectures it is important to bear these principles in mind. It is of paramount importance to avoid simply regurgitating what the cases say or the contents of a textbook or, worse, just reading off slides which may themselves be no more than a summary of the case law or the product of a slavish response to the textbook tradition. There is no more certain way of ensuring students' non-engagement, and no more certain way of ensuring they do no more than the bare minimum required to pass, than to deliver a non-reflexive, passionless series of lectures reinforced by seminars replete with closed questions or where the lecturer, in effect, redelivers the uninspiring lecture given last week.

But facilitating legal thinking must be balanced against ensuring they 'know the law' and the lecturer, through discussion with colleagues, must ensure that, at the end of their undergraduate studies, students know enough law to be able to hold conversations with potential lawyers who might be impressed by their having a law degree or with potential directors of postgraduate study; or ensure that those who commit to professional qualification are not left floundering by a lack of basic knowledge. The law school will want to know that students have sufficient opportunities to show they possess those skills, perhaps by ensuring particular modules are assessed by multiple choice exams or open-book exams where every question is a 'problem-type' question, or by the use of moots, while others adopt more discursive assessments such as 'discussion-type' exam questions, oral presentations and discursive coursework essays and still others seek a balance of the two approaches. Blended and distance learning might be explored too, but striking the balance will require a whole-school approach. The guiding principle is the need to move students away from assessment entirely or predominantly by the old staples of a two-hour closed-book exam and a 2,000 word essay, and decisions as to how any particular module is taught and assessed should be taken after consultation with colleagues in order to ensure the requisite level of variety.

Finally, our enthusiastic module tutor will need to grapple with the elephant in the lecture room; namely, the difficulty of ensuring that students remain engaged with their studies. Older, jaded colleagues may tell him of the insurmountable challenges presented by a culture of non-attendance whereby many students disengage from their studies once they have established what they need to do in order to pass. Colleagues of a theoretical persuasion might speak in terms of 'pragmatic non-reflexivity' on the part of students, pointing to behaviours 'acted according to collective idea of what is deemed socially proper … a routinized or even an unconscious acceptance, of taken for granted ideas about what is natural and expected' (Duncan 2011, 2.6). There is no easy solution to the difficulty and once a collective idea that classes do not matter has taken hold, it is difficult to loosen its grasp; but the lecturer must bear in mind that, for every student who falls into that category, there will be others who are eager to learn and willing to be creative. Podcasts and guided readings may be preferable to spending long hours preparing lectures that few students attend but, again, this is probably best approached through departmental or university-wide discussion.

The key messages for Nadia and other academics thinking about new modules:

1. At the initial stages, resist the temptation to focus solely on substantive legal content. The law you wish to cover, how you want to deliver the module and how you want to assess it need to be considered together.
2. Be creative. Your students will be creative if you give them the opportunity to be so, and a good manager/mentor will encourage your creative side.
3. Think about what your colleagues do. What works, or doesn't work, for them? Are there particular delivery and assessment styles that, as a department, you over or underuse?
4. Seek advice from people in other universities whose opinion you value. Every academic you meet will be bright; the best ones distinguish themselves by being nice – they will always make time to support and advise junior colleagues. Conferences are ideal for this. If they don't, give them a wide berth.

FURTHER READING

JOURNALS

Carrit, A. (2007) Teaching Research skills Outside the Curriculum: Lessons Learnt at Oxford University, *Legal Information Management*, 7(4), 239–243.

Greig, A. (2000) Student-Led Classes and Group Work: A Methodology for Developing Generic Skills, *Legal Education Review*, 11(1), 80–236.

Nicolson, D. (1997) Facing Fact: The Teaching of Fact Construction in University Law Schools, *International Journal of Evidence and Proof*, 1(3), 132–151.

Virgo, G. (2011) Why Study Law? The Relevance of Legal Information to the Law Student, Researcher and Practitioner, *Legal Information Management*, 11(4), 221–225.

CHAPTER 58

Challenges of International Students

DEVERAL CAPPS

According to the UK Council for International Student Affairs in 2012–2013 there were over 425,000 international students studying in higher education in the UK. With these students paying on average about £12,000 per year, and considerably more at our most well-known institutions, international students represent a significant income stream in the higher-education economy. In addition to revenue, international students bring cultural diversity, different legal experiences and new perspectives on our common law system. However, international students can also bring significant challenges to those who deal with them both inside and outside the classroom environment. This chapter will look first at why students choose to study in the UK, outline some of the challenges they present to tutors and offer advice on dealing with them.

There are a number of reasons why international students choose to study in the UK. The UK education system is of very high quality when compared with higher education in many other countries. As a result, students, or in many cases their parents, believe a UK qualification will all but guarantee high-level employment and perhaps a status impossible to access elsewhere, that is, barrister. Parents may of course simply wish to send their children to a UK university because they too studied in the UK and want their children to have a similar experience.

International students can face a number of issues when studying in the UK. Whilst the following may not arise with everyone – and some of them are certainly true for home students too – it is likely that at some point at least one will. As a result this will impact upon studies and performance overall. As a result of the following, tutors should, ideally, be sympathetic.

For the international student much of what we in the UK are used to doing will be completely new. There is the need to assimilate the sights, sounds and possibly smells of their new surroundings; get to grips with different systems of public transport; learn where to buy food – which might be very different to what students are used to at home. Students will have to get used to the British weather: the rain, the cold and perhaps even seeing snow for the first time. Even getting used to UK shopping hours, including limited opening hours on a Sunday might be significant.

The costs of studying in the UK are substantial and in addition to tuition fees, the cost of living must be considered. Whilst such costs vary depending on location, the UKBA estimate living costs of £1020 per month in Inner London and £820 per month everywhere else. Coupling tuition fees and living costs together, an international student could easily be looking at £20,000 per year of study. Whilst a good proportion of international students will come from wealthy backgrounds, many won't and it is not uncommon for relatives to re-mortgage their home to fund international study. Under such circumstances, the pressure on the student to pass and even save money wherever possible (sometimes through extraordinary house share arrangements) can be significant, which can impact on their ability to study.

Feeling homesick is something we all might have felt in our lives to either a greater or lesser degree. International students may find that the issues raised above mean that what might have been a very slight feeling of homesickness can be magnified dramatically and manifest itself in tears, non-attendance and ultimately in poor examination performance. When dealing with international students tutors should remember that this might be the first time a student has left their home and show compassion.

Dealing with overseas students on an academic level gives rise to challenges both inside and outside of the classroom. English language ability (or perhaps English language inability) is often cited as the greatest challenge for tutors. Students with poor oral skills may avoid engaging with classroom discussion for fear of appearing foolish and those with poor written skills struggle to coherently present arguments in their assessed written work and then fail to achieve anything other than a bare pass.

The United Kingdom Border Agency (UKBA) take English language skills seriously and in order to meet our visa requirements, students must be able to prove their English language competence and universities can be penalised if they admit students who do not possess sufficient language skills. Different courses and different levels of study have differing minimum requirements.

Coping with student language problems is difficult and must be dealt with sensitively. Students with poor English will know their communication skills are flawed and embarrassing students in the classroom is ill advised. The most appropriate way forward is for a private meeting with the student to offer support, counselling and perhaps referral to student services.

Clearly, practice is the best way to improve linguistic skills though this is often easier to suggest than to achieve. International students tend to live and socialise with students from their own country and too easily fall back into their mother tongue outside of university. Encouraging students to socialise with home students, developing mentor programmes and highlighting that 'practice makes perfect' is a sensible first step. Other possibilities are suggesting that the student finds a job that requires customer interaction. Improvements in language take time and when students are only on one-year programmes, significant improvement is difficult. For students who have particular difficulties with written work, the University of Bristol has developed a useful grammar tutorial – http://www.bristol.ac.uk/arts/exercises/grammar/grammar_tutorial/index.htm

Teaching styles and learning practises differ around the world and international students may arrive in the UK with the expectation they will be spoon-fed knowledge and given everything that they need. As a result they struggle with self-directed study and tutors may find that what is given out in class, comes back virtually verbatim in student work. Whilst this is a difficult habit to break, clear instructions to students warning of such dangers well before they submit is the best way forward.

As with home students, plagiarism and collusion is a growing concern – especially with the multitude of information freely available on the Internet. Given the heavy financial burden that students face, the fear of failure as well as their own language ability (in that they are unable to find different ways of presenting a point well made in a textbook, can lead them to difficulties). Again, as with spoon-feeding, clear instruction as to what is appropriate provides the greatest success, or simply informing a student that using quotes within their work is perfectly appropriate provided that full references are provided.

The key messages for Nadia and other academics working with international students:

1. Dealing with international students can be a really positive experience but it is different from interacting with home/EU students.
2. Use the opportunity of engaging with international students to reflect on your own assumptions about pedagogy from lecture style through to how you deliver seminar and tutorial instructions.

FURTHER READING

WEBSITES

International Student Barometer – http://www.i-graduate.org/services/international-student-barometer/

UK Council for International Student Affairs – http://www.ukcisa.org.uk

UKBA policy guidance on student visas – https://www.gov.uk/government/uploads/system/uploads/attachment_data/file/370866/T4_Guidance_11-14.pdf

CHAPTER 59

Applying for Research Funding

SALLY WHEELER

> Nadia has designed a research plan and now wants to apply for research funding.

Most academics, particularly at research-intensive institutions, have research targets both in terms of income generation and in terms of outputs. Research funding is increasingly a requirement for promotion at HEIs. Many institutions require funding applications to have been made in order to pass probation. HEIs, particularly research-intensive ones, have invested considerable resources in research offices dedicated to not only pricing research for applications but also in helping people find the funder for their projects. HEIs particularly like funding that attracts full economic costs (FEC). FEC allows HEIs to pass on the direct costs of a project (e.g. travel and time for the investigator(s)), estates costs and indirect costs. Indirect costs cover a contribution to the HEI's library and the running of its central services such as its finance management function, its HR function and its library.

It is worth remembering that some funders, for example Leverhulme and Nuffield, do not pay indirect costs and so, whilst funding from them still provides an opportunity to pursue research, it is perhaps not as popular a source as those funders which do. The addition of estate and indirect costs to a project makes it considerably more expensive than just time, travel and consumables costs. Estate and indirect costs can take a project over the financial limit for a particular scheme. You should look at the general shape of the costings for your project as you develop it. This will avoid exceeding the financial limit for a particular scheme. It is often hard to trim an idea back late in the day without losing its essential organising rationale.

You need to spend some time thinking about what you hope to get out of a funding application. This will influence the choice of funder and choice of scheme within a particular funder's portfolio. Good applications take considerable time to prepare, particularly early in a career. It might well be the case that it is a more efficient use of time in productivity terms, rather than career terms, to write an article or a book chapter than it is to prepare a case for support, an impact plan and a dissemination plan for a funder. A publication that does not get accepted by its target outlet can with the aid of referees' comments be turned into a successful submission at another journal.

The same is unlikely to be true of a failed funding application. Most funders do not permit resubmissions. Often applications are addressed to particular schemes or calls and funders have very different preferences and requirements.

You should apply for research funding to enable you to do something that you can't do within your normal workload. This might be a period as a visiting academic overseas or a project in a field that is new to you. You might wonder whether you need a track record of successful funding applications or publications in a particular area to apply for a grant. You are unlikely to get a large grant without having applied for smaller amounts of funding successfully on previous occasions. Funders need to be convinced that an applicant can deliver the research that they are promising. A reputation in a particular area is less essential as your application will be judged on the quality of the proposal you put together. There are numerous schemes that allow applicants to craft a relatively modest proposal (the British Academy is a popular place to start). You might think about looking at the various funders that support networks or seminar series as a way of drawing together a group of potential collaborators. Successfully running a venture of this sort within budget is a very good introduction to operationalising a research idea into a funding proposal. It also gives access to people in the field who you will be able to nominate as potential referees of an application. It might also give you some of the contacts outside academia that you will need to establish in order to create a convincing impact plan for the funding proposal.

The established route for academics coming into Law Schools is straight from doctoral study, unlike the other social sciences and the natural sciences where a period as a post doc or research assistant on a project is more common. Thus legal academics are unlikely to have seen how a project is managed, how emerging ideas from the research are captured and crafted into new applications and how dissemination and impact opportunities are created. You need a good, original idea on which to found an application. You need to take advantage of any training opportunities your institution or the wider academic community offers and to seek advice from successful grant winners. Some faculties and schools will have previous successful and unsuccessful applications available for consultation. Commonality of research area is not necessary to take advantage of this sort of assistance. What you should be looking at in those applications is how the idea is explained and what methodology is chosen and why. You need to think about the level of ambition the project displays for the amount of funding and academic time sought. Many less experienced colleagues try and squeeze an idea into a proposal that is just far too small to do justice to the idea. Once an idea is funded it is gone. If you are wary of submitting a very large proposal you should break a bit of the idea off and go with that.

You should also concentrate on developing your writing skills around your research idea. Most funding applications are reviewed at an early stage by subject specialists but as the journey towards success continues reviewers are likely to become much more remote in terms of area of interest match. Many applications fail at the latter stages of assessment because while they speak to subject specialists they do not engage with those in a broader field. Broader field here means legal study at its most general and the disciplines that border it. Avoid technical jargon and explain clearly what it is you intend to do and how you intend to do it. Get colleagues in the school and in disciplines related to law to read the proposal. They should be able to understand what you intend to do, how you intend to do it and why you intend to do it in that way.

Comparative elements need to be justified. Choice of interviewees needs to be explained. Potential access issues need to be acknowledged. Accounts of survey methodology need to include details of the sample frame and the response rate required for there to be a viable analysis. Collecting empirical data produces ethical issues. These need to be identified and an explanation for how they will be dealt with offered. The proposal needs to explain data collection, management and analysis. There are numerous qualitative data analysis packages available and it looks rather old fashioned not to be using one. You need to be able to explain its selection and what it will allow you to do.

A research proposal budget needs to be as accurate as possible. Get advice from the research administration at your institution about what you can include in the budget. Think about how to fund any essential items that cannot be included. A referee may comment adversely on a proposal that includes costs that a funder expressly excludes. It is not the case that paring a proposal cost down as low as possible makes it more attractive to a funder. Being cheap is not the same as offering value for money; if something fails because it is under-costed a funder has wasted their money. Submitting a proposal that is considered to be too cheap may be taken as evidence of inexperience in research management.

The key messages for Nadia and other academics considering applying for research funding:

1. Budget accurately.
2. Explain the idea and methodology.
3. Justify comparative elements.
4. Remember not every excellent well-reviewed proposal gets funded as there is just not enough sufficient funding for this to happen.

FURTHER READING

WEBSITES

http://www.esrc.ac.uk/funding-and-guidance/applicants/

https://www.vitae.ac.uk/researcher-careers/pursuing-an-academic-career/research-funding

Your own institution's guidance

CHAPTER 60

Presenting at Conferences

FIONA COWNIE

> Nadia now wants to present her research findings at a conference.

Presenting your research at conferences can seem like a terrifying prospect. But after you've done it once or twice, it gets much easier, and although it always requires some thought and organisation, there are lots of benefits from doing it, so it's worth the effort!

Choosing which conference to go to can be problematic, because there are so many. The easiest way to find out about conferences is to join one of the two largest legal academic associations, the Society of Legal Scholars (SLS) or the Socio-Legal Studies Association (SLSA). They both have email newsletters where lots of conferences are advertised.

Presenting at one of the big general conferences run annually by the SLS or the SLSA has the advantage that you can go to different sessions covering a wide variety of topics. But attending a specialist conference where papers will all be relevant to one area means that you might learn a lot about something you are very interested in, as well as meeting more of the other specialists in your field. Your decision will also be affected by the timing and cost of the conference, as well as the availability of networking opportunities. We'll go on to consider these issues in the rest of this section.

Once you've decided which conference you'd like to go to, you need to work out what it will cost and apply for some funding. Be careful to include costs of travel (and also subsistence, if it is not included in the conference fee). Generally, law schools have some funding available to subsidise conference attendance, but the amount and terms of the funding vary greatly from institution to institution. You therefore need to investigate precisely what the process involves in your law school, and especially whether there are conditions you need to satisfy before making an application, such as seeking external funding. You also need to clarify whether you should ask the conference organisers to invoice your law school, or whether you are expected to pay 'up front' and claim the cost back at a later stage (if the latter, don't forget to keep all your receipts).

When you apply to go to a conference, you will usually be asked for an abstract of your paper, which will be used to allocate you to a session in the conference timetable, and will often be included in the conference programme. Some people spend quite a lot of time thinking up an exciting title for their paper, in order to encourage others to come and listen to it. It is important to keep your abstract fairly short, and certainly within any word limit imposed by the conference organisers. Often, you have to write this abstract a very long time ahead of the actual conference, so it is best not to be *too* specific, in case, when it comes to it, you want to do something a little different from that which you first intended. You can often be over-ambitious in estimating the progress you will have made with your research by the time of the conference, and then live to regret an abstract which promises more than you can actually deliver when you present your paper.

Academic conferences are usually organised by a group of academics from the law school where the conference is being held, on a voluntary basis. They may have some administrative assistance, but they will usually be putting in a lot of effort themselves. Bearing this in mind, it is best not to be too demanding about the timing of your presentation, or your travel or accommodation arrangements. People who say 'I want to give a paper, but I can only do it at 11:00 on the second day of the conference' are a conference-organiser's nightmare!

When you present a paper at a conference, you never know who might be in the audience. Don't be upset if very few people are in the audience. This often happens when there are ten or twelve different sessions all going on at once. On the other hand, your audience might include several well-known experts in your field, whom you desperately want to impress! In either case, your audience is likely to be knowledgeable. Planning what you are going to say and how you are going to deliver it, is absolutely vital. The main thing to remember is how little time you will have. Conference sessions at law conferences generally last 90 minutes, and there are usually three speakers in the session. The usual format is: 'Twenty minutes each and twenty to thirty minutes for questions to any of the speakers at the end of the session'. A chairperson will be allocated by the conference organisers to chair each session, and it is their job to keep everyone to time. Always rehearse your presentation. Keeping to time is a really important part of conference etiquette; it is unfair both to the other speakers and to the audience (who want to hear all the papers) to exceed your allocated time.

Given the short time available, don't try to say too much. You will be surprised at how little detail you can communicate in 20 minutes. You really do have to focus on your main ideas and findings. Be ruthless in cutting out any background information, and don't waste time on a long introduction. PowerPoint slides can be useful to add interest to your presentation, but always remember that the technology may let you down, and make sure you can present your paper *without* the slides if necessary. Take along a few hard copy handouts for emergencies; if you have to use them it will make you look much more professional. Reading a presentation skills handbook, such as the Bradbury book below, is a good idea to ensure you don't make basic errors, such as putting too much content on your PowerPoint slides.

Giving a paper at an academic conference is a good way of getting feedback on your research before you write it up for publication. You can refine your article or book chapter in the light of the questions and comments you receive from your audience. You should also be able to network with your audience, and perhaps meet people who know more than you do about the field and who will be willing to read drafts of your work in the future, which can be really useful. You might also find that people direct you to information or ideas that you were unaware of, which you can later follow up yourself. Putting your name, institutional affiliation and contact details clearly on a slide or handout enhances your networking opportunities.

There is sometimes a temptation to give a lot of conference papers, but fail to publish anything. While understandable (writing a conference paper is much easier), it is a pity not to work out your ideas thoroughly and get them into the public domain. 'Never have an unpublished thought' might be a bit extreme, but there is certainly something to be said for balancing the number of papers you present with your published work.

The key messages for Nadia and other academics considering presenting at conferences:

1. Plan your attendance carefully, including how to fund it.
2. Make sure you keep to time when presenting.
3. Turn your conference papers into publications.

FURTHER READING

BOOKS

Blaxter, L., Hughes, C. and Tight, M. (1998) *The Academic Career Handbook*, Buckingham and Philadelphia: Open University Press, 65.

Bradbury, A. (2006) *Successful Presentation Skills*, 3rd edn, London and Philadelphia: Kogan Page.

Delamont, S. and Atkinson, P. (2004) *Successful Research Careers: A Practical Guide*, Maidenhead and New York: Society for Research into Higher Education and Open University Press, 148.

CHAPTER 61

Preparing Journal Articles for Submission

PHILIP A. THOMAS

> Following the successful presentation of her research work at a conference, Nadia is now looking to publish the research in her first journal article.

The good news is that it has never been easier to be published in an academic law journal. Paper journals are popping up like autumn mushrooms. The reason is that production costings have reduced thereby lowering the break-even publishing cost. Publishers need fewer subscriptions to make a profit and this has promoted niche subject areas with limited readership into print form. Additionally, and perhaps more importantly, electronic publishing has taken off big time. Electronic journals and alongside them university working papers offer virtually instant publication to a mass market. Many of these publications offer free access. There is also the commercial publishers' hybrid development of joint paper and online publication of the same paper. The online publication format has received the formal recognition and blessing of the REF Panel [2015] when it stated that papers published electronically were acceptable for submission alongside paper-based articles. However, if you are planning to publish via an online journal, ensure that all papers are externally refereed as this helps ensure quality control and academic recognition. Issues arising out of 'open access' remain unresolved but there is little doubt that getting into 'print' is something you can achieve. Your concern should not be getting published but rather, getting read. Today, the challenge is not too little literature but too much.

Assume you are preparing an article. Do you complete it and then look for a publication outlet? The answer, paradoxically, is no. You should decide once your writing idea is established where you should send your paper. This decision-making, chronological procedure is because your initial choice will direct and inform the style, length and content of your paper. For example, journals have word limits. Sending a paper of 15,000 words to a journal that tops at 12,000 will result in a rejection no matter how good or relevant a paper you submit. Read the journal's instructions to authors and follow those rules or guidelines. This information is found either on the website or printed in each paper issue of the journal.

Does the selected journal speak to a group of specialists, such as family lawyers, or is it a general journal that addresses a wide range of academic lawyers or indeed readers from other disciplines? Perhaps you seek to address legal or social practitioners. Your style, vocabulary and professional terminology should be shaped by that readership in order to retain their attention and involvement. For example, if you are an environmental lawyer writing for a specialist journal then you need not spell out what is the 'public interest doctrine' but you would need to do so for a more disparate readership. Another example is Foucault who is well appreciated in some circles but unknown in others. So, judge your potential readership and write accordingly.

There is a tendency to both overwrite and over-pack a paper. Overwriting involves prioritising the counting of words instead of focusing on clarity and content. Read a judgment by Lord Denning for an example of brevity and clarity. Dickens was paid by the word; you are not, so keep your paper tight, simple and meaningful. Prepare an abstract of your paper and block your paper into sections with useful sub-headings. Write your introduction and conclusion last and make them count. Some busy readers will look at the start and finish of your paper and then decide whether or not to read the entire paper. Your introduction should be a route map of the paper rather than asking the reader to be an explorer in a jungle of ideas and words. Explorers may give up or not even be prepared to commence such an intellectual adventure!

Do not over-burden your paper with several ideas. A multiplicity of thoughts can be confusing to the reader. One good idea is often sufficient. If you have further related ideas keep them for new papers. A sequence of complementary papers around a theme builds you a specialist profile and could possibly turn into chapters of a book or be submitted for a PhD by publication.

When you have 'finished' your paper accept that it remains 'unfinished' for the moment. Present the paper at a conference or at a staff seminar. Ask a trusted colleague to read and comment on it. What may appear blatantly obvious to you may be obscure or ambiguous to a fresh reader. You might even ask an experienced scholar to subedit your paper. Ensure you spellcheck the paper and complete all the footnotes. Some journals expect the footnotes to be in house style and others delay until an acceptance is offered before asking for this task to be undertaken. When your paper finally goes public you will be judged on it. Ensure it is your best work.

At the point of submission, normally electronic, request the editor to acknowledge receipt. If your paper is really topically 'hot', point this out in the covering note. It might ensure a quicker decision and possibly earlier publication. Should you receive a straight rejection ask for comments from the referees. This will help you review and rewrite the paper for submission elsewhere. A decision that offers comments and an invitation to resubmit should be taken positively and acted upon. When you resubmit ensure that your covering letter demonstrates how you have responded to the comments provided by the referees. If you have responded fully and appropriately then the editor may feel 'estopped' from rejecting your paper.

In some jurisdictions, including the USA, multiple submissions are normal. However, in the UK journals work on single submissions. If a multiple UK submission is identified the editor will return your paper forthwith. This means that you need to be careful in the selection of your journal to ensure the greatest chance of publication. An inappropriate choice will waste precious time whilst referees review and subsequently reject your paper. However, there is also an editorial responsibility to turn round the paper without delay. If you feel there is a delay then contact the editor and request a status update.

Finally, an 'article' for the purposes of this section includes case and legislation notes and also book reviews. In these journal sections speed is of the essence. For example, follow the progress of a case through the courts to its final appeal. Similarly, track legislation from the white paper, into its bill form and parliamentary passage. Book review editors find it difficult to convince senior academics to review texts so this is a prime opportunity for a junior academic. You should identify forthcoming books in publishers' catalogues. Contact your targeted book review editor and offer an on-publication review. Ask for the book to be sent in PDF format from the publisher so that you write the review even before it is on the shelves. You will be feted by the editor and publisher for your enthusiasm and innovation!

So get thinking, researching, preparing, organising, writing and submitting. Editors are waiting to publish your paper.

The key messages for Nadia and other academics preparing journal articles for submission:

1. Getting published is easy: getting read is your goal.
2. Select your journal and then start writing your paper.
3. Also consider writing case notes, legislation notes and book reviews.

FURTHER READING

BOOKS

Belcher, W. L. (2009) *Writing Your Journal Article in 12 Weeks*, London: Sage.

WEBSITES

10 Simple Rules for Getting Published, www.ploscombiol.org

How to Publish, www.roie.org/how.htm

CHAPTER 62

Book Proposals

Dave Cowan

> Nadia wants to publish her work as a book and is seeking advice on putting together a book proposal.

A book proposal is the academic's calling card. There is little that is more important – few people will actually read an academic book from cover to cover; on the other hand, your proposal will be pored over and considered often by five or more people. It is also a political process.

Let me start with some don'ts – this is partly because I have seen far too many poor quality book proposals.

(1) If the proposal does not make sense, is grammatically poor, or has holes in it (literally and figuratively), it will not get far. Get others to read and comment on it before sending it in.

(2) If you send your book proposal to two different publishers, the outcome may not be the same as with journal 'double dipping' (which is deprecated). Some publishers will understand. Some will only understand if you are honest and tell them what you are doing. Some will expect exclusivity. Just as with journal 'double dipping', if you do this, you should expect to be caught. The best approach is honesty and to ask upfront before submitting it – really, you should have a hierarchical list of targeted publishers not a scattergun. Actually, it may help you get a speedier decision.

(3) Many publishers will ask to see a specimen chapter or an example of your writing. Some aspiring authors will simply email their entire doctoral thesis. This might be welcomed but that outcome is unlikely. You cannot expect a second viva (if you are the sort of person who wants one) and nor can you expect detailed commentary on your thesis. The best response is to offer a paper based on your book's thesis which has been submitted to a journal. If there is no such paper, the publisher (and reviewer) may ask themselves whether there is enough to go on to give you a contract. The best guarantee of academic rigour and quality is for a potential book author to approach the publisher with a well-worked proposal *and* an accepted paper to be published in a quality journal which has peer reviewed the work. It is also helpful to a publisher to know who the external examiner was.

(4) The final negative point is that, if you expect a decent publisher to publish your doctoral thesis as it appears in your university's library, generally you will be in error. It takes a lot of time and patience to turn a doctoral thesis in to a monograph. This may be galling but the dataset may require expansion; the lit review and methodology chapters may require careful rewriting and paring down. The introduction and conclusion will need to be rewritten. It will need to be much more confidently and authoritatively written than your thesis which (rightly) should stress the limitations of the enterprise. Equally, the readership is likely to be general, so the key point is that your dataset should enable you to make general points for general readers. If you are intending to publish your doctoral thesis, it is absolutely critical that you explain up front that is your intention but that you are going to make a number of significant alterations to it in line with your expectations of the audience.

Now, let me be more positive.

The first thing an aspiring author should do is pick up the telephone or, if absolutely necessary, open their compose email. Talk to your external examiner, your target publisher, your colleagues and peers. Choose your publisher carefully. There are some key differences: most important is their reputation – publishers get reputations for a reason and you should always ask your colleagues what their experience is of any particular publisher; the price of their products; whether they will produce it as a paperback from the off (which few will do now), which will lead to bigger sales; whether they have a particular prominence in your field and whether they have series of books which interrogate your field; different publishers give different royalties although the differences are smaller now than they used to be (but no academic ever published a book to secure their futures); production values of the book (type of paper, font, covers *are* important). Some publishers will negotiate terms but these are often at the margins. Experience suggests that the key matter to negotiate is the production of the index. If you have never done an index before, hope that you never have to do one – it is tedious and, if you ask somebody else to do it, expensive. Try and get your publisher to throw it in with the contract. Some still will; most won't. Good luck.

Publishers often have series, with general editors and members of editorial boards, just like journals. We are at conferences; we are on the sniff for the next book; we talk to people; we publicise our series; we want to work with you. So, talk to us about what sorts of work we like to publish – our mission, if you like (and, if they don't have one, think again) – and whether your proposed work will 'fit'.

No publisher is going to say 'no' upfront. Many will talk to their academic colleagues for an initial view about the project. At this stage, it helps to be known, but that is not always the case (reputations are made and broken). Some publishers will also actively court early-career academics – they know that is where the major advances are likely to be.

The next thing is to complete the proposal form. This should be treated with loving care. To repeat the key mantra: it is your calling card.

- Set out your stall early on – tell the reader the types of literatures with which you are engaging, the thesis, and why it is important. What is the book's unique selling point?

- But, remember the other golden rule. The audience is likely to be general and the referees may not be in your field. Write it for that audience.
- Give chapter summaries that are coherent and work towards the theme(s).
- There are then the sections with which academics generally feel uncomfortable but which are particularly important to at least some publishers. These are competition for your book and market.
  - If there is no competition for your book, that can be a good thing (e.g. this will be the first book-length treatment of the Scottish referendum) or a bad thing (nobody wants to write about the subject because nobody wants to read about it – e.g. the law of forks). Distinguishing your book also helps you to restate its centrality in and to the literature.
  - Publishers want to know the potential size of the market – for what type of audience is it being written? There are some good indicators of market size – there are x number of academics who list y as their special interest in relevant academic directories. There are x number of students studying this subject at y number of institutions – this is where a little googling goes a long way. This section will also help the publisher think about how they might sell the book.
- Be honest about the length of the book. I am the worst offender here but, if you hand in a product which is twice the length of what you stated in your proposal, expect the publisher to refuse it or to publish it in a tiny font to get it within their page length. This last point emphasises something key: publishers tend to be profit-making enterprises; they will plan in advance for your book; turn in something different without advance warning (see below) and they will turn it away.
- If your book has pictures, tables or graphs, be up front about this. They are more expensive to produce. Publishers don't particularly like too many of them. Be careful also with copyright, and so on.
- It is also helpful sometimes to offer referees who can vouch for the quality of your work.

These same rules hold good for edited collections. However, there is one key difference. The proposed editors need to be crystal clear about the academic mission behind the collection and how the introduction and, preferably, conclusion will hold the collection together. Some publishers and series editors like to see a mix of chapter authors – from early to late career – but the key thing always is that the collection will cohere. This is no mean task and experience suggests that edited collections are not to be undertaken lightly.

Once you have delivered the proposal and accompanying documents, sit back for a bit. Expect to receive reviews. It is unusual in my experience for reviewers not to make salient points with which the author has to engage (or has forgotten to engage with). So, you should expect what in journal terms is referred to as 'revise and resubmit'. Just like a journal, this is not a commitment to publish your book, but it is a commitment to look at it again. Publishers will not do that unless they are interested in the product.

When you have finally got to the end of the process, there is the contract. I cannot comment too much on that, having never read a book contract. The academic rule is that books are always delivered late and things change over time. What is absolutely key, though, is what the relational scholars tell us – maintain your relationship with your publisher during its production. Things invariably go wrong – don't stick your head in the sand. Tell the publisher and the series editor – they will empathise.

> The key messages for Nadia and other academics putting book proposals together:
>
> 1. The proposal is your calling card.
> 2. Spend time on the proposal and draft it carefully giving as much detail in each section as possible.
> 3. Talk to colleagues, publishers and experts in your field to better understand which publisher might be your best fit.

FURTHER READING

WEBSITE

Publishers' Guidelines on Proposals – Usually Available on their Website.

http://getalifephd.blogspot.co.uk/2011/03/how-to-write-book-proposal-for-academic.html

CHAPTER 63

Managing Research and Research Teams

FIONA DE LONDRAS

> Nadia has been successful in securing research funding but must now manage the research including the team working with her.

One of the greatest challenges in managing research in an academic post is time, especially during term where teaching and administration demands combine with family and home and research can be forced out for practical reasons. You can counter this by blocking out a period of time every week for research and abandoning it only where something that truly requires your immediate attention arises.

The ideal might be to have a research day per week during teaching term, but for many that is unrealistic. A morning a week will suffice however to keep your work ticking over. Three simple steps help to make this work: (1) Close and lock your door for the assigned time; do not answer if someone knocks. (2) Turn off your email; if there is an emergency someone will ring. (3) Put the research time in your Outlook calendar so that if someone checks your availability they can see you are busy.

This approach still only buys you a three or four-hour block and so it is likely to work best when you are in the 'production' rather than 'creation' phase of your research. Using the summer months for creative research (planning out papers and projects and doing most of the thinking and reading) and term time for the production part (writing, referencing, checking, submitting) will help you to maximise productivity in those precious timeslots.

When managing a research team you must also build into your schedule the time to engage with them: discuss the work, write together, analyse data and discuss progress. Remember that your research team will also have time pressures: they need to be able to plan so you need to develop targets and timescales and to stick to them (put them in your diary!). People need to know what you want them to do, and when, and they need also to be able to get on with a piece of work without having you constantly changing expectations or parameters or throwing curveballs at them. If your project is well designed you should have monthly targets and timescales and share them with your team, clearly indicating what everyone is to do, so that they can then get on with that work. Few if any researchers need you to check in with them daily. A weekly meeting is usually a good general guide, although if your researcher thinks that is too (in)frequent it can be changed. Research relationships evolve over time so regular discussion of whether the dynamic is working well is important.

In this respect, as with solo research, good project planning is vital. Unless there is a clear plan, with clearly defined questions and milestones, assessing progress across the lifetime of a research project is difficult. In the context of a single project you are likely to have developed your plan before you hire your researcher(s), especially if the project is funded. This need not mean that the plan is set in stone. You are hiring collaborators, not service researchers. One presumes that you will hire experienced and professional researchers. I find it hugely productive to give new team members the plan on day one and ask them to come back in a week with an outline of how they would do it differently. For this to work you have to make it very clear that you see them as collaborators and partners and welcome their views. A fresh pair of eyes will almost always lead to improvement: to ideas that you have not previously thought of. If you have a big enough project to have both researchers and a project officer involved do not make the mistake of thinking the project officer exists purely for administration. (S)he will also often be able to come up with ideas to improve timeline management, innovate in terms of dissemination, or engage more diverse stakeholders. You must see all of your team as just that: members of a *team*. That is how the best collaborative research gets done.

A real challenge, both in managing your own research and in managing research teams, of course relates to quality: you must be vigilant about being demanding of yourself. This is another reason why splitting the creative and productive phases across non-term and term-time can help. It is difficult to be rigorous, original, insightful and significant when you are exhausted from teaching, marking and sitting in committee meetings and so using your non-term time wisely is important. But so too is being honest with oneself. We know what good writing looks like from the things that we read that provoke our intellectual curiosity. The truth is that we know when we have written something that just isn't very good. Our sense of this should sharpen as our careers progress, but at every stage we can and should use trusted, honest and constructive peers to get feedback on our work. The key to writing and doing better research is to accept being told that you are wrong, have missed something or are not sufficiently into the relevant literature. We must be open to this.

The same is true of our research teams. Researchers will sometimes present you with sub-standard work. In my experience the key to managing this is to give very detailed, very careful feedback – preferably face to face – on how and why it did not meet the standard you expect. Researchers cannot ascertain this by telepathy. You need to tell them. That is time-consuming but it is also part of making both the researcher and the research better. Your name will forever be associated with that piece of work and so, just as much as you would if you were doing the work yourself, you need to focus on it reaching the required quality level. Vague comments are not helpful; the first time a piece of work is handed over, schedule in a good period of time to go through it line by line, to speak about what kinds of literatures you would have expected to see and for the researcher to have engaged with, to suggest reading, to make the citation protocols you want used clear and so on. Make it clear that in the future you want all of the pieces of work to adhere to these standards. Once one is clear and comprehensive a harder approach is appropriate.

In relation to all of the above you can and should also look to how those you admire manage their research and teams and speak to them. What may look easy is inevitably challenging, but they will have found ways of managing those challenges and will almost always be happy to share.

The key messages for Nadia and other academics considering managing research and research teams:

1. Isolate time for research during term-time and be strict with yourself in using that time only for research. Use your non-term time for creative research processes and your research-slots during term for 'production'.
2. Plan your research well both individually and within a project. Enable your research team to also plan and do not micro-manage them in between settled timelines.
3. Concentrate on quality. Invite and take on board robust but constructive critique from other scholars to make you better, and provide similar critique to your research team. Be clear about your expectations of yourself and your team and work hard, together, to meet them.

FURTHER READING

BOOK

Blau, Peter M. (1994) *The Organization of Academic Work*, 2nd edn, New Brunswick, NJ: Transaction Publishers.

JOURNAL

Rahman, A. (2007) Why Do Collaborative Research? *British Medical Journal*, 335(7614), 3034.

WEBSITE

Muller, N. 'The New Academic' (blog). www.nadinemuller.org.uk

CHAPTER 64

Battling the Exclusive Research Culture

CHLOË J. WALLACE

> Nadia is keen to balance her research commitments with teaching but feels there is an 'exclusive' research culture.

Debates as to the balance between research and teaching within universities are a perennial feature of modern academia. The 1963 Robbins Report into Higher Education refers to the debate, and advocates the importance of the research environment to university education. 34 years later, the Dearing Report considered a distinctive feature of a higher education institution to be engagement in research and scholarship as well as teaching. Ideally, both research and teaching are placed at the heart of university activity, and given equal priority. The reality, however, is somewhat different.

The ideal view starts from the premise that both research and teaching concern a single fundamental academic activity: scholarship and its dissemination. Increasingly, however, this is not how academic activity is managed. Universities treat teaching and research as distinctly different activities requiring different qualifications. They are funded from different streams and subject to different institutional strategies and targets. They thus become different activities, which individual academics have to combine, and often reconcile as competing priorities.

An 'exclusive research culture' starts from an assumption that these competing priorities ought always to be resolved in favour of more and better research, rather than more and better teaching. This assumption is rarely articulated externally, as student recruitment increasingly depends on the perceived quality of teaching offered within an institution. It nevertheless remains a pervasive part of academic experience. A central manifestation of this, which is also part of the cause, is the different ways in which quality of research and of teaching is evaluated. Put simply, the most visible evaluation of teaching (the National Student Survey) requires a baseline standard of good teaching which will keep students satisfied, whereas the most visible evaluation of research (the Research Excellence Framework) requires and rewards excellence. Thus, in appointments and career progression, teaching quality can be 'satisfactory' whereas research output must be 'excellent'. Individually, a truly excellent teacher with a mediocre research profile will often be less successful than a good-enough teacher with an excellent REF profile.

There are two issues, distinct but related, embedded within this 'exclusive research culture'. The first is an assumption that teaching and research are distinctly separate activities. The second is an assumption that research is the most important. The second assumption is hardest to resist, because academic contracts are premised on expectations of output which may conform to it. In terms of appointment and promotion, you are dependent on the expectations which your employer places on you: 'excellent' research and 'satisfactory' teaching. For some, one option may be available in institutions where 'teaching and scholarship', or 'teaching-focused' career paths are offered. These paths exempt academics from research expectations in terms of outputs, impact and REF inclusion, but require instead an enhanced contribution to 'scholarship', including the writing of textbooks, curriculum development and/or development of innovative teaching materials and methods. They may also include substantial roles involving leadership and management of student education.

These teaching and scholarship routes are distinct from teaching only/teaching fellow roles, which are often hourly paid and tend to be less secure. They retain an assumption that teaching within higher education requires a scholarly background, but allow for the dissemination of that scholarship through teaching and other pedagogic activities, which are not recognised by the REF and thus not classed by universities as 'research'. As such, whilst they might appear to exist within the paradigm of research and teaching as distinctly different activities, they are in many ways a resistance to the narrow definition of 'research' as limited to REF-recognised activities.

Such routes primarily exist in pre-1992 institutions, and not in all of those. They are rarely recruited to for permanent posts. However, it is worth investigating whether such a route, or something similar, is available in your institution. You need to assure yourself that promotion routes, up to professorial level, are supported, to avoid being seen as a second-class academic by your institution. You probably cannot avoid, however being seen as a second-class academic by some of your colleagues. That said, the teaching and scholarship route can be a satisfying academic career pathway for those whose skill set and inclinations lie in this direction.

This will not, however, suit those for whom research in the form of publication, funded projects and impact activities remain a central feature of their academic ambitions. Here, resistance to the exclusive research culture may come from a rejection of the view of teaching and research as distinctly separate activities. It is difficult to attain a balance between research and teaching if you treat them as wholly different activities. Whilst institutional policy may not encourage this, a holistic approach to the academic role is more effective in enabling an academic to achieve that balance.

Hattie and Marsh (1996) present evidence that the quality of research output is connected with the amount of time devoted to it in a way that is not true for teaching, and many academics would agree. One cause of 'accidental' prioritisation of research is taking on too many research projects, which require a lot of time to do to a sufficiently high standard, and thus push out teaching projects. Quality, however, is more important than quantity. If you want to make time for good teaching, you need to make hard choices to limit the quantity of research you do, in order to maximise its quality.

Seeing the academic role as a holistic one means making what connections you can between your research and your teaching. To do this you should insist on doing at least some of your teaching within your research interests. Traditionally, in law there has been an assumption that everyone should be able to teach at least one 'core' subject, whether or not that is your field of research. This is reasonable, but avoid taking on the work which colleagues who are inflexible on this matter are unprepared to do, particularly if this involves being pushed out of teaching in your own research area.

It is unrealistic to ensure that that all of your teaching derives from your research, however. Thus you should also think about what value you can add to your other teaching, in terms of scholarly activity and/or career progression. In particular, avoid thinking about teaching activity solely in terms of classroom contact hours, and consider the development of innovative approaches; leadership experience, or new directions for research. Such broader scholarly activity or leadership may be recognised within your career progression; ensure that you are familiar with what your promotions criteria actually are, rather than what they are rumoured to be, and take advice from a mentor who equally pays attention to their teaching.

This kind of resistance to the exclusive research culture is not easy, precisely because it is a culture. Such cultures are not only embedded institutionally, but also filter down into the attitudes and behaviours of academic colleagues. In most institutions, an academic career which focuses on teaching rather than on big research projects will be seen as less prestigious and may attract fewer internal and external plaudits. However, one antidote to the high levels of stress experienced by many academics is a career path which matches your values and preferences. Finding the right balance, for you, between research, teaching and scholarship can improve job satisfaction, and for most of us this balances out the disadvantages.

The key messages for Nadia and other academics considering battling the exclusive research culture:

1. Investigate whether your institution offers a teaching and scholarship career path and consider whether that would be a satisfying route for you to take.
2. Look for ways to see your research and teaching as part of the same scholarly endeavour, by allowing the one to inform the other.
3. Add value to your teaching activity, through innovation or leadership, so that it contributes towards your career progression as much as your research does.

FURTHER READING

JOURNALS

Coate, K, Barnett, R and Williams, G. (2001) Relationships Between Teaching and Research in Higher Education in England, *Higher Education Quarterly*, 55(2), 158–174.

Greenbank, P. (2006) The Academic's Role: The Need for a Re-evaluation?, *Teaching in Higher Education*, 11(1), 107–112.

Hattie, J. and Marsh, H. W. (1996) The Relationship Between Research and Teaching: A Meta-Analysis, *Review of Educational Research*, 66(4), 507–542.

Locke, W. (2012) The Dislocation of Teaching and Research and the Reconfiguring of Academic Work, *London Review of Education*, 10(3), 261–274.

Robertson, J. (2007) Beyond the 'research/teaching nexus': Exploring the Complexity of Academic Experience, *Studies in Higher Education*, 32(5), 541–556.

CHAPTER 65

Promotions in Higher Education

JESSICA GUTH

Nadia has been doing well. She has had a journal article and book chapter accepted for publication and work is progressing well on her book. She has been able to secure a small research grant for a pilot project and has just received her teaching evaluations for her second year of teaching. They are positive. Nadia is now thinking about promotions and moving up the career ladder but she knows very little about what the next step is or how the process works.

Research suggests that many academics have little or no idea how promotions work in higher education institutions (HEIs). They often do not fully understand the criteria used to decide promotions nor are they familiar with the process. There is also quite a lot of evidence that university processes can be unnecessarily opaque and complex. Most universities have a career structure which is based on lecturer, senior lecturer/ principal lecturer, reader, professor but these titles do not necessarily mean the same thing across the sector. Old universities often have two levels of lecturer which may be referred to as lecturer A and B or junior lecturer and lecturer or they may just be called lecturer but be split into two different grades on the pay scale. In some cases promotion from the lower lecturer scale to the higher is automatic, for example on completion of a probationary period; in other cases an application is required. New universities often make a distinction between the more teaching-focused, principal lecturer and more research-focused, senior lecturer. The first thing to do when thinking about promotion therefore is to work out exactly what the career structure in any given institution is. Human resources (HR) departments or more experienced colleagues can help.

Promotions criteria and the way they are applied can also vary from institution to institution and there is often a lot of confusion and rumour about exactly what the requirements are. Guth and Wright (2008) suggest that there is a three-way mismatch between what the criteria are, what academics think they are and how they are applied. There is no easy solution to this. Academics seeking promotions need to, as best they can, find out what the criteria are that they are measuring themselves against. One way to do this is to look at job descriptions and person specifications published when new jobs are advertised. However, there is some suggestion that the criteria applied to applications for promotions rather than applications for new appointments are more stringent or at least more stringently applied. There is a lack of research in this area but many academics report that they found it easier to move up the career ladder by moving institutions and others provide anecdotal evidence that promotions have been gained by securing job offers from other institutions and using them as bargaining tools.

Another way to get a sense of the criteria is to be able to look at successful applications and to talk to colleagues who have been through the process or have other experience of it about the expectations. Having a good mentor or mentors (whether formal or informal) as well as good networks can be really important in this regard. Where mentoring works, established academics can provide guidance and support through the process and give invaluable feedback on strengths and weaknesses leading up to a formal application. Networks will also help in a number of ways. Talking with colleagues can help clarify where gaps might be on the CV and what can be done to fill those gaps. Networks of course also lead to opportunities which in turn lead to a stronger CV overall. However, mentors and networks also carry risks when it comes to understanding promotions criteria. Because there is still a lack of transparency around promotions in HEIs, there are lots of rumours and misconceptions and it can be difficult to separate fact from fiction.

Generally speaking all institutions work on the basis of re-grading rather than promotion so the applicant will need to demonstrate they are working at a higher level than their current job level actually is. Also generally speaking, institutions will look for competence in teaching, research and administration and external activities but the emphasis on these can vary considerably and there may be more than one path open to academics at the same institution. Discussions with HR, mentors and heads of school should help clarify the criteria.

Research also suggests that academics perceive the promotions process as time consuming and involving complex paperwork and it is true that finding the time and headspace away from the 'day job' to work your way through the process and paperwork can be difficult. In some institutions there will be a form to complete, in others a statement and current CV will do the same job. In some there is a defined timescale in which applications are invited and considered two or three times a year, in others you can apply as and when. In any case, HR should be able to advise and give guidance on the required paperwork, timescales and stages.

A fair amount of research has considered the gender implications of promotions processes and criteria in higher education. Based on this research, the importance of networking, mentoring and positive leadership cannot be overestimated. It seems clear that in many HEIs promotion relies on academics pushing themselves forward for consideration and only in the rarest of circumstances will academics be told 'you should really apply for promotion now'. Research confirms that women are less likely to do this or do this only when they are sure they meet each single criterion and can demonstrate that with ease. This puts them at a disadvantage when compared to academics who submit speculative applications. The research demonstrates clearly that promotions are gained even where not all criteria are fully met and even where this is not the case, feedback on an unsuccessful application can only be helpful in developing the next one.

There are other (often gendered) factors which are cited as barriers to promotion and progression in higher education. Things like caring responsibilities, work–life balance issues and family leave (all discussed elsewhere in this book) together with a long-hours culture and increasing pressure on academics' time can lead to a feeling of not being good enough or never being able to meet the criteria for promotion. However, thinking about promotion and progression early, mapping skills and experience against the criteria for the next step up and actively seeking opportunities to fill gaps and reduce weaknesses can go some way to mitigating against these barriers. Having a clear career plan will of course help all academics be more strategic in their own career development.

In Nadia's situation as outlined at the start of this chapter, Nadia seems to be progressing well in terms of research and teaching but we know little about her administrative duties or external activities. Depending on the career structure at her institution, an application for promotion may be too early (if for example the next step is a senior lecturer post). If there is a split lecturer scale though, she should be encouraged to find out what the process is and map out her skills against the criteria and apply unless there are significant weaknesses. If she is unsuccessful, the feedback can help her develop a more strategic career plan on which a future application can be based.

The key messages for Nadia and other academics considering promotion:

1. Do not wait until you want to get promoted to think about promotion, actively plan your career all the way through.
2. Find out exactly what the procedure, including timescales, is.
3. Find out what the criteria are; map your CV against them – but don't wait until you can demonstrate you meet all of them three times over – have a go.

FURTHER READING

JOURNALS

Bagilhole, B. and Goode, J. (2001) The Contradiction of the Myth of Individual Merit, and the Reality of a Patriarchal Support System in Academic Careers, a Feminist Investigation, *The European Journal of Women's Studies*, 8(2), 161–180.

Doherty, L. and Manfredi, S. (2006) Women's Progression to Senior Positions in English Universities, *Employee Relations*, 28(6), 553–572.

Parker, J. (2008) Comparing Research and Teaching in University Promotion Criteria, *Higher Education Quarterly*, 62, (3) 237–251.

Various Authors (2006) Special Issue on the Advancement of Women in Universities, *Employee Relations*, 28(6).

WEBSITES

Guth, J. and Wright, F. (2008) Women in the Higher Education Sector – Confronting the Issues for Academics at the University of Bradford, *Project Report*, Bradford: Bradford University Law School. www.brad.ac.uk/management/lawinbrief

CHAPTER 66

Editing Special Issues

CHRIS ASHFORD

> Nadia has seen a call to edit the special issue of a journal in her research area.

Your first experience of journal editing may be through producing a special issue of an established journal. From the journal perspective, special issues can help to raise the profile of the journal, reach out to new authors, attract new readers, and ensure that the journal utilises the energy and ideas of the wider academic community. It also enables the journal to highlight a particular area of scholarship or a particular issue that needs further investigation. It's a powerful tool for journals to promote and stimulate a field of study.

It can also be an opportunity for you to raise your profile in a particular field or specialism as well as creating an opportunity to build new networks and work with colleagues who share the same interests and research passions as you. These special issues can give structure to your CV, setting out your specialism and your networks. Special issues can also sometimes be published simultaneously or shortly after as a book, further enhancing your publishing record.

Journals will often issue calls for special issues via academic networks and/or through their own circulation lists. This may be an open call or it may be around a particular theme. An open call provides an opportunity for you to select a specialism that aligns with your own interests and which you believe will be of interest to the journal's readership.

Whilst most academic law journals tend to be general in scope – their broad focus sufficient to define the contents – a special issue is typically much more specific, identifying a theme or time-sensitive topic that they would like to dedicate journal space to exploring.

Whilst this might be a law-focused journal, it could be another discipline-based journal (for example in psychology, sexualities, theory such as feminism, sociology, history, geography, economics and so on) that is addressing a legal issue from a theoretical, socio-legal/interdisciplinary or multidisciplinary perspective. Opportunities to edit special issues may exist beyond the narrow range of law journals.

Ensuring you are on journal alert mailing lists will help to ensure you find out about potential calls but you should also monitor disciplinary and subject-based mailing lists in your field for calls to edit special issues.

In responding to a call, you should ensure that you pay careful attention to the call and respond to it in full. If it's an open call, you need to justify not only why the subject should be investigated (with reference to appropriate literature/evidence) but also clearly set out why that journal is the right vehicle for the specific proposal. If it's a responsive call, the focus will inevitably shift to being more about what you will bring to the issue (skills, experience, perspective), and the overall approach of the issue to the subject at hand.

Some calls will want you to provide an indicative list of authors to give some idea of the potential shape and structure of the special issue alongside your substantive proposal. This might necessitate you contacting people before submitting a proposal to get some individuals 'lined up' but a journal will recognise that any indicative list may change (but not be completely different) in the course of developing an issue. If you're linking the special issue to a recent conference or event, the pool of authors are likely to be self-selected to some extent and a network/community already created which can make for a supportive environment in the production of a special issue.

Journals also typically have some flexibility in the number of articles to include. Ensure that you suggest at the upper end of the range if one is given as you may find that one or more authors drop out or are unable to meet deadlines.

Attracting and selecting your authors can be a challenge and will vary on the approach to the issue you're taking. If you're assembling 'experts' your collection is unlikely to consist merely of those undertaking doctoral study. If the collection is intended to showcase 'new thinkers', it is unlikely to include senior academics who have been writing in the field for 30 years. Once again, subject specialist mailing lists can help you to recruit authors along with the regular bulletins from the learned societies. However, you will probably also need to draw upon your networks established through conferences and your research and teaching activity to assemble your authors.

Working out a realistic schedule is key and will be a question that your authors are likely to ask along with asking for a clear brief about the issue. Setting out not just the final submission date (allow yourself at least a couple of months to turn around any submission before you submit to the journal), but also a timeline: the deadline for an abstract, the article draft, deadline for the final manuscript draft and also an indication of when the author can expect proofs and final publication. Many journals make material online first, before print publication (assuming you're not editing an online-only journal). You may also find yourself responsible for ensuring that authors return copyright forms and organise any copyright issues that may arise (for example, if an image is used in an article). In most cases, the journal editorial team and publisher will be able to assist you in these tasks.

It might be tempting to think that you can wait until the deadline for the submissions to roll in. You may be lucky and have some academics who send you their manuscripts on time or early without promoting. However, the reality for many academics is that there are an increasing array of demands on our time and your journal may drop down their priority list. This is all the more likely to be the case with senior academics who may have unexpected and sudden additional demands placed on their time. You should schedule regular 'check-ins' with authors to make sure that they are progressing appropriately. This will help bring the journal contribution back to the forefront of their mind and make a timely delivery more likely. It also enables people to identify potential late submissions early on and then manage those submissions more closely.

You may also be responsible for identifying the reviewers for a special issue either through your own suggestions or via the journal's database of reviewers. Just as with your authors, you may find some reviewers are late or forget completely and require managing to ensure reviews are timely and that your authors can respond to their suggestions. Many journals now use software such as ScholarOne or Editorial Manger which help to support this with automated reminders and the ability to pre-select alternative reviewers if first choice reviewers decline the invite to review or miss deadlines.

Do not underestimate how time-consuming the process of producing a special issue can be, but nor should you underestimate how rewarding an experience it can also be.

The key messages for Nadia and other academics considering editing special issues:

1. Think about the focus of the journal you are publishing in/aspire to publish in. Pitch your special issue appropriately for that audience.
2. Carefully consider the mix of authors you are seeking to include.
3. Give thought to the timing of your special issue.

FURTHER READING

WEBSITES

Muller, N. (2012) Editing Essay Collections & Special Journal Issues. http://www.nadinemuller.org.uk/the-new-academic-guides/editing-publications/

Nicholas, D. (2015) Publishing Special Issues, *Taylor & Francis Editor Resources*. http://editorresources.taylorandfrancisgroup.com/publishing-special-issues-2/

CHAPTER 67

Editorial Boards/Being an Editor

Chris Ashford

> Having recently gained insights into the editing process following the editing of a special issue, Nadia is now keen to join an editorial board and has ambitions to one day be an editor.

Joining an editorial board can be an extremely rewarding experience. It's a public statement of your expertise within the academy and can create new and important opportunities to develop skills and networks. However, it's also a role that comes with responsibilities. You are likely to have joined following an open call and selection process or after being invited to join following board deliberations.

Even the most respected and well-known academics are not members of a board just because of their name. It is expected that you will be a reviewer for the journal, typically a number of times each year, and you will also be a champion for the journal. In practical terms, this means promoting the journal amongst colleagues and the wider academic community, ensuring that it is known and respected for its area of focus. It also means soliciting high-quality material for the journal through existing contacts and networks and through new links forged at conferences and events. It's important that you seek clarification of what will be required from you (for example, typically how many reviews you might be required to undertake in a given year), whether you've been appointed for an indefinite term or a fixed term and so on. It's also useful to talk to the editor to get a sense of the direction of the journal, new initiatives that might be being developed (but which aren't yet public) so that you can get an idea of whether this is a project you want to be part of and champion.

Being part of an editorial board coupled with perhaps guest editing a journal (see elsewhere in this handbook) can serve as excellent preparation for taking on the role of an editor-in-chief or associate editor, or it might be enough to tell you that those roles are something that you desire.

The experience of being an editor will vary from journal to journal. There are also particular strands of journals, for example the growing number of online open access journals, those that are well established and with a big funding base to employ staff and support grants and prizes, through to those that are largely voluntary run but with some funding from a learned society or other organisation and professional publisher support through to those that are entirely volunteer based but have a traditional paper-based format. The experience of leading and managing a team and journal will vary in these different contexts.

It can be a tremendous support to have employed staff serving as an initial point of contact, managing day-to-day enquiries and more administrative-facing tasks such as chasing copyright forms and suchlike. However, the chances are that you won't have this kind of support. Instead, you're likely to be reliant upon a combination of fellow academic volunteers and perhaps the support of a professional publisher. Whatever the case, it is worth exploring what support is available to you via these channels.

Rather than acting as an editor-in-chief or general editor, you might undertake the role of associate editor or editor of a particular section such as book reviews. These roles will give you more responsibility with a journal and may involve greater control over soliciting and managing journal material but you'll have the support of the main editor. As with joining a board, it's important that you're clear about what the expectations of the role are, and additionally it's useful to gain some shadowing experience if possible.

If you're the main editor, sometimes called a general editor or editor-in-chief, you have overall responsibility for the journal, and lead the journal with the support of your editorial board. You will inherit a board and a composition which you may wish to change. Where people are appointed for fixed terms, there's a natural moment when both parties can move on but it can be more difficult to change a composition if this isn't the case. Having different opinions can enrich a board but conflict and/or board members who don't fully contribute may ultimately mean that you need to have some difficult conversations to get that colleague to re-engage or ultimately to depart the journal. Getting the support of the rest of the board is important when faced with these challenges. Such occasions are the exception rather than the norm and boards will typically be a tremendous source of support and guidance.

As editor, your primary focus will be on ensuring sufficient quality submissions are coming through, a robust peer-review process is in place, articles are effectively managed from first submission through to production, and your board is working effectively. However, in addition to this, you will be tasked with developing a broader programme of journal activity subject to your specific resource context. This may include annual prizes/seminar competitions, calls for guest issues, expanding and refreshing the composition of your board, expanding your reviewer database, or developing and promoting your journal through new technologies such as social media.

Acting as a journal editor or as a member of a board is a rewarding and enriching experience. In both cases, many academics perform the role for a considerable period of time. In some cases, term lengths lead to people naturally moving on but in other cases, people can remain in their role for decades. In a climate of increased academic metrics and a demand from universities for their staff to produce outputs and meet their own key performance indicators, devoting many years to activity such as journal editing may prove more difficult than in the past. Whatever the reason, the moment will eventually come when it's time to pass the baton to a new editor. Your last duty is to find and support the appointment of your successor. They will bring fresh ideas and a new approach to the journal, but they will – if they're sensible – also want you to support and advise them as they undertake their new role.

The key messages for Nadia and other academics considering editorial boards/being an editor:

1. If joining a board, be clear about the expectations of your role, and for how long you're committing to the tasks.
2. If taking over as an editor, ensure that you've shadowed the previous editor(s) for some time and keep the previous editor(s) involved with the journal. They will be a constant source of great advice and experience.
3. Work closely with your publisher and your board to gain new insights into publishing and the field. Drawing on creative and insightful voices is vital to the success of a vibrant journal, but ultimately you are the one who must lead the journal.

FURTHER READING

JOURNAL

Duncan, N. (2006) Pro Bono Legis Doctorum: Forty Years of the Law Teacher, *The Law Teacher: The International Journal of Legal Education*, 40(3), 313–330.

WEBSITE

Taylor & Francis provide a number of reflections from various editors on their Editor Resources website. http://editorresources.taylorandfrancisgroup.com

CHAPTER 68

PhD Supervision

SALLY WHEELER

> Nadia has received an application from a potential PhD student and is considering
> whether she should take on the supervision of this student.

First you will need to decide whether you have the time and the intellectual confidence
at this stage in your career to take on the supervision responsibility for a graduate student. This is likely to be a cost-benefit analysis by of the situation. Factors you might
take into account are whether supervising a PhD student to completion is a promotion indicator or even a requirement at your current institution, and where this sits as
an institutional priority for advancement in comparison with, for example, successful
funding applications and publication outputs. You would need to think about what is
important to your career plan now and in the next three years in terms of what goals
you have set yourself. Undertaking to supervise someone is a huge responsibility and
supervising 'well' is a large time commitment. It will also take up some of your intellectual and creative space if it is to be an enjoyable experience for both parties. Across
your career you are likely to get more PhD students wanting to work with you than you
have room to accommodate so deciding to supervise one now is not an all or nothing
choice. There will be other opportunities.

Every HEI has rules about who can undertake doctoral-level supervision and what
the shape of that supervision is; for example whether is to be done as a team-based
exercise with more than one supervisor and, if it is, what the respective roles of those
team members might be. The amount of supervision, the record-keeping responsibilities for that supervision and the milestones that PhD students need to achieve to maintain their PhD status will be set out as institutional requirements. The PhD experience
and the institutional and departmental training that goes with it is becoming more and
more structured as institutions realise that PhD students are likely to pursue careers
other than academia on completion. Employability concerns are very much part of the
PhD process. As a supervisor it is your responsibility to find out what those rules are
and then to use them to help you decide whether this is something that you want to do
and have time to do now. You are likely to only be permitted to be a second supervisor or a supervisory team member until you have had a successful student completion
in that role. In this case you will need to find a colleague with whom you can form a
working partnership that allows you to take on a PhD student.

PhD supervision offers an opportunity to create the beginnings of a research group within a particular school but it is not absolutely necessary that a potential PhD student be very close in terms of their chosen area of study to their supervisor. It is perhaps more important that there be an intellectual connection around the approach taken to a subject and a shared theoretical and methodological position than a precise subject matter match. It sometimes takes young academics a while to accept that precise subject area fit is not always a good thing for PhD supervision and certainly not something to be waited for. By this I mean that the closer in subject area a PhD topic is to one's own area of interest, the harder it is to see that student move away in intellectual terms as they develop their own ideas. There is a temptation to pull them back to one's own preferred intellectual journey in this area rather than to let them develop their own position.

PhD supervision involves at the very least co-production of the PhD candidate's foundational intellectual development. There is something of this in UG and PG teaching but to a much lesser extent. The one-to-one relationship or the supervisory team relationship with a PhD student can be a very intense and intellectually rewarding one; it can also be a deeply unhappy and frustrating experience for both parties. In fact it is quite likely that the journey to PhD completion will include periods that reflect both of these emotional tropes and you should be prepared for this. A supervision relationship is not something that should be embarked upon without a first meeting or at least a Skype conversation to explore common ground and determine whether there is an intellectual chemistry.

Your own PhD experience might not be that far behind you but you may well not have committed to memory the feelings of fear and isolation often experienced in the early days of PhD study. What you should have got from your supervisor and what you need to give new students is a road map that sets out what needs to be achieved in each academic year and the incremental steps that will get the student to each of these points. Courses on supervising research students are offered by many institutions, try to attend one. This will help you decide on the approach to important issues like how soon a new student should start writing and what form that writing should take, when data collection should start and what ethics approval is needed. Be prepared to set deadlines for written work to be submitted and be clear about the level and timeliness of feedback that the student can expect. Endorse the training that a PhD student has to do within an institution as your endorsement validates the training in the eyes of the research student.

What you are doing by setting out expectations on written work and its timely submission and giving commitments on feedback is providing a structure in which the PhD and the supervisory relationship can develop and hopefully flourish. The presence of this structure with goals and expectations on both sides will give you something to fall back on if the PhD does not progress at the rate that it needs to do to reach completion. You need to remember that your role is one of guidance on the quality and structure of the thesis – to challenge the depth of its argument and the evidence produced by fieldwork and so on, and not to provide exhaustive reading lists of materials. A PhD student should have moved beyond a supervisor's in-depth knowledge of the literature in the first few months of the PhD and be independent in this respect. The closer the subject matter of the PhD thesis is to your area of interest the more tempting it is to intervene the process of iteration and refinement that is a PhD. This slows down the student's progression to intellectual independence.

The key messages for Nadia and other academics considering PhD supervision:

1. Remember that your role is to guide the student to intellectual independence.
2. Familiarise yourself with the policies and processes relating to PhD supervision and PhD study so you can help your student navigate the institution.
3. A very close subject interest fit is not essential and can sometimes be unhelpful.

FURTHER READING

BOOKS

Dunleavy, P. (2003) *Authoring a PhD: How to Plan, Draft, Write and Finish a Doctoral Thesis or Dissertation*, Basingstoke: Palgrave.

Morris, C. and Murphy, C. (2011) *Getting a PhD in Law*, Oxford: Hart Publishing.

Phillips, Estelle M. and Pugh, Derek S. (2010) *How to Get a PhD: A Handbook for Students and Their Supervisors*, Maidenhead: Open University Press.

CHAPTER 69

The Law Subject Associations

BECKY HUXLEY-BINNS

> Nadia is keen to get involved in one or more academic association but does not know which ones might benefit her most.

Imagine that you had a question about a particular teaching method, or an opinion about the effect of a recent judgment, or a concern about the implications of a white paper. Where might you go to share your thoughts? Your immediate colleagues may offer you a kind ear, or a devil's advocate's response, but for a wider audience and perhaps a range of views and experiences, we suggest you become an active member of a law subject association. Collegiality and friendship are often undervalued in higher education and the law community benefits greatly from the kindness, generosity and quality of its academics, best exemplified through the workings of its law subject associations. It is the unequivocal advice of this handbook that each reader joins at least one law subject association; which one is up to you. We suggest you go along to the annual conferences and see which one (or ones) is the best 'fit' for you and your subject interests.

Membership of any of the associations brings great benefits including:

- the opportunity to be in a community with like-minded and similarly motivated academics
- (usually) receipt of a regular newsletter or bulletin
- (usually) receipt of a learned journal
- (usually) the right to participate in and/or bid for funding for research grants
- (sometimes) the opportunity to host a seminar or series of funded seminars within the remit of the organisation
- (sometimes) eligibility for awards, prizes and bursaries for papers, conferences and reports
- (sometimes) discounts with publishers
- access to and reduced rates for the association's workshops, symposia and annual conference.

Each organisation has a constitution and is run by a council and/or executive committee operated by officers (executive committee members), volunteers who donate considerable time and energies to support their society. The summaries below are taken from the organisation's websites and for further information, please refer to the relevant website(s).

The main UK-based law subject associations, in alphabetical order, are:

ALT – The Association of Law Teachers

http://lawteacher.ac.uk
The Association of Law Teachers (ALT) is made up of law teachers from both higher and further education, and for almost 50 years has played an active role at the heart of legal education. It has an international membership and maintains close links with other national and international organisations pursuing similar interests.

bileta – The British and Irish Law Education and Technology Association

www.bileta.ac.uk
Formed in 1986, bileta's aim is to promote the use of technology in legal education throughout the UK and Ireland. Membership is usually by organisation but individual membership is permitted. The website above details those organisations which are members.

LERN – the Legal Education Research Network

http://ials.sas.ac.uk/lern/lern.htm
Not a subject association, per se, LERN is a network of researchers interested in legal education. It hosts workshops and regularly makes available small grants for research into legal education. LERN is mainly supported by the Association of Law Teachers (ALT, above) and the Society of Legal Scholars (SLS, below), especially in terms of their financial support for the Small Grants. It also receives support from the Institute of Advanced Legal Studies (IALS), the Law Publishers Association and the Higher Education Academy (HEA).

SLS – The Society of Legal Scholars

www.legalscholars.ac.uk
Founded in 1908, the Society has over 2,900 members who teach law in a university or similar institution or who are otherwise engaged in legal scholarship. Its aim is the advancement of legal education and scholarship in the United Kingdom and Ireland.

SLSA – The Socio-Legal Studies Association

www.slsa.ac.uk
Formed in 1990, this association's aim is to advance education and learning and in particular to advance research, teaching and the dissemination of knowledge in the field of socio-legal studies.

In addition, there is the Committee of the Heads of University Law Schools, or CHULS. CHULS was founded in 1974 and represents law schools through their heads. It focuses on issues of concern to law schools. Its website address is http://chuls.ac.uk

The British Academy also publishes a Directory of Subject Associations and Learned Societies based in the UK which is available at https://www.britac.ac.uk/links/uksahss.asp where you will find information on some of the more specialist associations, such as, for example, the association of women barristers, the UK environmental law association (UKELA).

Other international legal education focused associations include:

The Association of Legal Studies in Business
www.alsb.org
This association hosts an incredibly welcoming good annual conference (in my opinion) and it also advances legal studies in business education; it is the professional home for legal studies researchers and educators, fostering collegial relationships and productive collaboration with researchers, educators, and organisations throughout the world.

The Australasian Law Teachers Association
www.alta.edu.au/
This association represents the interests of law teachers in Australia, New Zealand, Papua New Guinea and the Pacific Islands.

The Canadian Association of Law Teachers – L'association Canadienne Des Professeurs De Droit
www.acpd-calt.org
CALT brings together law teachers from across Canada in pursuit of common interests and concerns, including legal scholarship, teaching and overarching issues of law and policy which relate to academic and professional interests.

The Society of American Law Teachers
www.saltlaw.org
SALT is committed to advancing teaching excellence, social justice and diversity. SALT is a community of progressive law teachers, law school administrators, librarians, academic support experts, students and affiliates.

The key messages for Nadia and other academics considering joining subject associations:

1. Check out what each of the subject associations offer, online and by going to their conferences if you can (time and cost are factors of course).
2. Be an active member; read the newsletters, support colleagues' contributions, perhaps even become an executive member.

FURTHER READING

BOOK

Cownie, F. and Cocks, R. (2009) *A Great and Noble Occupation*, Oxford: Hart.

CHAPTER 70

Dealing with the Media

PAUL BERNAL

> Nadia finds herself fielding an increasing number of media enquires about her research.

Academics should, in theory, be good at dealing with the media. We're supposed to be knowledgeable, to be good thinkers, to write well, and be able to speak to an audience. If we can write journal articles, why not newspaper articles? If we can lecture to students, why can't we speak authoritatively on the radio? The answer of course is that we can – but often we don't. It's not in our comfort zone. That is something that legal academics should change. We can and should be good at dealing with the media.

There are many reasons to engage actively and positively with the media. Universities love the exposure – it raises their profile, makes them more attractive to students and even potentially to funders. Academics can benefit personally – it can improve their reputation, lead to invitations to conferences and so forth. Further, interaction with the media is engagement and can potentially lead to impact. Politicians, for example, are much more likely to read a piece in a newspaper than they are to come across anything published academically.

Once the nervousness and inhibition is overcome, working with the media can be very enjoyable. It can be an opportunity to talk about the subjects that you know, to explain your views and to put them across to a much wider audience. Legal academics should relish that opportunity.

There are some particular times when the opportunity to deal with the media can come up. When a new law is being contemplated – or when it is passed. When a critical event – a key case, for example – happens in your field. When someone – a politician or even a fellow academic – says something particularly controversial. When you yourself write something important – having a book published, for example. When you're going to present your work at a conference or give a public talk. All these occasions may elicit media interest. If you are ready for it, and know how to get the attention of the appropriate people, the media will want to talk to you.

Getting their attention is one of the keys to engagement with the media. There is no simple solution, but there are two particularly important routes. The first is to work with your university media office – all universities have them, though the names and forms vary. They have contacts with journalists, can put out press releases, and often get calls from journalists looking for expert comment. Let your press office know who you are, what fields you cover, how you can be contacted and so forth, and then when a call comes in, they can forward the information to the journalist. The second is through the active use of social media: journalists are very active on Twitter in particular, and if you have a Twitter presence and use it well, they may contact you directly. If you write good blog posts, they may read them, quote them, or even ask you to let them use them directly in their newspapers and magazines.

There are different considerations for different forms of media. The print media is very different from the broadcast media, television from radio, online media from more traditional media. Within those categories things can vary substantially. Local radio and local newspapers are very different from their national equivalents. One, however, may lead to another – if an event is really newsworthy you may have many requests to deal with, one after another. The media tend to appreciate a fast response and a quick turnaround of written work.

With print media, you may be asked to comment on an issue – a case, for example – and that may mean a long conversation with a journalist by phone, resulting in just a few sentences appearing in print. A good journalist will want to understand the underlying story, and will be willing to spend time in order to do so. If you give them the time, they are not only more likely to quote you well, but more likely to come back to you later when other stories come up. You may also be asked to provide whole pieces – in which case it is helpful to learn how to write in 'journalistic' style: referring to official style-guides can help (see references below). These pieces will probably be edited, however, and you are unlikely to have control over the headline on your piece. This can lead to misunderstandings – but they go with the territory. Print is different from online too – there are generally tight limits in the length of pieces in print, and often a longer lead-time.

Broadcast media is qualitatively different – being interviewed or being part of a panel means being succinct and pithy, keeping things simple and getting right to the point. There's rarely space for the kind of caveats and qualifications that academics require in their writing – it often sounds like uncertainty or prevarication. Interviewers and non-academic panellists may not have the kind of patience that fellow academics have – and you can end up 'losing' an argument just by being too complicated. There's also the distinct possibility of seeming boring – interviews on radio are likely to be cut short if you seem boring. What's more, they won't ask you back: with broadcast work you need to be lively and as natural as possible. The broadcast media tends to want opinions and sound bites – if you are uncomfortable with that, it may be better to avoid it. With TV, there are other considerations such as body language – this is one area in which training can really help. Universities will often be able to provide you with specific media training – and opportunities to practice with mock interviews and so forth.

There are other possible pitfalls. Sometimes you can feel as though you are being ambushed – you believe that you're being interviewed about one thing and in practice the interview seems to be about something quite different. You may be put on a panel with someone who is slicker, faster and more 'in tune' with the media than you. Again, this just goes with the territory. Similarly, with the print media, it's possible to be misquoted – or to make mistakes that are then out there for all to see. Any academic who engages with the media in this way has to grow a thick skin. The rewards, however, can make it well worth it.

More serious than being embarrassed can be if media work comes into contact with the law. Defamation law, for example, needs to be taken into account, as does contempt of court in certain circumstances. Any legal academic expecting to engage with the media would be advised to read up about these areas – see the Quinn reading below.

One final point. Sometimes it may be possible to be paid for media work – pieces written for magazines and interviews on national radio stations may well attract a fee, and where relevant academics should avoid working without being paid, as they can at times be used as substitutes for paid journalists. These fees, however, are unlikely to be significant: media work should be undertaken for other reasons, not for the financial rewards.

The key messages for Nadia and other academics considering dealing with the media:

1. Engaging actively and positively with the media can bring benefits for legal academics and for the institutions at which they work.
2. Though there are pitfalls and potential risks, from being misquoted or misunderstood to some legal risks, these are generally outweighed by the rewards.
3. Working with your university's media office can really help.

FURTHER READING

BOOK

Quinn, F. (2013) *Law for Journalists*, 4th edn, Harlow: Pearson.

WEBSITES

Associated Press Style Book. www.apstylebook.com

Guardian and Observer Style Guide. www.theguardian.com/guardian-observer-style-guide-a

www.journalism.co.uk

National Council for the Training of Journalists. www.nctj.com

CHAPTER 71

Readerships/Professorships – How to Get There

PHILIP N. S. RUMNEY

Nadia is mapping out her future career path.

The criteria for high-level research appointments can vary to some degree between institutions. However, there are a number of factors that influence career progression to reader or professor and should be considered important irrespective of the institution in question.

Just as when starting out on an academic career, becoming a reader or professor requires long-term planning and making sure that appointment criteria are understood. When planning a career path to reader or professor the various strands that lead to progression need to be identified. The most important factor is a record of excellent quality research published in highly regarded journals. The quality of research is crucial and it is worth noting that quality outweighs quantity. Everyone at some point in their career suffers CV anxiety or searches the web profiles of other scholars to see what they have written. A long list of publications, however, does not in itself signify quality.

Scholars working in a given field and those who sit on shortlisting panels quickly spot web profiles or CVs dominated by mediocre articles and books. In the case of aspiring readers or professors, where there is little evidence of a significant amount of higher-level work of international quality then shortlisting panels and other scholars will see such a person as having 'topped out' – that is, they will be seen as unlikely to produce work of the very highest standard in the future. No-one expects a young scholar to start producing world-leading research from the first day. However, by the time they are in a position to apply for a readership a scholar should have produced some Research Excellence Framework (REF) 3–4★ quality work and be on an upwards trajectory in terms of research, funding and other activities.

An aspiring professor should have already reached a consistently high standard of research which would score 3–4★ in the REF, have successful funding bids and engage in other activity, such as being a journal editor, being invited to give keynote papers, or engaging in knowledge exchange activity. It should be acknowledged that a scholar seeking a professorial appointment should also be able to show evidence of leadership. Readerships and professorships are not so much a reward for past work, but a springboard for further high-quality work.

No scholar should underestimate the importance of personal qualities. It is important to be willing to reflect on past work and see areas for development or improvement. Seeking advice can be very useful, and any aspiring reader or professor should be willing to listen to good advice. Who is approached to give advice is important: some people give terrible advice; it is only worthwhile taking advice from people who are knowledgeable, supportive and honest.

Collegiality is an essential personal quality for senior researchers, as is patience – there are no short cuts. People seen as being in a rush are not necessarily viewed favourably, particularly when their scholarship is weak or infrequent. A scholar with a strong record who applies for a readership or professorship may not be successful for a whole host of good reasons – not least, because of the strength of other candidates. Learning from the experience is crucial. Likewise, responding to disappointment with bitterness is never a good idea and makes it less likely that such a person will be successful in the future.

Some scholars see their research as so important that they become selfish. Every legal scholar has come across selfish colleagues who place research and their own ambition above everything else. It is one thing to be career minded; it is quite another to treat colleagues and others poorly. It leads to dislike and a poor reputation. It should not be assumed that members of shortlisting and interview panels will be so blinded by high quality research, research grants and the like, that they will not take into account, perhaps unconsciously, how applicants treat their colleagues and students.

Securing research funding has become an increasingly important part of academic life. In the past this was the domain of old universities, but in recent times much more focus is given to this issue in the post-1992 sector. Scholars who wish to become readers or professors should actively seek research funding and all institutions offer advice and help in identifying funding opportunities.

Aspiring readers and professors should also have a sound understanding of research impact and strategies for securing impact. They should be able to identify which of their own research outputs are likely to have external impact and must be able to formulate a clear impact strategy. Similarly, scholars who wish to be readers or professors should always have a clear research, impact and funding plan.

There is an increasing focus on teaching quality in all institutions. Readers and professors are not immune from the reasonable expectation that they can teach to a high standard. Indeed, in a growing number of institutions professors and readers, however good their scholarship, are expected to demonstrate a commitment to teaching. The very best scholars are respected by their students and colleagues for their teaching skills, as well as ideas.

The move from reader to professor requires a recognition of the difference between the two positions. Professors are expected to lead. Authoring world-leading research or bringing in research grants may show leadership, but leading is much more than that. A leader is someone who can identify new opportunities, think strategically and can work out ways of implementing strategic plans. It is also about bringing other people along in the sense of supporting colleagues and helping them develop their careers. These are all skills that can be developed over time. Readers who engage in such activities show clear evidence that they are developing the necessary skills to be a professor.

One of the other distinctions is that a professor should be an established authority in a given field or subject area, not just one of many – someone who can offer original thoughts and contributions. This may include groundbreaking empirical or theoretical insights published in high-quality research outputs or work that changes the way others see a particular issue. In many institutions attracting regular research grants is also seen as important, along with knowledge exchange and community engagement activity. A reader should be able to show that (s)he can meet at least some of these criteria and be working on the others.

There is one final lesson for those who are ambitious and wish to become a reader or professor – do not rush. The former boxer, Nigel Benn once commented that fighters who are in a rush to be a success often make bad decisions that destroy their careers. He observed that when fighters are patient and fight for titles, the success and money comes along automatically. Leaving aside the issue of money, the point is that becoming a reader or professor takes time, patience and above all, it necessitates doing the right things in the right way.

The key messages for Nadia and other academics mapping out their future career:

1. Becoming a reader or professor will take time and it requires planning as to what will maximise the chances of success.
2. The quality of scholarly publications is more important than the number of publications.
3. However, it is not all about publications. Research funding, teaching, knowledge exchange, showing leadership and being an excellent colleague, may also be important factors.

FURTHER READING

BOOK

Cownie, F. (2004) *Legal Academics: Cultures and Identities*, Oxford: Hart Publishing.

Glossary

24-hour technology: a term to capture 'always-on' technology and the impact of this accessibility on academics

a citation advantage: the idea that you get more citations if something is published open access

academic board: sometimes also referred to as senate. Key senior decision making forum of a university

ALT: Association of Law Teachers – http://www.lawteacher.ac.uk

appraisal: a regular opportunity (typical annually or bi-annually) for staff and their manager to reflect on staff activities and performance over a defined period of time

article processing charges (APCs): the charge made by a publisher for making a publication available via Gold Access

article-level metrics (ALMs): indicators which measure the overall performance and reach of published research articles

ASA: Advertising Standards Authority – an independent regulator across all media

Asperger syndrome: a form of autism with a triad of impairments: difficulties with social communication, social interaction and social imagination

auditory learner: someone who prefers to learn through listening

Aurora: a leadership programme for academic women – see www.lfhe.ac.uk/en/programmes-events/you/aurora/

BILETA: British and Irish Law Education and Technology Association www.bileta.ac.uk

BIS: Department for Business Innovation and Skills www.gov.uk/government/organisation/department-4-buisness-innovation-skills

black letter: a term used to refer to a body of scholarship which is typically focused on doctrinal aspects of law

BPTC: Bar Professional Training Course – the vocational stage of training for aspiring barristers

Browne Report: independent review by Lorde Browne – making recommendations to UK government on future of higher education (HE) fees policy and financial support for undergraduate (UG) and postgraduate (PG) students www.gov.uk/govenrment/publications/the-browne-report-higher-education-funding-and-student-finance

chair: professorship – personal or institutional

chancellor: ceremonial figurehead of a university

clinical legal education: a learning-by-doing teaching methodology which engages students through participation in authentic legal activities including law clinics or placements

constructive alignment: the idea that teaching and assessment are aligned

course leader: someone who manages a programme or part of a programme

Dearing Report: a review undertaking by Lord Dearing in 1997 also known as National Committee of Enquiry into HE which proposed significant changes to UK tuition fee funding and went to inform the Teaching and HE Act 1998 which introduced tuition fees – www.educationegnaldn.org.uk/documents/dearing 1997/dearing1997.html

degree awarding powers: institutions authorised by government to award undergraduate and /or postgraduate qualifications

Destination of Leavers from Higher Education (DLHE) survey: survey of higher education leavers six months after graduating https://www.hesa.ac.uk/stats-dlhe

doctrinal: see **black letter** – an approach which suggests a focus on legal institutions and the law as laid out in legal text(s)

dyslexia: a learning difference which affects the learning process in reading, spelling, writing and sometimes numeracy. There may be weaknesses in short-term memory and information-processing speed

embargo period: a period of time imposed by publishers during which a publication cannot be made freely available

empirical research: an approach to research which focuses on obtaining data directly or indirectly through, for example, interviews, questionnaires, or ethnographic research or archive-based research

employability: a policy agenda encountered in HE which seeks to align programmes/ modules with skills and or knowledge development perceived to be aligned with employer needs

equality and diversity: equality – the idea of a common benchmark of opportunities across characteristic (e.g. race etc.) and diversity seeks to recognise richness and variety of these difference

ethics: a term used in a number of situations – including legal ethics and ethical conduct of lawyers and research ethics – doing ethical research as outline in the ALT or SLSA research ethics statement

faculty: could be part of structure of university – usually larger than a school or department encompassing more than one discipline or term used to refer to academic staff

FHEQ: *Framework for Higher Education Qualifications* in England

flipped classroom: the idea of providing information online prior to teaching sessions and using sessions for more interactive work

formative assessment: formative assessment is assessment carried out during a course of study for the purpose of improving learning. Its main purpose is to provide feedback to make adjustments to students' learning

Full Economic Costing: a method of costing a research grant which includes all costs associated with it including items such as staff costs, estate costs and other institutional overheads

GDL: Graduate Diploma in Law

glossary: a painstaking process that nearly sent us both mad but we hope it is useful!

gold access: reference to open access publishing; gold access refers to the article being made freely available by publishers (online) who will then usually charge an author processing fee. Green Access refers to an article being made available by the author in pre-proof format via a repository. No charge is made by the publisher but embargo periods may apply

graduate tutor: typically a PhD student funded (f/t/or p/T) with an emphasis on teaching delivery

green access: see gold access

HEFCE: Higher Education Funding Council for England

HESA: Higher Education Statistics Agency www.hesa.ac.uk

impact: a term with increased predominance post REF 2014 designed to capture real-world consequences of research activity and outputs

impact factor (IF): a metric applied to journals to denote reach based on average citations of articles published in that journal

law clinic: a university-based legal service involving students providing assistance to live clients, as distinct from Street Law and simulated clinical activities

law in context: term defined by William Twining to research and teach law in a broader political, social environment/context

learning outcomes: a statement of skills/knowledge a students will have gained through studying a particular session, module or programme

lecturer: typically the first step of an academic career synthesizing research, scholarship and teaching. In pre-1992 university this is often divided between two grades lecturer A and B, in post 1992 between two grades – L and SL

lecturer A: see lecturer

lecturer B: see lecturer

liberal: see liberal law degree

liberal law degree: a contested term which seeks to describe law degrees which seek to offer a liberal education in the discipline of law without being tied to any particular vocation

literature review: stage of a research project during which existing published scholarship on the topics in question is reviewed and evaluated in the context of the current project

LLB: Law Degree Legum Baccalaureus – UG bachelor level degree in law

LPC: Legal Practice Course – professional stage of training for solicitors

method: the specific tools to be deployed in undertaking research

Million+: university think tank predominantly made up of post 1992s www.million+.ac.uk

module: a discrete subject forming part of a programme of study

module leadership: see course leader

National Student Survey (NSS): annual survey of students at the end of their course of study to evaluate their course and their time at university and college

new university: an institution established as a university in or/after 1992

OFFA: Office for fair access www.offa.org.uk

OFT (now replaced by CMA): see CMA – www.gov.uk/government/organisations/competitionn-and-markets-authority

old university: university established pre 1992

open access (OA): see chapter on this subject

Ormrod Report: published in 1971 offering a comprehensive overview of legal education with a focus on England and Wales

pedagogy: practice of teaching

peer-review: research evaluation by appropriate experts within the academic community

performance review: see appraisal

PGCert for HE: see chapter on this subject

plagiarism: academic misconduct in which work is represented as the author's work when it is not

principal lecturer: post-1992 university term referring to a position which is more senor than senior lecturer (SL) – duties often focused on management and admin alongside teaching

pro bono: also referred to a pro bono publico meaning 'for the public good'. In the context of clinical legal education pro bono services involve providing legal advice or representation free of charge. A formal definition can be found in the Pro Bono Protocol at https://www. lawworks.org.uk/why-pro-bono/what-pro-bono/pro-bono-protocol

problem-based learning (PBL): see chapter on this subject

problem-based learning (PBL): a pedagogy which is student centred and which posits a problem which students solve independently

professor: the most senior academic role, usually an expert in their chosen field

programme leader: see course leader

QLD: qualifying law degree – UG level qualification which meets professional body regulations

QR: quality related research funding awarded to institutions based on REF results

qualitative: a methodological approach in which the focus is on words either written or spoken, or images: anything not quantitative

quality assurance: internal and external processes through which standards are monitored and upheld in HE

Quality Assurance Agency: the UK body tasked with ensuring quality in UK HE institutions

quantitative: a methodological approach in which the focus is on numerical data

RAE: see Research Excellence Framework

reader: academic position senior to SL (both pre and post) higher education institutions and junior to professor. A teaching and research post typically with a focus on research activity and sometimes with a leadership component

redbrick: type of university – usually old university – universities developed in response to industrialisation and expansion of HE in the 19th and early 20th century

REF: see Research Excellence Framework

reflective learning: a pedagogic approach in which value is placed on the recall and evaluation of experience and progress made

repository: a virtual institutional storage space for academic outputs typically making them publically available

research assistant/associate: a role which is typically junior and often undertaken during or post PhD which typically supports a specific programme and is often fixed term

Research Excellence Framework (REF): a peer-led auditing exercise which seeks to measure scholarly outputs impact and environment in UK HEIs to determine rigour, significance and research of that scholarship with a view to determining financial governmental support for that research activity

revalidations: see validations

Robbins Report: 1963 report heralding a significant expansion of universities – Robbins principles seeking to ensure that students get instructions in skills, promotion of general powers of mind so as to produce not mere specialists but rather to maintain research in balance with teaching and to transmit a common cultural and common standard of citizenship

Russell Group: a group of 24 universities www.russellgroup.ac.uk

school: an institutional structure which is smaller than a faculty reflecting a department or discipline

senate: see academic board

senior lecturer: an academic role in post 1992 in contrast to Lecturer(B) in pre-1992 university it is a term comparable to principal L pay/grade but usually with less emphasis on leadership

SLS: Society of Legal Scholars – http://www.legalscholars.ac.uk

SLSA: Socio-Legal Studies Association – http://www.slsa.ac.uk

socio-legal: an approach to teaching and research in which law is placed on a broader social, economic and political cultural context and which draws upon methodologies and methods from other social science disciplines

STEM subjects: science, technology, engineering and mathematics subjects

tactual learners: a learner who learns by touching or handling something or by relating to other people

UKVI: UK visa's and immigration – https://www.gov.uk/government/organisations/uk-visas-and-immigration

university alliance: a group of universities bringing together innovative and entrepreneurial universities – http://www.unialliance.ac.uk

unaligned: university not part of one of the groups of institutions

validation: a programme approval process

vice chancellor: the leader of a university

virtual learning environment (VLE): a virtual repository organised on programme/module lines which may be used to support and enhance interactive learning

visual learner: a learner who uses images, pictures and diagrams to help them make sense of data and learning

vocational: an approach to learning and scholarship in which the needs and desires of professional and commercial stakeholders are prioritised

Index